DANCING IN THE
NO-FLY ZONE

Young girl at a displaced persons' settlement in Baghdad, October 2003

DANCING IN THE
NO-FLY ZONE

A WOMAN'S JOURNEY THROUGH IRAQ

HADANI DITMARS

OLIVE
BRANCH
PRESS

An imprint of Interlink Publishing Group, Inc.
www.interlinkbooks.com

First American edition published in 2006 by

OLIVE BRANCH PRESS
an imprint of Interlink Publishing Group, Inc.
46 Crosby Street, Northampton, Massachusetts 01060
www.interlinkbooks.com

Library of Congress Cataloging-in-Publication Data
Ditmars, Hadani.
Dancing in the no-fly zone : a woman's journey through Iraq / by
Hadani Ditmars.
p. cm.
"Parts of this book have already appeared in articles written by the
author for the Independent and the Globe and Mail."
Includes bibliographical references and index.
ISBN 1-56656-634-7 (pbk. : alk. paper)
1. Iraq War, 2003– —Personal narratives, Canadian. 2. Ditmars,
Hadani—Travel—Iraq. 3. United States—Foreign relations—Iraq.
4. Iraq—Foreign relations—United States. I. Title.
DS79.76.D57 2005
915.6704'443—dc22
2005019542

The author and publishers gratefully acknowledge permission to reprint lyrics from *Stories of
the Street* by Leonard Cohen, © 1968 Columbia Records and Leonard Cohen, from the album
Songs of Leonard Cohen.

*Cover photo: An Iraqi bride and groom are greeted by a US soldier as they pass through a
security checkpoint outside a Baghdad hotel on their wedding day Saturday, September 27, 2003
(AP Photo/Khalid Mohammed)*

Printed and bound in Canada by Webcom

To request our complete 40-page full-color catalog,
please call us toll free at 1-800-238-LINK,
visit our website at **www.interlinkbooks.com**, or write to
Interlink Publishing
46 Crosby Street, Northampton, MA 01060
email: info@interlinkbooks.com

To all my Iraqi friends and to all good friends of Iraq

Baghdad, the City of Peace

The city of Baghdad has been famous since its establishment by the Abbasid Caliph Abu Ja'far al-Mansur who ordered the building of the celebrated "Round City" in the spring of 145 AH (AD 762) on the right bank of the Tigris. The planning of this city is considered by researchers as the ideal example of urbanism and it is, indeed, a superb evidence of Arab achievement. Later Abbasid caliphs and emirs competed in enlarging and developing Baghdad by building luxurious palaces and parks, impressive edifices such as mosques, hostels, schools and intellectual centres which remained for centuries the focus of world learning.

Various dark periods have overrun Baghdad and it was diminished considerably through repeated coups and civil wars. Consequently all the institutions were badly neglected and daily life was almost paralyzed. Sieges and wars by foreign nomadic hordes who had no cultural understanding added much to the calamities. On top of those sad circumstances were the invasions of the Mongols under the command of Hulagu in 656 AH (AD 1258) and of Tamerlane in 795 AH (AD 1392) which resulted in destroying the city's fortifications and buildings, palaces, mosques, colleges and libraries, causing all of the beautiful monuments in Baghdad to vanish. But these were not the last invasions in the long history of the city. Later attacks and counter attacks by rival governors and rulers who attained supremacy in Baghdad — e.g. the Jalairids, Safawids and Ottomans — each in turn contributed to further devastation of the city's artistic and cultural treasures. Very little remained of the once fabulous Baghdad. However, the brave city withstood all those hard days and soon overcame its conquerors who, influenced by the spirit of Arabian culture, all wanted to have Baghdad as the seat of their Kingdoms.

— FROM *TOURIST GUIDE OF IRAQI ANTIQUITIES*, PUBLISHED IN 1972 BY JUMHORIAH PRESS, WHEN HASSAN AL-BAKR, SADDAM'S PREDECESSOR, WAS PRESIDENT

Sara, a girl at the displaced persons' settlement in Baghdad whose father was wounded during the invasion, October 2003

Contents

Preface

I am going to light a fire in Paradise and to pour water on to Hell,
so that both veils may vanish altogether.
— Rabia, an eighth-century Iraqi woman poet and Sufi saint

WHEN I FIRST WENT TO IRAQ, in November of 1997 — on assignment
for the *New York Times Magazine* — the "news" was the latest
confrontation between U.N. weapons inspectors and Saddam Hussein.
But my interests lay elsewhere. The piece I did for the magazine on "a
day in the life of a Baghdad hospital" described the destruction six years
of sanctions had wrought on average families. I wrote of new mothers
so malnourished they could produce no breast milk; of parents who had
sold their last household possessions to pay for their children's penicillin;
of toddlers dying of preventable diseases in a country that had once had
the best health-care system in the Middle East.

The U.S.-backed U.N. embargo was the harshest ever imposed on a
modern nation. After two decades of war, despotism, and sanctions,
Iraq was an ailing land, with a few good doctors fighting the rising tide
of despair like characters from Camus's *La Peste*. None of which
stopped my editor in New York from rejecting my piece for being
"too soft on the Iraqis."

I persisted, and ended up writing a series of features for the daily
newspaper, including one on the growing humanitarian crisis, the first
ever published in the *Times*. The Iraqi pooh-bahs at the Ministry of
Information — the government agency that did its best to control
journalists — did not appreciate this, as they thought my account of a
suffering populace reflected badly on the regime. They promptly
expelled me, on Christmas Eve, 1997.

For six more years, the American government remained apparently unmoved by the suffering the embargo was causing. The U.N. "oil for food" program, introduced in 1996, staved off starvation but not malnourishment. A U.N. committee controlled by the U.S. and U.K. banned the importation of "dual-use items," anything that could conceivably have a military purpose: these included oxygen bottles, many pharmaceuticals, chlorine for water treatment, and science textbooks. The Baathist elite had access to smuggled goods, but the poor and middle classes, who just a decade before had benefited from a generous welfare state, did not. Confronted with the horrifying UNICEF statistic that 500,000 Iraqi children under five had died — mainly through water-borne diseases that resulted from a U.N. prohibition on investment in the country's war-ravaged infrastructure — Clinton's secretary of state, Madeleine Albright, famously replied, "I think it is worth the price."

Meanwhile, the international arms and petroleum industries — even American firms such as Chevron and Mobil — continued to do business in Iraq, under the guise of third-party "silent partners." As the three thousand percent devaluation of the dinar wiped out the country's middle class and the state-issued ration card became a bargaining chip in the struggle for survival, any possibility of dissent declined dramatically. Sanctions and the black market economy they fostered only emboldened a government that had been unpopular and weak at the end of the Gulf War. The state had become both Scourge and Savior.

I RETURNED TO IRAQ several times over the next six years, filing stories for publications such as *Newsweek*, *The Independent*, *The San Francisco Chronicle*, and *Wallpaper**, as well as for the BBC and CBC. I would marvel again and again at the Iraqis' stoicism and ability to survive. Yet there was so much more to the former "cradle of civilization" than stories of misery and suffering. In the midst of despair I found art, beauty, architecture, music. I discovered a world of orchestras that played wonderfully impassioned symphonies on wrecked instruments, playwrights who pushed the limits of censorship, artists who spent their last dinars on paint and canvas, who lived for a higher experience that transcended consumerist definitions of success.

But no one could escape the regime's oppressive nature. As an exiled friend in Vancouver would tell me later, "We can only blame the Americans for so much. After all, Iraqis killed Iraqis, and they still are killing." This sad phenomenon of neighbors and even brothers turning on each other may well be one of the most tragic aspects of Iraq's long saga. Even in the art world, friends spied on friends and betrayed one another. The situation was far from romantic. "When will the sanctions end?" was the mantra, which was also code for, "When will this regime end?"

No one expected both to end so brutally.

Many contend that the embargo was slowly being destroyed by trade with Europe and Asia and that when it was over, a resurging middle class would have spelled the end of Saddam Hussein's regime. The U.S. only invaded, they say, for economic reasons, to make sure the lucrative post-embargo oil contracts did not go to the Russians, French, and Chinese. The fact that Marines guarded the Ministry of Oil but stood by while the other ministries and the National Museum were looted did little to dispel such theories.

I was unable to witness the actual invasion because, for reasons I may never know, I had been blacklisted by the former regime and could not get a visa. I did not reach the new Iraq until the fall of 2003. This book describes the country I saw then, as well as the one I remember from the days of the *ancien régime*.

I have come to realize that, despite the chaos and violence, the fall of 2003 was a unique time. Any lingering euphoria about the spring invasion was fading fast. During the course of my stay, an Iraqi politician was assassinated; the remnants of the U.N. headquarters were bombed a second time; foreign journalists and Iraqi policemen were targeted; and attacks against U.S. soldiers — and the corresponding U.S. counter-attacks — grew more intense. In the weeks after I left, a restaurant I'd frequented was blown up, an embassy across from an art gallery where I'd heard a children's choir was bombed, and the hotel I had stayed in was hit by a missile. And yet all this was but a foreshadowing of what was to follow. In retrospect, fall 2003 was a special window of opportunity to witness post-invasion Iraq without being totally locked down in a safe house or walled compound.

While some Iraqis still voiced support for the toppling of Saddam's regime, many others spoke bitterly of the U.S.'s real motives. And the American policy of ignoring the plight of ordinary Iraqis continued. The occupiers lived behind concrete barriers, cut off from the harsh reality of life for millions of citizens. Most knew little of power cuts, water shortages, kidnappings, unemployment; but they would learn.

Other things had also remained the same. My old Ministry of Information-appointed "minders" — so-called "guides," whom we'd once had to pay for the privilege of being spied on — were still at work, this time as fixers and translators for American TV crews. The businessmen who had done oil deals under the old regime were now in the "security" game, trading in international mercenaries. And the everyday reality for Iraqis, once difficult to document owing to government control, was still being ignored by the mainstream media, often because it was simply too dangerous to cover. Westerners heard about kidnappings and killings once the criminals started targeting foreigners, but Iraqis had been victims of the same crimes from the day the invasion began. The transition from tightly controlled police state to stateless anarchy left average citizens afraid for their lives.

The old fear of being informed on had given way to a more general anxiety about the safety of walking outside to buy a loaf of bread. As one old friend told me, "We don't know who to be afraid of ... Once there was only one Saddam — now there are dozens." Twenty years of war and sanctions, of waiting for some Godot-like liberation, and only this.

If my book can do anything, if there is anything left to say about a tragedy that seems to worsen every week, it is to pay tribute to the Iraqis I came to know over seven years. And to pay tribute to a culture that invented writing and architecture and survived invasions and conquerors, to a place that manages to be surreal and funny and heartbreaking and beautiful all at once. To a land that deserves a better fate than that offered up by presidential television, spiraling violence, and the missionaries of the petroleum industry — a land that spawned both Ishtar, the Babylonian goddess of love and beauty, and Rabia, the saint and poet who wrote:

The source of my suffering and loneliness is deep in my heart.
This is a disease no doctor can cure.
Only Union with the Friend can cure it.

With a fervent wish that the Friend will find Iraq again soon.

Two men and a woman at al-Gaylani mosque in Baghdad in 2000, shortly after Friday prayers

Prologue

AND SO I FOUND MYSELF once again on that familiar flight route from Vancouver to Heathrow to Queen Alia airport in Amman. It looked newer and slicker, with fewer wandering feral cats, every time I arrived.

Mohammed, who lived at the villa of Ali Maher, an eccentric architect friend I was to stay with, was waiting for me. He worked nights as a DJ at one of Amman's popular new nightspots and had come to pick me up at 6:00 a.m., right after work. As we drove through rush-hour traffic to Swaylah — the village turned suburb where Ali's father, General Fawaz Maher, had acquired land in the fifties — I noticed a few more BMWs and Range Rovers than on my last trip to Jordan a year before.

Every time Iraq has a crisis, Jordan prospers. First it was the Gulf War, then the U.N. embargo with its oil-for-food trade and smuggling profits in banned goods. Now the money was in hosting American military convoys and providing accommodation for Western NGOs and frightened U.N. personnel, biding their time until "security" was re-established, resolutions passed, deals made, destinies changed. In the meantime, Halliburton profited every time a newly rich Jordanian bought an SUV.

All the while Mohammed, a young Bedouin with a pierced nose, spoke to me about hip hop, the latest New York street fashions, and the tribe his grandfather came from. We drove past Bedouin villages on the side of the highway that looked like afterthoughts, thrown together with a certain military-meets-campground style. Goats nibbled desert shrubs as we crawled by in clouds of exhaust.

Mohammed thought that I could easily pass for one of his tribespeople and — like so many Middle Easterners — did not quite buy my claim to Canadian-ness. And so I began my story, whose emphasis and parameters would change every time I told it, depending on who was asking the perennial question: So, where are you from?

I told Mohammed about the great-grandparents from Lebanon, who had fled the Turks and landed in Canada in 1908. I did not get into my father's Anglo-Danish-French-Mohawk pedigree. I downplayed the Orthodox Christian bit and mentioned my mother's conversion to Islam when I was ten. Sometimes the whole process was so exhausting that I would just answer, "I'm from Vancouver" — as good and honest an answer as any. But I was in a fine traveling mood that day and up for a little local solidarity, which Mohammed soon obliged me with.

"*Ochti*," he said, half smiling: *sister*. I had passed the test.

WHEN WE ARRIVED AT THE VILLA, I was greeted by Ali, an architect renowned for his hospitality to young artists. Over tea, I explained that I was planning to look up old Iraqi friends in Amman, and mentioned Karim, the principal cellist in the Iraqi National Orchestra, who — the last I'd heard — had taken a teaching job at the Jordanian Academy of Music. "You mean Karim Wasfi?" Ali replied. "He lives at my place when he's in town!" It turned out that Karim even slept in the same ornate bed, specially built for King Farouk by Ali's father, that would be mine for the night.

The coincidence — it seemed that Ali and Karim had met a few years before I'd met them, in Amman and Baghdad, respectively — became weirder when I learned that Karim was now in Baghdad. He had forsaken his cello and taken a job as the director of a new American-backed NGO, the Iraqi Institute for Democracy.

As I lay on the bed that had once cradled an Egyptian monarch and a brilliant Iraqi musician, I tried to get my head around Karim's abrupt shift from fierce Iraqi nationalist and defender of Saddam to poster boy for the "democratic" fruits of regime change. As I dozed off, I noticed something plastic and colorful on the floor. I reached out and drew it near. It was a Sears card with Karim's name on it.

I put it down immediately. What kind of ominous talisman was this? What had happened to Karim? What was happening to Iraq? I fell asleep and dreamed of cars driving slowly down burning highways.

Chapter 1: War is Over

Oh Baghdad, Baghdad, You are in my blood

AMMAN, JORDAN, SEPTEMBER 2003. The headline concert for the Souk Ukaz Music Festival. Kazem al-Saher, Iraq's most famous pop star, crooned the rousing chorus of the song he had penned during the American invasion of his homeland. The voice of the handsome young singer reverberated throughout the ancient stone amphitheater, built by Roman hands two thousand years earlier. But on stage he was a tiny figure, dwarfed by his large orchestra and the huge crowd. His fans held up Iraqi flags as they clapped and chanted the lyrics with him:

Oh Baghdad, suffer no more ...
You are the Mecca of intoxicated lovers
You carried your pain alone for too long
Throw your wounds onto my chest and embrace my little heart.
Civilization will not survive without a soul and a conscience
Oh Baghdad, you are in my blood

Swaying, shouting, singing, the roar of the crowd almost drowned out the Iraqi star.

This was downtown Amman, home to the city's ever-changing refugee population. Most of the Palestinians had settled by now, and it was fleeing Iraqis who currently lived in the tenements near the bus station (while their wealthier countrymen resided in gated uptown villas), taking low-level jobs in the nearby souks. They were Amman's latest underclass. And tonight they were angry. They could never have afforded the $100 entrance fee to see their idol, whose mix of traditional *makam* love songs with Western-style pop had induced a nostalgic frenzy in the thousands of young Iraqis now swarming the theater.

Trying to cover my cleavage and cameras as best I could with an old Uzbeki shawl, I pushed my way through the mob. I was accompanied by a ragtag group of festival organizers as well as Noura Jumblatt, the wife of the Lebanese politician Walid Jumblatt, who was a special guest. We had barely made it inside before fighting broke out between angry young Iraqis, Jordanian police, and the fine, upstanding ticket holders of Amman. Crowd-control methods were rather brutal, but the sounds of batons thwacking flesh were drowned out by the loud, incessant chanting of Kazem's name by the thousands of fans already cramming the stadium.

When the superstar finally came on stage and launched into his hit, "Baghdad La Tatallamy," the crowd exploded. Out came the Iraqi flags. Whole families began dancing in the aisles. The *shebab* (youth) poured in from everywhere, even jumping over the steep walls at the top of the amphitheater. Outnumbered, the police tried in vain to stop them. There was a feeling of great emotion and great danger. It felt like anything could happen.

Al-Saher began another song about Baghdad, "Too Much Talk," a romantic ballad that spoke of the city as a jealous lover:

Oh Baghdad, will God ever again create such beauty?
You are closer to me than my heart

The mood of the crowd hovered somewhere between religious ecstasy and frenzied love.

When the English diva Sarah Brightman came on stage, her long hair flowing over an elegant evening dress, to perform the duet "War is Over" with Kazem, her voice was barely audible. As she mouthed the words, "In morning dew, a glorious scene came through, like war is over now ... I feel I am coming home again," no sound was heard, so the crowd shouted Kazem's name and chanted patriotic Iraqi slogans. Who was silencing the British singer? Conspiracy theories blossomed, until it was revealed that the enthusiastic mob had accidentally ripped out her mike cord.

We all knew that the war was far from over. Still, there were always moments when it seemed to be waning, offering brief glimpses of joy and peace. I recalled my second trip to Iraq, back in 1998. The three-day American bombing campaign, codenamed Desert Fox, coincided with Christmas and Ramadan, so there was a heightened sense of celebration when it stopped. I remembered Christmas Eve, when an air-raid siren sounded at midnight, just as I was coming back from Mass in a Baghdad church. At the al-Rashid Hotel, two French journalists (one was Georges Malbrunot, who would be kidnapped in August 2004 and released four months later) were just weaving their way in from a champagne-soaked party at the French embassy. When they heard the siren, one called, "*Qu'est-ce qui se passe?*" and his friend replied, "*C'est encore la guerre!*"

As it turned out, it wasn't war again. It was just a false alarm. All the hacks made tracks to the Press Center hoping for another good story, but all we found were a few sleepy Ministry of Information officials drinking chai and watching Fashion TV by satellite. Only a few days later I would stay up all night in those same claustrophobic rooms to break the story of the first firefight in years between Iraqi and American forces (which would mark the escalation of the no-fly zone bombings by the US and UK), but tonight things were relatively calm. Since it was midnight and Christmas to boot, the motley crew of French, Italian, German, Japanese, American, British, Canadian, and Gulf Arab journalists all headed over to the ABC TV Christmas party to unwind. There were even some Iraqis among us, mainly translators and fixers.

After a few drinks, someone put on a Tom Petty CD and a few of us started dancing. But somehow, the music didn't seem to fit the occasion. So I went off to wake up a Palestinian cameraman who I knew had some CDs of Umm Kulthum stashed in his suitcase. Ten minutes later, with the great Egyptian diva's full-throated alto booming through the night, some of the Qatari TV reporters got up to dance. I joined them, moving my hips and hands in the serpentine way I'd honed after years in the Middle East.

And then, in room 810 of the al-Rashid Hotel in Baghdad, on Christmas Eve and the first Friday of Ramadan, something vaguely miraculous took place. A tall, blond American TV reporter got up and started to dance with us. Slowly, different nationalities joined in: first the French, then the Japanese, then the Italians. Eventually, even the Iraqi translators were dancing. Time seemed suspended. I remember passing pomegranate seeds around, squeezing them from the fleshy pulp of a ripe fruit in a quasi-communion. World peace may have been a long shot, and the bombing in Baghdad had only stopped a few hundred hours earlier, but here was an American dancing with an Iraqi. I was momentarily high on belly-dance diplomacy. With the right stomach muscles and a bit of grace and rhythm, it seemed, anything was possible.

From then on, my dancing skills opened all kinds of doors in Iraq. At a New Year's Eve wedding, guests who had previously been suspicious of my pidgin Arabic and vaguely foreign look came around when they saw me dance. The right hip movements seemed to speak more powerfully than any words. Soon I found myself dancing with a group of Iraqi women and children who accepted me, at least while the music was playing, into their circle.

Five years on, in the amphitheater in Jordan, I could not watch from the sidelines as homesick Iraqis danced with their hearts and hips. I made my way down towards the center of the stage, framed by fans and menacing-looking military police. Tottering in my heels and balancing two cameras over my shawl, I somehow managed to jump five feet down from the last row of ancient stone seats and join the dancing in the mosh pit.

As I watched the young Iraqis dance, I reflected on all that their nation had endured. In the twentieth century, it had survived British occupation, the installation and dissolution of a monarchy, a CIA-backed coup that had brought the Baath party to power, the rise of Saddam Hussein, and a harrowing war with neighboring Iran. Then, after eight years of hellish conflict that left hundreds of thousands dead on both sides and almost bankrupted Iraq, Saddam invaded Kuwait. George Bush Sr. used the opportunity to "bomb Iraq back into the stone age" in an $85 billion crusade. Far from the glorified video game it appeared to be on Western television screens, the Gulf War was a violent assault on an impoverished nation that left an estimated 150,000 Iraqi civilians dead and violated several Geneva conventions. Thousands of retreating Iraqi soldiers were massacred by American troops, and water-treatment plants were deliberately targeted.

But what followed was worse. Ten years of the harshest sanctions in the history of the U.N., exacerbated by Saddam's despotism, left half of the Iraqi population without access to clean drinking water and thirty percent of adults suffering from anemia, the majority women in their child-bearing years. Before the embargo, Iraq's socialized medicine and great oil wealth had meant that the biggest health issue was obesity; by the mid-nineties, infant mortality was on a par with sub-Saharan Africa. The Iraqi dinar was devalued by more than a thousand percent, and almost overnight, the lives of most citizens went from comfortable to desperate, with many women forced to prostitute themselves to feed their families. The education system, once the envy of the Arab world, was in ruins. The resulting "brain drain" saw a fifth of the population emigrate, many to neighboring countries, the luckiest to Britain and America, the same countries whose fighter planes were taking part in regular bombing raids in the so-called "no-fly zones."

While a small number of Iraqis — including Saddam's family and cronies — were enriching themselves through sanctions profiteering, life for the majority was grim. The middle class disappeared and the gap between rich and poor grew into a gulf. People with Ph.D.s drove taxis while uneducated smugglers drove Mercedes. The Baghdad book market was full of exquisite Arabic and English volumes, family heirlooms being sold for a few dollars by parents hoping to scrape together enough money to buy medicine for their children. In the absence of any cultural, social, or economic development, a whole new generation of angry, unemployed, and unmarried young men was seduced by the lure of Hollywood action movies and the promise of fundamentalist Islam.

This was the legacy the Americans inherited when they invaded in 2003. Their motherland was in dire straits, but still the young Iraqis danced, a sense of violence and despair hanging over their ecstasy. I noticed that, as the night wore on, the few young women in the crowd — mainly dressed in jeans and T-shirts and often waving Iraqi flags — began to edge away from the stage, retreating back to the seating area. The crowd was wild, and grew even wilder when the last song ended. Before I knew it I was caught up in a swarm of young Iraqi men, grabbing, pushing, and shoving me in all directions. I started to scream and kick my way out. A Jordanian policeman stepped in, and a male festival organizer had to accompany me all the way outside, standing behind me the whole time. As a taxi carried me away, al-Saher's melody was still ringing in my head:

Oh Baghdad, Baghdad, You are in my blood

My own connection to Iraq was beginning to feel inescapable. After six years of reporting from the troubled but fascinating country, I felt somehow joined to it, as if our destinies were entwined. It seemed to be with me always, not only in neighboring Jordan but even in faraway Vancouver, where I was forever meeting Iraqis who told sad tales of exile and longing.

In less than a decade I had witnessed crisis after crisis, writing of doctors and dying children, missiles and wrecked infrastructure, but also of hope and happiness, of music, theater, poetry — even dancing. After this latest invasion, I had decided to return to find all the people I'd come to know over my last five trips to Iraq: the actors, the writers, the mothers, the children, the minders, the doctors, the imams and priests, Sufis and poets, hotel clerks and floor cleaners and even bureaucrats. I wanted to write the epilogue to their stories. I wanted to see if they were still alive, if their families were safe, to see how they were doing after the latest trauma that had swept through their land like some rampant fire, destroying everything in its path while the arsonists promised redemption, freedom, *democracy.*

I knew I might not even find them in the post-war chaos, with no telephones, no electricity, no security. But at least I could tread in their old footsteps, and in mine as well, in the hopes of finding some sliver of illumination, some momentary epiphany to calm my fears about the future. I wanted people to know about the real Iraq, not the superficial televised version, but communicating that reality had always been a Herculean task, fraught with racism, ignorance, and cultural blind spots.

I had received a message from Ramzi Kysia, the tireless humanitarian from North Carolina who has worked for years in Iraq with a group called Voices in the Wilderness. In it he warned me of the dangers of the "new Iraq," the kidnappings, rapes, and murders that had now become commonplace. It was a grim portrait of life during (continuing) wartime, and I immediately thought of all the times I'd walked alone and unhassled down al-Sadoun street, shopped in the souks and gone to the theater at night.

I shuddered to think that Iraq might end up as another Afghanistan: invaded, then abandoned and forgotten. I did not want Joe Public to read yet another grisly news item about *terrorism in Iraq* — the self-fulfilling prophecy of the American neo-con cabal — and shake his head and say, "*Tsk tsk*, those crazy Iraqis."

I'm not sure why I care so much about Iraq. Perhaps it has something to do with my mixed Middle Eastern and North American ancestry. But I think that anyone who has spent more than a few months in the country gets hooked, in an almost masochistic way. It is a land that stretches the very fiber of your being, pulling you between despair and euphoria, pushing your spiritual and psychological limits until you're convinced there really is a God, or at the very least, some benevolent goddess, some behind-the-scenes Ishtar pulling strings beyond the parameters of your usual mortal existence.

Cradle of civilization, birthplace of Abraham, capital of the Islamic world under the great caliph Haroun al-Rashid, and more recently a center of pan-Arabism and artistic and intellectual life, Iraq is not a place to be considered lightly. It is a place to read poetry, a place to study holy books, to ponder the meaning of civilization. It is a place to dance, a place to sing *makam,* the eternal expression of love and longing. It is a place you remember, not just for its long-dead gods and kings and architects, but also for their descendants, the men and women and children who live on its ancient earth, despite the land mines and depleted uranium and heartbreaking violence.

And so perhaps that's what I *can* do. After all, I am only a writer. I eke out an existence in dollars and words. But — somewhere between the fire and the garden — I can remember.

Oh Baghdad, Baghdad, You are in my blood

Chapter 2: Fly Me to the Moon

A FEW DAYS LATER I found myself flying into Baghdad, thinking not of poetry or love but of surface-to-air missiles. I tried to relax and block such thoughts from my heat-oppressed mind, but it was hard when I was sitting next to the head honcho for the American Coalition Provisional Authority (CPA) in Baghdad.

If it hadn't been for my friend L, a Canadian businessman whose uncanny skills had helped him prosper under both the old and new regimes, I never would have made it onto the flight. On most of my previous trips to Iraq I had come by car along the treacherous highway that runs through lunar-like desert terrain from Amman to Baghdad. This was always a difficult voyage, but more so since the war, with murderous bandits now lurking among the Bedouin villages and vast stretches of no man's land.

Susan, a contact of L's who worked at a security firm with the unlikely name of Custer Battles, had arranged the plane ticket for me. "There is one thing that you must never do," her travel agent had told me when I booked. "You must never let anyone know that you are a journalist." It seemed these flights, organized by the CPA, were then off limits to anyone but CPA staff, military types, a few select Washington-backed NGOs, and what remained of the U.N. presence in Iraq.

"What should I say if anyone asks me what I'm doing?" I asked her.

"Just say that you work for Custer Battles." The company was in charge of security at the Baghdad airport; several months later the U.S. State Department would charge it with massive fraud.

Now, I'd met some "security" fellows. There were some staying at my hotel. I'd had dinner with them the night before. Big burly guys with Manchester accents, ex British military types who'd probably seen action in Northern Ireland. You wouldn't want to mess with them.

They had tattooed biceps but got all sentimental when they talked about their mums. They were working for ABC news.

When I went to purchase my ticket later that day from the Royal Jordanian office, a motherly type named Nafisa looked me up and down. "Who do you work for?" she asked.

"Uh ... Custer Battles," I demurred, my head suddenly full of cowboys and Indians.

"Are you sure you're not a journalist?" she inquired. "You know, they're not allowed on these flights."

I looked at Nafisa. I put my hand to my heart and offered up an earnest expression that I hoped would convey, "No, of course I'm not a journalist. Do I look like one? A journalist would be taller and blonder and wear a flak jacket and have more money and always be an American no matter what side of the 49th parallel they came from. A journalist would also be a man and carry much neater notebooks than mine. He would have a small silver flask of whisky in his back pocket and his name would never be Hadani."

"I work for Custer Battles," I repeated. "I'm in, um ... accounting."

After a sleepless night, I took a taxi at 4:00 a.m. the next morning to Amman's military airport. I slumped into a chair in the tiny waiting room and surveyed the scene. Nattily dressed RAF officers chatted discreetly while uniformed Americans fiddled with their hand luggage. This was already a very different experience than the midnight Iraqi border one. Instead of the usual visitors from dodgy regimes, international "businessmen" and the odd peace activist, here I was surrounded by English-speaking men in uniform. I was somewhat of a novelty.

The middle-aged blond man sitting next to me had taken me by surprise, striking up a conversation in the waiting lounge. "Where are you from?" he had wondered with an American twang.

"Um, Canada," I had mumbled. "And you?"

"I'm from Virginia. My name's Hank."

I introduced myself and then Hank asked, "What are you doing in Baghdad?"

"I, um ... am working for an NGO," I managed, which seemed a good answer.

"Oh, yeah," said Hank casually, "which one?"

Quick: think, I told my sleepy self, wracking my brain for NGO names. Finally, after what seemed an eternity with Hank's unblinking military gaze staring me down, I blurted out, "SAPED."

SAPED was the actual acronym of a small, grassroots NGO I'd recently become acquainted with. They were hippies from the Shuswap area of B.C. who worked with peasant co-operatives in Guatemala and had expressed some interest in assisting the women's center in Gaza that I'd written about for *Ms. Magazine*. We had also spoken before I left Vancouver about the possibility of starting a woman's project in Iraq, so my narrative was not entirely fiction.

"I'm uh ... looking to .... um ... identify ways in which we can support appropriate women's projects .... um, women's and children's projects. And what are you doing in Iraq?" I added, before he could ask me any more awkward questions.

"Well," he smiled, "some people call me the mayor of Baghdad. I'm the regional director for the CPA in Baghdad." And he pulled a red lollipop from his knapsack and began to suck on it.

Hank had just come from a week's vacation, a fishing trip with his daughter on the Potomac. "It was really relaxing," he told me, his blue eyes sparkling, "and we caught lots of mackerel." I asked him how long he'd been on the job. "About a month," he replied, with a tone that still suggested a hint of eagerness.

"Isn't it hard to tell who the real Baathists are?" I asked Hank after we'd put on our seatbelts in the plane. "I mean, the ones that gave orders, not the ones that followed them?"

Hank smiled. "Oh, no. The 'have-nots' were pretty quick to tell us who the 'haves' were under the old regime." (Soon afterwards, the CPA admitted that they were recruiting former *mukhabarat* — Saddam's intelligence officers.)

Hank was an old US-AID hand who had worked in El Salvador and Bolivia. Like many in the CPA, he had far more experience in Latin America than in the Middle East; his Spanish was fluent but he spoke no Arabic. I wondered later if the American adventure in Iraq had failed in part because they had assumed the country was just another banana republic that would be swayed by fistfuls of dollars and armies of mercenaries.

Hank seemed bright and personable, like the sunny side of the world's most lethal military force. I played my NGO role by bringing up the plight of Iraqi women, whose status had once been among the highest of women in the Arab world. I mentioned that before the first Gulf War, forty percent of Iraqi doctors were women, and that the first female government minister in the Arab world had come from Iraq. Now, thanks to decades of war and twelve years of sanctions, Iraqi women were still dealing with massive unemployment, high infant-mortality rates, skyrocketing cancer rates and — especially since the U.S. invasion — a total lack of security.

Hank seemed genuinely interested and listened to much of what I had to say as if it were totally new information.

"Does the CPA have a specific program in place to deal with women's issues?" I asked him.

"Ummm ... We're looking into some possibilities," he mumbled.

New ideas began percolating in my mind. Perhaps I really *would* start a project for Iraqi women, I thought. My book research could double as research on Iraqi women. I would even enlist the help of the old hippie NGO. It was all meant to be: the plane ride, meeting Hank. I was going to help save Iraq! But first, I was in desperate need of some sleep.

"Well," said Hank, "I'd be interested to hear the results of your research. If you can find a local NGO to work with, we might be able to help you out. You should come by the palace sometime for a chat." He meant Saddam's old Republican palace — now in the heart of the fortified American "Green Zone" — which had been appropriated as CPA headquarters.

As we approached Baghdad airport, I thought of all the times I'd been there before. The first time, in 1997, I had been waiting for the Russian nationalist politician Vladimir Zhirinovsky, who was supposed to defy the sanctions and pay a visit. The welcoming party included a large troupe of dancing Bedouins, who waited for hours with a herd of sheep ready to be slaughtered in celebration. But Zhirinovsky never came, and the sheep were spared their fate. Then there was the time in 2000, when a sanctions-busting flight arrived from Spain and hope was high for an end to the decade-long siege. I had interviewed Khaled, a young floor cleaner who had never been up in a plane before, but dreamed of flying somewhere, anywhere.

Now the Saddam International Airport, after being looted and stripped bare by U.S. soldiers, housed a prison and a Burger King. It even had a new name: Baghdad International.

Once we landed in Baghdad, we were immediately enveloped in the 110-degree heat. "It's much cooler now than it was last month," Hank told me, as we walked onto the tarmac. My computer bag had morphed into a 400-pound monster and I felt like I was walking underwater. Somehow I made it through, past airplane hangars and military barracks and rooms full of young Americans in uniform, to the "customs area." The weirdest thing about the new Iraq, I thought, was not just the shock of hearing so much American English, but the sight of so many clean-shaven blond men in shorts. In the old Iraq the traditional Baathist ensemble of double-breasted Italian suit and heavy moustache was *de rigueur*, summer or winter.

We were greeted by a group of multiracial Marines as well as a small contingent of Iraqi "trainees." I half expected them to be wearing name tags. One of the trainees fiddled with a small digital camera and eventually took my photo. An African-American corporal stamped my passport with a kind of entry visa that simply said: Baghdad International Airport, September 5, 2003. At the bottom, almost as an afterthought, it said: Iraq 1404 CPA.

The area we were in was a hundred yards away from the old Saddam International Airport, a kind of Iraqi Charles de Gaulle designed by a French architectural firm in the relative prosperity of the late seventies. That was where I had waited for Zhirinovsky in 1997 with the dancing Bedouins and the sheep, and where the departures board had been frozen in time for years, flashing "flight 376 now boarding for Cairo" — the last flight to be scheduled before the Gulf War, on January 15, 1991.

Then, I had written about the airport as a kind of Sleeping Beauty, kept alive for years by dedicated staff who, despite the no-fly zones and the total lack of flights, came to work every day. Iraqi Airways employees watered plants, cleaned floors, practiced their English over coffee and, best of all, took simulated flying lessons, hoping that one day, their prince would come — perhaps not Zhirinovsky, but some kind of international flouting of sanctions that would open them up to the world again.

In 2000, sanctions-busting flights began to arrive from Turkey, Morocco, Spain, and Greece, and internal flights began again to Basra and Mosul, in defiance of the no-fly zones. I flew to Basra economy class and upgraded on the return flight — for an extra ten bucks — to first class. I remembered the leather bucket seats and the incredible lounge muzak — Tom Jones singing "Fly Me to the Moon" and "Viva Las Vegas," as if the entire flight were unintentionally retro-cool.

A stewardess served us fluorescent orange drinks and reminisced about flying to Rio and Rome in the seventies. Now it was just back and forth to Basra — but at least she was working. The heavily mustachioed party in front of me puffing away on Cohibas turned out to be the president's nephew and his entourage. I remember looking out the window and thinking of all the long-suffering Iraqis below, and then turning to my minder, Ali, and saying, "Why can't the Americans and the Iraqis just sit down together and make some kind of deal?"

Ali turned to me and said, *sotto voce*, "They already have."

But something had gone wrong somewhere along the way. Saddam was now in hiding, his sons were dead, and Tariq Aziz was being held at the infamous airport gulag — reportedly in the old terminal, which had once housed hundreds of Iraqi Airways employees and welcomed all those sanctions-busting flights. In addition to being used to hold prisoners indefinitely in inhumane conditions, part of the old terminal had become a money-printing factory.

As I stepped out into the harsh daylight of the new Iraq, I thought again of young Khaled, the floor cleaner from my 2000 trip, who had been so in awe of all those newly arrived international flights. "It's my dream," he'd told me shyly. "To fly."

Chapter 3: Welcome in Baghdad

A FAMILIAR IF SOMEWHAT haggard face was waiting to greet me at the airport. It was L. He had come to pick me up complete with driver and SUV. His face was ashen, as if he had been up all night; later I would learn that he had, and that his evening had involved mortar fire. But for now, even an exhausted-looking acquaintance with dubious business partners was a comfort. I was glad I wasn't encountering the strange new landscape of post-invasion Iraq all alone.

L greeted me with a half-hearted "Welcome to Iraq" and a slightly bemused chuckle. He looked much older than the last time I'd seen him, in 2002. "Listen," he said as I put my bags in the SUV, "I've got some business to do. Omar will take you to the hotel I've booked. I'll send a driver round later to bring you to my place for lunch." A few seconds later, we were off, Omar and I, into the wild blue yonder of "liberated" Iraq.

As we drove past American tanks and barbed-wire garrisons, I realized that the entire area around the airport had become a giant army encampment. Alongside the highway — now called "sniper's road" because of the almost daily attacks on U.S. soldiers — I saw men with donkey carts full of petrol cans. "They are selling gasoline," Omar explained, gesturing to the huge line at the nearby petrol station, "for those who don't have time to wait in line." Next to the Alabaman accents and the short pants, this was the most curious thing I'd seen so far. But as Alice once observed in another upside-down world, things would get curiouser and curiouser.

"Lots has changed," I said to Omar.

"Yes," he agreed. "L has gained a lot of weight since the last time, don't you think?"

"Must be the American diet," I mused.

"Yes, yes," agreed Omar. " The Americans, they drink so much Coke. We, we drink water."

Omar told me he'd been up all night with a sick child. "My daughter," he began. "It was something she ate, or something she drank, we don't know." The doctors at the hospital, overwhelmed by the wounded and the dozens of other children with often-fatal water-borne illnesses, had given her a few aspirin to calm the fever and sent the family home.

We entered a residential neighborhood, which looked relatively normal, except for a burned and looted bank and a few sandbagged buildings. We were not far from Qadisayah, where one of the last big battles of Baghdad had been fought before the city fell to the Americans. Then we passed an area close to the Amaryiah bomb shelter, where an American bomb had incinerated four hundred people during the first Gulf War. I had visited the site in 1997, with a group of Americans from Voices in the Wilderness. I remembered that two of the Americans had broken down in tears at the horrific sight of human skin grafted onto concrete walls. A woman whose daughter had died in the attack was the unofficial guide to the site, which had become a kind of shrine to the dead. She spoke of temperatures that had reached over four hundred degrees Fahrenheit and said that many had been boiled alive when the bomb struck the water system.

My reaction had not been as emotional as the two Americans'. I felt slightly disgusted that this tragedy, like so many others that had befallen innocent Iraqi civilians, was being exploited by a regime that had little respect for the rights of those same victims. My minder from the Ministry of Information that day had been a young Kurdish fellow. It was my first trip to Baghdad, and indeed my second day on assignment, so I asked him point-blank: "Don't you think it's a bit hypocritical of the regime to make so much of this, after what they did to your people? What about Hallabja [the Kurdish village gassed by the Iraqi army in 1988]?"

"Officially," he replied, "it was the Iranians that committed that particular atrocity." His tone hinted at his real opinion.

Not much has changed that way, I mused — both sides blaming each other for atrocities. Now for every mass grave the Americans dug up they had to contend with the specter of thousands of civilians killed during the invasion; for every "resistance" bombing, the ghosts of all the Iraqis killed in the first Gulf War and by the ensuing sanctions.

Just as my thoughts were turning black, Omar reached for his glove compartment and pulled out not a gun but a Britney Spears CD. "You like?" he asked, smiling. He was trying to make me feel at home.

As "Oops, I Did It Again" coursed through the SUV's sound system, we passed the main power station, with its four smokestacks.

"This is how you can tell how much electricity there will be," explained Omar. "If you pass by in the morning and there is only one going, then you know you will have only a few hours. If you see a second one, like today, then maybe you will get five or six hours."

Omar told me a bit of his life story. He had been working for L for the last six years. Trained as an orthopedic surgeon, he ended up taking a job as a driver at the al-Rashid Hotel because the money was better. "Is it true that the drivers there were part of the *mukhabarat* [the secret police]?" I asked. Omar looked at me and smiled. "Only about ten percent of them, not all."

"Baghdad doesn't look so different," I said as I gazed through the window at familiar riverbank scenes and distant monuments.

"Maybe," Omar replied. "But you will see that the people have changed. They are bad now. There are many bad people." This was not the usual "Welcome to Baghdad" speech I'd come to expect from my previous visits. "Maybe one thousand people a day are killed in Iraq now," he continued, "because of the security situation, the crime. Before, maybe these crimes happened once in a while. But now you will see that most of the people are carrying guns."

I asked him if he had a gun, looking for one out of the corner of my eye.

"No, I don't carry a gun," Omar replied, "because I have a different policy. If someone comes to take the car, I will give him the key and say, 'take it.' He may have a thousand reasons to kill me. If I shoot him, I may shoot in the air, but he will shoot straight. My life is not worth it."

It was nice to know someone had his priorities straight, even if it was a one-time al-Rashid *mukhabarat* driver who now worked for a "collaborating" contractor who had once done business with Saddam Hussein. After all, SUVs are hardly worth dying for.

"That was a police station," announced Omar matter-of-factly as we passed a bombed building. I gazed at the black shrouds announcing dead loved ones, and then at dozens of shops selling satellite dishes, refrigerators, and air conditioners. Finally we reached the Hayat Tower, the hotel L had booked for me in Karradah, a middle-class residential area in central Baghdad. It was an oddly Andalusian-looking fortress, next door to the Hotel Sindbad — the headquarters, I would find out later, of a Kurdish faction, complete with dozens of Kalashnikov-toting *peshmergas* ["freedom fighters"].

I entered the faux-marble lobby, with its elaborate chandelier, and checked in.

"Is there a phone in my room?" I inquired.

"Yes," said Ali, the smiling front-desk man. "But there is no outside telephone line." As I entered one of the hotel's two semi-functioning elevators, a group of armed Ghurkhas arrived in the lobby. Later I would find out that these genuine Nepalese warriors had been hired by the Americans to guard the airport.

I had been given a room on the third floor, directly underneath the Ghurkhas. (A few months later, a single cruise missile would pierce the hotel's sixth floor.) Beyond exhaustion, I sat on the 1970s sofa and switched on the television. What a surprise! There were dozens of channels: Al Jazeera, BBC, Al Arabiya ... I felt a pang for the Iraqi state television — propaganda with a disarming sense of naivety — I'd come to know and love. I fell asleep in front of an episode of Arabic-subtitled *Dynasty*.

I AWOKE SEVERAL HOURS LATER to a jarring sound. I thought perhaps the air conditioning had broken down, but it was louder than that, a kind of hard, sustained rattling. I went to the window and looked out. On one side was the hotel's heart-shaped swimming pool. On the other was an empty yard where a man kept pigeons. Maybe sixty feet from the pigeon coop was a busy street, where traffic had slowed to allow the advance of five huge Abrams tanks. I looked at the Americans, absorbed in their mission, and then back at the man, absorbed in his pigeons. I couldn't sleep for the noise, but the bird man seemed oblivious.

Chapter 4: Crossing Borders

A NOVELTY OF THE NEW IRAQ, my Andalusian fortress tower had an internet café. When I went to check it out later that evening, I thought that the fellow behind the desk looked vaguely familiar. Perhaps it was just that weird traveling feeling. But then I noticed that a kindly faced woman in an abaya sitting near him also looked familiar. We smiled at each other and after a minute realized that we did know each other. Incredibly, this was the woman with whom I'd shared a service taxi to Baghdad on my first trip to Iraq in 1997. She was a Jordanian who'd married an Iraqi, and the man behind the counter was her son, whom I'd met briefly when we'd stopped at her house on the outskirts of Baghdad. In a rather startling coincidence, he was now running the internet café at the hotel.

I said hello to the lady in the abaya — whom I only knew as Umm (mother of) Marwan — and greeted her son. It had been six years and a regime change since we'd met, so it was hard to know where to start.

"Remember when we crossed the border?" Umm Marwan asked me.

How could I forget? It had been quite a trip. We had been traveling with two medical students, a Jordanian Bedouin named Khalil and a young Iraqi called Ali. Then, as now, most journalists wanting to enter Iraq had to pay a lot of money to travel in a private car. At the border, you then had to fork over copious amounts of baksheesh to get your equipment past the series of charming border guards and various "computer inspectors." But for reasons of both economy (mainly) and adventure (partly), I had chosen the group-taxi route and gone in as a "civilian."

For this honor I had enjoyed the attentions of some particularly B-movie-looking mustachioed border guards. They had come for me at the baggage checkpoint and, separating me from my traveling companions, had led me to a dark little room several hundred yards away. They turned out to be rather friendly thugs, and even offered me sweet tea as they rifled through my things and examined my passport. Above us, the ubiquitous portrait of Saddam Hussein surveyed the scene.

One of the policemen found a few photographs I had brought with me on my journey and pointed to them accusingly. One showed me in my grandparents' Lebanese village in the Bekka Valley, standing on a hillside next to the village shepherd, who is playing the pan pipes and wearing a kaffiyeh wrapped around his head. This seemingly innocent, rather pastoral snapshot — brought along, ironically, as a kind of visual proof of my "Arab solidarity" — was suddenly the object of intense scrutiny.

"Where is this?" demanded the policeman with the slightly thicker moustache. I told him about my recent visit to my ancestral Lebanese village, but to no avail.

"Aha!" said the man with the thinner moustache. "You say you are Canadian, but here you are in Lebanon!" He smiled with great satisfaction, as if he had caught me in a trap.

"I think," said his colleague, "this is not Lebanon, this is northern Iraq ... And you are a Kurd!"

"But no," I protested, "I am a Canadian," knowing full well that a discussion of the relative merits of multiculturalism *à la canadienne* versus the Iraqi version would get me nowhere. Somehow I now found myself in the absurd position of having to prove my Canadian-ness to two Iraqi border policemen. I briefly pondered singing the national anthem, but decided against it.

And then came the *coup de grâce*: exhibit B, the second snapshot. This one was of me, dressed in *shalwar kameez* standing next to my Pakistani/Afghani ex-boyfriend in his Singapore home. How would I ever explain this?

"Who is he?" the policemen asked.

"Ah ... my boyfriend," I replied with a sudden feeling of dread.

"No," boomed the thickly-mustachioed one in a loud voice, "I am your boyfriend now." The two moustaches smiled and then broke into great gales of laughter.

In the end, the forces of global capitalism were stronger than any identity politics; the whole affair was settled for five dollars.

WHEN I FINALLY MADE IT to Baghdad in 1997, I found another, less penetrable border. The American journalists occupying several floors at the al-Rashid Hotel had erected huge psychological barricades. Apparently indifferent to the very real suffering around them, they dismissed any talk of soaring infant-mortality rates and growing malnutrition as mere "Iraqi propaganda." They lived and worked in their hotel rooms and their only contact with Iraqis seemed to be with their minders and drivers, all appointed by the Ministry of Information.

After spending my first few days in Iraq with a group of well-meaning but slightly paranoid Christian Americans on a "humanitarian mission," who would only eat bread and salted pistachios ("The meat might be contaminated" they whispered, "the vegetables lethal"), I started to go a bit strange myself. It wasn't until a French writer and gourmand whisked me away to a wonderful Baghdad restaurant and encouraged me to dig in, dismissing the humanitarians' concern as an obsessive American fear of germs, that I began to feel human.

After five weeks in Baghdad, I was virtually expelled by the Ministry of Information. I use the term "virtually" because it was more like an insistence that I leave very quickly rather than an actual expulsion, and because I still don't know the reason — whether it was because I was "suspicious," or because I had pissed off a Ministry notable who worked for CNN, or because I wasn't paying the minders enough baksheesh, or perhaps all three. The bottom line, I knew, was that I had transgressed boundaries; I had crossed certain borders that I shouldn't have.

In spite of this, I found myself back in Baghdad the following December, with a visa issued within hours of the first Desert Fox airstrike. And so I crossed the Iraqi border a second time, this time not in a group taxi but with an Associated Press (AP) photographer from Barcelona in a roomy utility vehicle. At pit stops during the ten-hour drive across the desert, people assumed he was my husband; even at the border, the company of a man with a Spanish passport seemed to facilitate my "passing" as a European. Instead of taking tea with the policemen, this time I sipped chai with Javier in the "VIP lounge," a comfortable space complete with sofas and satellite TV. We entered

Baghdad on the last night of American bombing, quietly checking into the al-Rashid Hotel. "Separate rooms," we insisted, much to the bewilderment of the desk clerk.

During my three-week stay in Baghdad, I did not avoid the Americans, who, together with media from around the globe, had congregated at the al-Rashid. In fact, while visiting the bombed-out homes of civilians, fasting for Ramadan and celebrating Christmas, I managed to fall in love with an American. He was a tall blond TV correspondent from New Jersey who got up to dance at the Christmas Eve party, and at some point that night, it happened. Somewhere in between a Tom Petty song ("Refugee," I think it was) and an Umm Kulthum lament, I fell hard.

The "secret police" were on to us immediately.

The American accompanied me to my room one night, and the next morning, everyone at the Ministry of Information seemed to know. "Must have been the elevator guards," I said to Mr. American Television, when he told me that a senior minder had taken him aside and said, "I know where you were last night" with a salacious smile. I later learned that, in the pre-embargo years, hidden cameras in the rooms of the al-Rashid had allegedly filmed foreign correspondents' follies for the amusement of minders and for possible blackmail purposes. Luckily, the budget for videotape seemed to have been another victim of sanctions-induced austerity.

But all in all, considering my cultural treason, the minders were pretty cool about the whole thing, with one exception. "Why?" one of them asked me incredulously one afternoon, "with all these fine specimens of Iraqi manhood around, did you choose that American? You will only regret this."

In the end, the minder was right. Mr. American Television looked good on screen, but in reality, all his shiny promises fell flat. It was just another war-zone romance.

IN 2000, I CROSSED INTO IRAQ ALONE, with a driver who spoke none of my languages. I contemplated the desert night in silence, occasionally sleeping, then waking to miles of empty sand and a sky full of stars. At the border, my driver did not have the correct baksheesh technique, so I was subjected to a midnight computer inspection and a mild interrogation.

"What are you doing in Iraq?" Should I explain about the *Wallpaper** magazine assignment on modern architecture in Baghdad?

"Journalist," I said bluntly. This time, ten dollars was required. Then a "team" of inspectors searched my luggage. They asked for the *Vogue* magazines in my suitcase. I tried to make a joke, retelling a Mullah Nasrudin story about donkeys and smugglers, but language got in the way and the joke fell flat. "Are you calling us donkeys?" asked an irate inspector. I distributed a few more magazines and was mercifully delivered from the whole weird scene.

Once in Baghdad, I was joined by a German photographer. English-speaking minders were in high demand so, based on our common rudimentary abilities in Spanish, we were assigned a stern but affable Spanish-speaking minder. We cruised the streets of Baghdad in our big old Buick, on the prowl for Bauhaus buildings. With my basic Arabic and German and my experience of Iraq, I was the cultural and linguistic go-between, striking a delicate balance between Kais, from the old, Stalinist school of Iraqi minders, and Daniel, the organized photographer from Frankfurt.

The faces of the women we passed on the streets, taking children to school, walking to work, struggling to survive in an economy ruined by war and sanctions, reminded me of the Lebanese side of my family. A woman's head would turn and I would see a cousin; we would round a corner and I would spot my grandmother. What was I doing in that big car? they seemed to be asking me with their gaze.

ON MY NEXT TRIP TO IRAQ in the winter of 2000, on assignment for *Ms. Magazine*, my mission was to find some of these women and report on their reality. If Iraqis in general were invisible to the Western eye, Iraqi women were that much harder to see. Although their presence in public life had diminished since the first Gulf War, they were still active in many areas of society. But as a traveler, there was a threshold that had to be crossed before you could really get inside the lives of women. In fact, the road to Baghdad was a man's world, conspicuously absent of any sign of womankind. From my hotel in Amman, full of hookers and tourists, to the venerable al-Rashid Hotel in Iraq's capital, it was just a blur of desert highway, roadside stands run by men and male border guards, occasionally interrupted by strategically placed rock piles created by Bedouin to mark the landscape according to the stars.

And once I got to Baghdad, my encounters with women felt almost clandestine. Every interview had to be arranged through a minder, who might have been tall or short, good-humored or stern, but who was always a man. This absence of the X chromosome factor threw me into a kind of gender amnesia; I traveled in psychic drag. Sitting with my driver in the roast-chicken joint on the last Jordanian pit stop before Iraq, where men sat smoking and eating and watching soccer matches on TV, and wild cats waited in silence for the right opportunity to pounce on unfinished dinner plates, I was one of the boys. Although I squatted afterwards in a separate Turkish toilet, outside of which a man waited holding a bar of green soap, and I wore a long black dress, I was free to comment on the soccer match and make jokes with the Jordanian and Iraqi men whose wives were waiting at home. After all, I was the one paying the dinner bill for my driver. My status as a foreigner outweighed the baggage of my sex.

I WAS JOLTED BACK to my present trip by the sound of gunshots outside the café. "Come away from the window!" shouted Marwan. He led his mother and me to the back of the room, where we crouched down next to empty cartons of 7-UP. Some of the foreigners in the café continued reading their e-mail; finally, after a few more rounds of gunfire, they joined us in the back.

Marwan drew a heavy iron gate across the café's front entrance. A tall African-American mercenary named David was dispatched to "check things out," and Umm Marwan and I continued to catch up. She was clearly accustomed to the phenomenon of gunfire after dusk.

"Do you remember when we crossed the border," she began again, "and poor Khalil had to have that AIDS test?"

"Yes, poor Khalil." The young Bedouin student did not want to fork over the fifty dollars that would have spared him the "blood test" administered by a "doctor." There was never any actual lab follow-up; it was just a way to bring hard currency into the crippled economy. I had narrowly escaped the test by screaming a lot and waving my Canadian passport around.

"He acted so tough in the car," said Umm Marwan, shifting her position slightly so that her abaya spilled gracefully over her knee, "and then he almost cried at the border. Me, I would have come for you, if you had been held by those police even one minute longer! I would have gone in and screamed until they released you." Evidently I had been on to something with that screaming technique.

We were both sitting cross-legged on the floor now. The sound of ricocheting bullets reverberated through the café. I seemed to be the only one who flinched at the gunfire; by the time I left a month later, the sound would seem as normal as traffic in the street.

"I spent the war at home," Umm Marwan told me. "I figured, if something happens to me, I'd rather have it happen where I live, not on the road, fleeing as a refugee." I suspected the real reason was that like so many Baghdadis she could not afford to abandon her home and re-establish herself in another country. "There were missiles falling in my neighborhood, but I never left. We had some water, but no electricity during the fighting. And things still aren't back to normal. The summer almost killed us, it was so hot. But who is responsible for this delay, we don't know."

I mentioned to her that some Iraqis I'd met complained that Saddam had been able to restore electricity only three months after the Gulf War.

"Well, yes," said Umm Marwan, "he knew how to do things. He had his ways. There are a lot of problems now. Everyone blames each other. People are stealing pipes and wires, cutting them, we don't know exactly what's happening. Everywhere people are living in fear — of kidnapping, bombs, thieves. My friend's son was held for ransom last month — 25 million dinars [$20,000 U.S.]. Someone on our street even stole a money-making machine. It's crazy now in Baghdad."

Her descriptions were worlds away from my memories of Baghdad under Saddam, a city so carefully controlled that I felt safe enough to walk certain streets at night alone. Now, it seemed, women were being abducted in broad daylight.

"It's so much more dangerous now," Umm Marwan explained. "I never used to lock my door while I was at home. Now I do. Thieves are everywhere. Once last month at 9:00 p.m., I wanted to take a cab home from the market. Someone tried to pull me into a car, but I screamed and managed to escape." It seemed that even middle-aged women in abayas were now fair game.

"So what's the hardest part of living in Baghdad now?"

"Everything is hard. At night we hear gunfire, there are thieves, American tanks ... At the beginning of the war, we were happy to see them. We thought things would get better — but in Iraq, you know, it's not easy. Now we have hundreds of different political and religious parties, everything is expensive, salaries are low. My husband is too old to work. Thank God Marwan has this job."

Marwan, a plump, good-natured graduate from the University of Technology, certainly looked like a good son. He was also increasingly a good Muslim and, as I would learn, used his contact with foreigners at the café to proselytize — in the friendliest of ways — about the virtues of his born-again faith.

He would later advise me to avoid swimming in the heart-shaped pool outside the café, as it was "not good" to attract attention. In fact, every time I did swim — in my modest and decidedly unsexy Speedo, goggles, and bathing cap — scores of idle waiters, clerks, and hitherto invisible "pool attendants" would magically appear and stare unrelentingly for my full twenty minutes of lengths. Sometimes I wondered if they had some kind of arrangement with Marwan. It was enough to make a girl turn to hijab.

Marwan described how his university had been burned and looted after the invasion. "Equipment was stolen," he said, "libraries robbed. I saw thieves stealing all our work and projects. I felt like my house was being destroyed."

Marwan was a genuine techno-geek who liked his job. His main worry was that the cost of connecting to the internet lines — previously state-owned and available to Iraqis for $15 a year — would go up with privatization.

But what about the censorship of e-mail? I asked him. Hadn't that been a worry?

"It's true the internet was monitored before," said Marwan, "but only to protect people from the bad sites." It was hard to tell if he was referring to pornography, *The New York Times* online or some kind of Trotskyite chatline.

"Didn't you ever worry about people reading your e-mail?" I inquired.

"No," he replied. "They only read the e-mail of people who were suspicious." You can take the boy out of the Baathists, but never the Baathist out of the boy.

"Yes, and before we had internet at home, through our phone lines," piped up Umm Marwan. "Now we have no phones!" There was no problem with censorship these days, it seemed, but you might get killed en route to the internet café. The Americans and their cronies, of course, had their own mobile-phone service, completely unavailable to average Iraqis. Routed through a 914 area code (somewhere near Buffalo), it was virtually free, and you could call anywhere in the world. Provided you were one of the lucky ones who had a phone. For the less well-connected, there were always Thuraya phones, which almost never worked and cost about $2 a minute when they did.

"When we will have this phone service they promised?" asked Umm Marwan. "When will the electricity be restored? When will the new Iraq come? When? Now Iraq is a jungle — you can't do anything. There is no security, no jobs, families can't be supported. What will happen? Nobody knows. All we can do is wait, just wait. We are all waiting."

More gunshots rang outside. "This *is* the new Iraq," laughed Marwan.

"That was a Kalashnikov," observed Umm Marwan, "an Iraqi gun. The guns, you know, they are in the streets with the people."

But this is a residential neighborhood, I said. Isn't it safer than other areas?

"Maybe, sometimes," shrugged Umm Marwan. "We don't know where is safe. Something could happen in the middle of the day, anywhere, any time. I want to buy a weapon for my home, to protect myself," said the moon-faced matron, who looked like she would have trouble killing a fly. "A pistol is expensive — two hundred dollars at least — but a Kalashnikov is cheaper, maybe only one hundred dollars. Anyway, I will try. I have to keep one at home. My husband is old, he has heart disease." Perhaps she would be determined enough to visit one of Baghdad's new open gun markets. Perhaps the Americans wouldn't arrest her for carrying an unlicensed weapon; as under the old regime, licenses were only available to those with "connections."

At that moment the American mercenary came back into the café with a blond, blue-eyed colleague. "It's all right folks," said the blond with an Alabama twang. "At first we thought it might have been an assassination attempt. Barzani [the Kurdish leader] was next door for a meeting. But it was just a couple of thieves."

One of Marwan's colleagues, an older man with a thin frame and a curly moustache, shrugged his shoulders as the Americans left the room. "Barzani," he said. "Thieves. Americans. What difference? Same same."

Chapter 5: Karim

THE NEXT MORNING, after a fitful sleep interrupted by the sound of gunfire and the rumble of tanks, I pondered what to do on my second day in the new Iraq. As I read my fortune in the grounds of my strong Arabic coffee, the telephone rang. It was Karim, the principal cellist in the Iraqi National Orchestra. I had e-mailed him from Amman to say I would arrive that week, but how had he known the exact time I'd be in my hotel? This felt a bit like the old Iraq, where people would just turn up "by accident" at the most opportune moments.

"Karim," I said on the phone. "It's so nice to hear your voice."

"Can I come up?" he replied.

This was new. In the old Iraq there had often been elevator guards at each floor, there to thwart dangerous liaisons or espionage, but more than happy to turn a blind eye for a few dollars. "Are you allowed to?" I asked. "Of course I am," said Karim. "I'll see you in a minute."

As I waited, I remembered the last time we'd seen each other. It was in early 2001, and I was about to leave Baghdad in a service taxi. Karim had given me a bag of oranges and chocolate and pistachios for the road and wished me a safe journey. "Take care," he'd said, as if I were the one that needed looking after, not him, a young, orphaned artist trying to provide for his two younger sisters in a sanctions-plagued city. He'd played the host that visit, even inviting me to stay with him and his sisters at their apartment when my U.S. dollars started to run out.

Amazingly, the minders at the Press Center had apparently never discovered my alternate lodging arrangements, even though foreign journalists staying with locals was more or less forbidden and the apartment was right in front of the Ministry of Information. The Wasfi family apartment and the ministry were part of a complex of bland state-owned buildings in an area that was now close to the "green zone." The area also included the al-Rashid theater and the Mansour

Melia hotel, the latter a cavernous behemoth from the eighties that hosted mass weddings (a Baathist gesture of goodwill for cash-strapped Iraqis) and B-list foreign dignitaries.

It was Ramadan, and I would come back home — after a frustrating day interviewing people who would take one look at my minder and offer up nothing but Baathist platitudes — to freshly cooked dolmas prepared by Karim's sisters and auntie. Photos of his parents, both of whom had died from mysterious post-Gulf War cancers, overlooked the comforting domestic scene. When the Press Center — a claustrophobic space full of mustachioed spooks chain-smoking black Sumer cigarettes — got to be too much, I would pop over to the apartment and listen to Karim practice the cello.

Karim was part Circassian and part Turkish: his mother had been Egyptian and his father a famous Iraqi actor. More than six feet tall and at least 250 pounds, he was not someone to take lightly, in any sense. When he played the cello, his huge frame wrapped around its shape and they fused into a giant being of sound. That sound had occupied such a huge space, reverberating in his apartment and then in my memory; it was such a contrast to the gloomy Press Center that sometimes it was hard to believe that the soaring spirit of Karim's cello and the depressing pettiness of Baathist apparatchik bureaucracy occupied the same country.

But they did. And that was part of the attraction, what kept me coming back for more: how to bleed that unexpected greatness, that astonishing depth of meaning out of concrete walls of suffering, out of days spent with stone-faced minders. Somehow, I always managed. Indeed that's how I'd first met Karim. One evening after a thunderstorm during my 2000 *Wallpaper** visit, exhausted by two weeks detailing the excesses of brutalist Iraqi architecture, I'd wandered accidentally into the al-Rashid Theater. I was feeling dead inside, crushed by the weight of the regime and the heat of the long day, and I walked into a room full of the most beautiful music. It was the orchestra playing *Heartbeat of Baghdad*, a symphonic poem by a young Iraqi composer. My affair with the city was rekindled.

I'd stayed in touch with Karim by telephone and e-mail. On February 17, 2001, the day after Baghdad had been bombed by U.S.

warplanes, he'd phoned me to wish me a happy birthday, not even mentioning the bombing until I brought it up. He'd been performing Beethoven's Sonata in G minor in the garden of the Orfali Cultural Center when guided missiles lit up the night sky. He'd paused for a moment, he told me, and then calmly said to the audience, "Go if you must, but I'm staying. I came here to play music." Almost everyone remained seated until he had finished his performance.

But the last time I'd spoken with Karim, things had changed. It was May of 2002 and I was in Barcelona. I had $10,000 worth of assignments riding on a visa that still hadn't come through. I was getting desperate. I phoned Karim, thirteen times, the line cutting out every time after a minute or so. When I finally got a stable line and told him about my plight, he responded like one of those impenetrable minders: "I'm sure that whoever denied you the visa had a good reason for doing so." He didn't even sound like Karim, but instead like his alien pod-person self, like something out of *Invasion of the Body Snatchers*. There was no emotion in his voice at all. I knew the lines were tapped and that I might have been blacklisted, but there was something else, something different that I couldn't quite put my finger on. Not until I'd spent some time with Karim in the new Iraq would I be able to name it.

"HELLO, HADANI!" We embraced in my doorway and I invited him in. Over cans of Pepsi, we caught up. Karim told me about his sisters, who had resettled in Sweden, and his auntie, who was still holding up in her Mansour apartment. He spoke of his new job, as director of the Iraqi Institute for Democracy. "I don't have much time to play the cello any more," he admitted.

Karim looked different. Gone were his formal, double-breasted suits; now his look was casual, American. He was wearing Tommy Hilfiger jeans and a baseball cap, backwards. And there was something in his eyes — a harder look, or perhaps just a tired one. It was difficult to tell.

"You know, the nights are the hardest here," he told me. "They are lonely. There's nothing to do. I miss ..." he sighed and looked out the window, "I miss everything. You know, being able to go out at night to the theater, to a friend's house, to a party. Now I just sit at home at night. Sit and think ... It's not good."

"What do you think about?" I asked.

"Oh, well ... my life. This job I have. It's so crazy trying to work in Iraq now. I think about my sisters in Sweden. About my career." Karim started to smile. "Hey. I have to show you something." He reached into his wallet. It was his passport. His *American* passport.

"I'm a U.S. citizen now," he proclaimed, half self-mocking, half proud.

Looking at his passport photo I felt a slight chill. I knew that Karim had studied at the University of Indiana, under the legendary cellist Janos Starker, and that he had gone back recently to try and get a teaching position. But I had never really imagined him as an American.

"Double agent," I said, only half joking.

"Hey, they can't arrest me now," he laughed. "I'm one of them."

But I knew that — beyond the baseball cap and jeans — Karim would never be an American. He was absolutely and essentially Iraqi. He was not naive; he was a survivor. I couldn't imagine him subscribing to any Pollyannaish belief in liberal egalitarianism. He was not comfortable with informality. He was never frank, often speaking in coded, cryptic ways. And he had never, as long as I'd known him, expressed the slightest interest in or concern for the state of democracy in Iraq or anywhere else. But his new job at the Iraqi Institute for Democracy paid $1500 U.S. a month.

"So, how is it going with your new job?"

"You mean, why am I depressed, even though I have an NGO badge?" he replied, playing with the laminated photo ID card that was now the symbol of legitimacy in Baghdad — even though there was no central authority issuing them and it was easy enough to make your own from a business card. "Well, we're selling democracy, but it's not a product that does too well in this market."

"Why not?"

"Well, even before Saddam," he answered, in a more serious, rehearsed tone, "the regime wasn't truly democratic. We're not fighting a decade or so of dictatorship and oppression here; it's at least a century. People are just angry and frustrated. They have no vision of their future. It's just disorganized chaos. At least under Saddam it was *organized* chaos — now it's worse. Everyone is suspicious of one another and fighting amongst themselves."

"Do you feel impotent?" I asked him.

"At least I can try ... Something has to happen ... Something has to start." He sounded like he was desperately trying to convince himself. "It's almost like the situation with Saddam. No one ever thought that he would be overthrown, but it happened. For many people, this dream came true." I noted his positive spin on regime change and wondered how sincere it was. "So for us to have a truly free society will take some time. And the tools that the society uses for expression of that freedom are different than in the West. But we're starting and within a year or two we can see some change, I'm sure."

I thought of what Nehru had written in 1934 about the real motives of the British in the areas of the former Ottoman empire they claimed to have "liberated": "The novel feature of the modern type of imperialism is its attempt to hide its terrorism and exploitation behind pious phrases about 'trusteeship' and the 'good of the masses' and the 'training of backward peoples in self-government.'"

"But we're trying. And we're different than all those political parties," Karim added with contempt, "all these newly varnished and clean-looking thieves who came back."

"But how did you go from being a cellist to directing an NGO?"

"Well, it's a long story," he sighed. "I still believe in culture as a tool for reconstruction, but I can't support myself as an artist. I need some kind of base to work from."

"But do you still play at all?"

"Not much." His last performance had been a year earlier in Amman.

"What really brought you back here?" I asked.

"What brings *you* back?" he retorted. "The same thing ... searching and re-searching ... searching for truth, for stability, for refinement ..." His train of thought seemed to have derailed. "Amman was too ... limited. Besides, I think Baghdad needs me more."

But most of his old friends had left the country, he said, and the orchestra had been receiving anonymous death threats from fundamentalists who objected to their perceived "Western" bias. I remembered Karim's brilliant interpretation of Elgar's Cello Concerto, which he performed on the tenth anniversary of the Gulf War in Baghdad. Then he had considered himself an "ambassador for peace," and had told me, "Culture knows no borders. Here I am, an Iraqi who studied in America, playing a concerto written by an Englishman about a war that happened over eighty years ago in Europe." And yet the concerto had been a meaningful and relevant expression of Iraqi life. When I first heard the orchestra perform it, I felt as though the musicians were playing on their own heartstrings.

"What piece of music would you like to play in response to the current situation?" I asked him.

"I'd like to do improvisations," he replied. "When I first came back I wanted to just grab my cello and play in Bab el-Sharj [a downtown market]. I tried once in August but I was almost shot and kids were throwing rocks. It was a disaster."

"Would you ever try again in a more secure place?" I asked "Like maybe, beside the swimming pool here at the hotel?" I pictured the mercenaries from many countries gathered around. Could music still soothe the savage beast?

"Well, maybe," said Karim. "Perhaps Prokofiev's Cello Concerto in E minor. It's powerful, cohesive ..." He searched for the right adjective in English. "Effective. And ..." — he returned to a tone that suggested the old artist Karim I'd known and loved — " it's one of the most beautiful pieces for cello."

KARIM WAS EAGER TO SHOW ME his new office, so we set off for the Iraqi Institute of Democracy in a car supplied by the hotel. Passing through Karradah, there didn't seem to be too much damage from American bombing.

"It was the looting that really caused problems," explained our driver, an affable Shia man in his late thirties named Ali. I had wrapped a scarf around my head and put on my baggiest clothes, in deference to warnings I'd received about modesty in the new Baghdad. The effect was vaguely "peasant girl from Falluja." Ali laughed at my disguise, pointing out a bare-headed woman walking alone through the streets in jeans and a T-shirt. "You see!" he exclaimed. "All *that*," he gestured towards my getup, "is not necessary." Still, the casually dressed woman was one of maybe eight that I'd see over the next few weeks. Better hijabed than abducted, I figured: I had heard many stories of "uncovered" women being kidnapped and assaulted in a perverted form of "Islamic" justice. As I would soon find out, many women were hijabed *and* abducted.

In the unrelenting September sunlight, I caught glimpses of Haroun al-Rashid's old city in sharp new relief. We passed a familiar-looking Bank of Baghdad, blackened from looting, and then the National Theater, also burned and ransacked. Beneath a banner advertising an old musical comedy was the theater's entrance, barricaded with sandbags and barbed wire. A forklift stood frozen in mid-air, awaiting further instruction. Across the street were the bombed-out remains of the Iraqi Air Force headquarters; a constructivist-style statue of a brave pilot in uniform still stood proudly outside the flattened building.

"There are squatters living in the old ministries now," explained Karim. "And the villas that belonged to former ministers are now occupied by the Americans — and their friends." He said this last bit with a kind of controlled rage in his voice. It was not easy to tell where Karim's loyalties lay.

A couple miles later, we passed by the statue of the "father of Iraqi democracy," Abdul Mushin al Sadoun, who was prime minister in the 1920s. A nationalist and idealist who fought against British occupation, he had revived the phrase *al iraq lil iraqayeen* — "Iraq for the Iraqis" — first used against the Ottoman Turks. But eventually, caught between difficult negotiations with the British and feuding Iraqi groups, he had killed himself, despairing of any kind of democracy taking hold in Iraq. Karim pointed out that this was actually a plaster copy of the real statue, which had been looted soon after the invasion.

SOON WE PULLED UP in front of the Iraqi Institute for Democracy. We were greeted by a small Arabic sign that looked as if it had been designed by a twelve-year-old for Hallmark. A stylized flower emerged from a wobbly-looking map of Iraq. In front of the door, a man sat on the ground, idle, sullen.

"Is the office secure?" I asked Karim.

"Yes," he replied. "We have a guard ... ah ... but he's not here today."

We walked up two flights of darkened stairs to arrive at the office. A good-looking man in his forties stepped out to greet us. Karim introduced him as Hussain Sinjari, the president of the institute and his boss. Sinjari had been an MP in Iraqi Kurdistan and was married to a pretty Belgian woman named Sonja who, Karim said only half jokingly, "runs everything here."

The "institute" consisted of two rooms, furnished in a familiar if somewhat Spartan Baathist style. A strange plastic tableau of galloping wild horses hung over Karim's desk. "Hey, we're not responsible for the artwork," he smiled sheepishly.

Karim began a discussion with Sonja about a grant he hoped to procure from the CPA. He'd had a successful meeting with an American official a few days earlier and was eagerly awaiting the verdict.

"But don't we need to give them documentation?" Sonja asked. She was from Brussels.

"No," said Karim. "He trusted me, he trusted my word. He wants to use us as a model for other organizations. Of course," he continued, lighting up a Marlboro, "they would be more comfortable to sponsor us once we are more established. But they want to use *Iraq Today* as a link between the CPA and Iraqi society."

Iraq Today was a weekly newspaper that the Institute sponsored. Sinjari was the editor. But it was in English. How many Iraqis would that reach? An Arabic version was apparently almost up and running.

Karim took another long drag of his Marlboro. "A grant," he mused, "will give us credibility. But we need to have a clearer mandate, so then they would know whom they are supporting." With their record, I wondered how the Americans discerned genuine democrats.

I glanced down at the *Iraq Today* front-page headline: "In Wake of Hakim Assassination — Sorrow and Fears of Looming Civil Strife," it announced of the recent killing of the Shia cleric and more than eighty of his followers. An almost painterly photo of the mosque in Kerbala exuding plumes of black smoke and framed by dazed bystanders stared out at me. It was Goya in Iraq.

BUT UNLIKE THE CHRISTIAN fundamentalists in the Bush administration, I was not a great believer in the apocalypse. In fact, I was still something of an optimist. So I decided to tell Hussain about an idea I had. I didn't mention that I'd only come up with it that morning.

"I have this idea," I began, "for a project that would help women and their children."

"Yes, tell me," said Hussain, sounding quite sincere.

"Well, it's kind of a community garden meets women's center meets cultural project. I'm calling it 'Garden of Peace.'" Community gardens were all the rage in development circles in North America. I wondered if they would work in Baghdad.

"It seems that these days, there's much less public space for women and their children," I continued. "I mean, women can't go out of the house much because of crime. And where do their children go to play? The streets aren't safe any more. So," I explained, really getting into it now and hoping that Hussain would too, "the idea is to locate areas of urban green space — like maybe, say, an old villa with a garden."

"Yes ..."

"And then, give the women some land to work with. Gardening will be therapeutic, but also practical. The women can grow vegetables to feed their families and maybe even to sell in the market. There can be a playground for their children, and also cultural activities for them, like painting, music, even drama games — ways they can express themselves and their experience of war. And for the mothers, it would be a place to meet, discuss their problems, maybe get referred to medical clinics ... and there could be literacy classes for them too."

Hussain smiled. He knew, of course, that the kinds of women and children I meant were from the poor areas of Baghdad, not the middle classes.

"I think," he began slowly, "this is a wonderful idea! We would love to work with you on this."

"Did your mother keep a garden?" I asked him, picturing some lush Kurdish village in the north. Kurdistan had been a great agricultural area before Saddam's forces had wreaked havoc there. I imagined a woman with a headscarf planting zucchini and pomegranates.

"Er ... ah ... she had a gardener," he replied.

I realized that Hussain came from an old, land-owning family, and my mental image of his mother's garden changed quickly to that of a country estate in genteel disrepair.

Soon, it was all settled over chai. The Institute would be my supporting NGO. I would go to the palace and explain it all to Hank from Virginia to try to win the necessary US-AID money with which to hire armed guards for the garden of peace. Democracy in action!

If only there were still some benevolent goddess to appeal to, I thought, some gracious Ishtar bestowing grants, instead of lollipop-sucking middle-aged Americans with a warped sense of Protestant mission.

As we walked outside into the noonday brightness, I noticed a boy standing on the sidewalk selling live *mazgouf*, the special fish from the Tigris that Baghdadis love to barbecue in their gardens. As SUVs whizzed by and beat-up jalopies farted petrol, the boy tried in vain to revive the fish, who lay half dead in his shallow cartload of water. He splashed water on his catch and a few managed half-hearted flip-flops.

"I'm sorry," I told him. "I'm not buying."

Chapter 6: Theater of the Absurd

THE NEXT DAY, I WENT to look for my old friends at the National Theater. One of the last semi-functioning theaters in Baghdad, it was a ten-minute walk from my hotel, but everyone discouraged me from walking there alone with a camera, even though I had done so many times before on previous visits. So I went with my driver, Ali.

Most of the theater's exterior walls were blackened from fire but some hardy landscaping — mainly palm trees — had survived. Sandbags and barbed wire surrounded the main entrance, but I saw a small crowd gathered at a side door. I walked towards it and found half a dozen armed guards at the entrance. They wore badges issued by the new Ministry of Culture.

As I entered the theater's cavernous lobby, I thought back to all the times I'd been here in the past. I had discovered Iraqi theater almost by accident. While on assignment for an American paper that wanted meaty political stories, I'd been invited to see a play. To my surprise, I found that theater in Iraq strode bravely where the state-run press dared not tread. The plays — primarily popular musical comedies — were forums for jibes at everything from American air raids to government corruption. In a society where information was tightly controlled, far more was revealed in the nuances and humor of theater than in any official Ministry of Information statement.

There wasn't much that could capture the natural surreality of life in Baghdad — except perhaps for its theater. I remembered the morning I'd received my first invitation to the National Theater. Later, I'd entered the dining room of the cavernous al-Rashid Hotel and witnessed an unforgettable scene: as Bing Crosby crooned a slightly distorted version of "White Christmas" (well into January) and vaguely Babylonian-looking Santa Claus figurines looked on, dozens of dinner-jacketed waiters hovered around a group of Egyptian notables eating

A circus scene from My Love is the Moon *at the National Theater, 2002*

cornflakes. Their groaning breakfast table was dominated by a massive centerpiece: a cake in the shape of the tower of Babel flanked by two ceramic tigers, their faces contorted into snarls.

But the innate drama and surreality of Iraqi life weren't the only explanations for Baghdad's flourishing theater scene. Under the draconian, decade-long embargo, films and film-processing chemicals were being blocked at the border as so-called "dual-use items" — materials that an American-led U.N. committee claimed could be used for military purposes. So most cinemas had closed, reopening as forums for an art that required only human passion and ideas.

My guide to Baghdad's cultural scene had always been Sadiq Ali Shaheen, the aging film and theater star who looked like an Iraqi Maurice Chevalier. We communicated in our common language of broken German. He knew everyone and took me around Baghdad in his beat-up old Lada.

One night in early 2002, the last time Sadiq took me to the National Theater, was especially memorable. Built in the seventies, the theater still had an air of grandeur, with a marble lobby and a huge portrait of Saddam Hussein to welcome theater-goers. But the smell of sewage leaking from the bathrooms — like so many in Iraq, wrecked and unrepairable owing to a lack of spare parts — diminished any lingering sense of glamour. And Wolfowitz's latest threats of air raids, conveyed via a CNN broadcast I'd seen that day at the Ministry of Information, were not far from my mind.

The performance that night was of *My Love is the Moon*, a play by Haidar Monather, the 30-year-old actor/director and one-time star of Baghdad's theater scene. It featured grand surrealist tableaux that seemed fantastic at first, yet somehow managed to capture the essence of Iraqi life. The play, which mixed historical eras as well as film clips and theater, told the story of a young man named Faraj, played by Monather himself, who visits one of Baghdad's historical museums with a group of friends. There he gets caught in a time warp, and enters the world of the Ottomans shortly before the British occupation of Iraq.

He soon falls in love with Kamar, a beautiful young woman being preyed upon by the palace madam, Regina, who wants to sell her to the sultan. By mixing pre-recorded video with live theater, and Ottoman rituals with modern pop-culture references such as Santana songs, Monather seamlessly blended past and present. Eventually the young lovers are reunited and somehow end up in modern Baghdad, but not before some incredible scenes. One finds Faraj dressed in a monkey suit, performing in a circus in Istanbul. When he complains to the ringmaster that he is a man, not a monkey, he is told, "The people have paid to see you dance — so dance!" At which point the sultan, Regina, and entourage emerge on a rotating stage, watching as young Kamar dances for them. But when she collapses in exhaustion, they begin to laugh, shouting, "Long live the Empire."

It wasn't too difficult to make the leap from Haidar's portrayal of the corrupt Ottoman court, on the verge of collapse and British occupation, to modern-day Iraq, standing by for the next round of American bombings. And the long-suffering audience seemed to identify with the caged animals caught in a circus of the absurd.

But despite the play's anti-imperialist theme ("First the Turks, then the British, now the Americans," says one character), for many patrons a trip to the theater was simply a pleasant diversion from the daily grind. For a mere 2000 dinars (about $1 U.S.), they could enjoy an evening of escapism and catharsis. The audience, a mix of young theater students, Haidar fans, and whole families out for a night on the town, was clearly enthralled by *My Love is the Moon*.

Samir, a 21-year-old theater student, liked the way Haidar mixed elements of modern and classical theater as well as traditional Iraqi and Western pop music. "Haidar is my hero," he'd told me. "There's no one like him in today's theater scene. He's unique."

Alia, a young mother at the theater with her husband and two young daughters, said she liked Haidar's plays too. "They reflect Iraqi reality — I can relate to them." But if she were to write a play, she said she would write one about the plight of women in Iraq, about the daily struggle to survive and keep their families together. "My little girl has leukemia," she confided, "and she loves going to plays. We go to the theater much more often now than before the embargo."

WHILE MUSICAL COMEDY was hugely popular — even Saddam Hussein's novel, *Zubaida and the King,* was turned into a musical — the humor was barbed and usually about the embargo. That night, Sadiq had also taken me to a theater across town, in Baghdad's former warehouse district, where *I've Seen It With My Own Eyes,* a comedy about the sanctions, had been running for two years. In the play, residents of a poor Baghdad neighborhood build a rocket ship and head for outer space, where they encounter extraterrestrials. As they try to explain their life back home to the aliens, the dialogue is rife with ironic comments. One young man wants to marry a "space-girl" but complains that he can't afford to pay for the wedding, and, being unemployed, cannot support his future bride.

In another scene, there is the sound of a loud explosion. A character comments, "You see there was a bombing — tomorrow eggs will be twice as much. We must unite in the face of 'beastly powers.'" With nuance and timing, he conveys a double meaning immediately understood by the audience: the "beastly powers" are both the "imperialist bombers" and the black marketeers. In other scenes there are similar simultaneous references to civilians suffering in Afghanistan and Palestine, and the corruption so rampant in sanctions-plagued Iraq.

The theater, a converted cinema hit by a missile during the Iran–Iraq war, was even more rundown than the National Theater. Sadiq introduced me to the owner, a portly, mustachioed man in a double-breasted suit, who said that his theater had been the first of the formerly state-run theaters to privatize. Business was booming, he told me, and there were full houses almost every night.

"Under these difficult circumstances, people come here to vent some of their feelings about their hardships," he explained. "Our theater is the first one in Iraq to receive an actor from another country — Younis Chalabi from Egypt — to act with our actors in this play," he told me proudly, adding, "And this is a break with the sanctions, which were meant to cause psychological and cultural isolation."

The crowd spilled into the lobby at intermission. Most of the theater-goers were young men without families, Iraq's lost generation of angry teenagers who had come of age knowing only war and sanctions and who couldn't even afford to get married. This was their big night out. I was one of the few women there, and had to stand between Sadiq and my minder at all times.

I tried to find someone who could tell me their favorite joke from the play. One young man said he'd really liked the line about the Baghdadi guy not having enough money to marry the alien girl. She'd said something like, "I'd never marry him, he doesn't have enough ration cards." But no one else was forthcoming.

I talked to the young man who worked at the cafeteria. He couldn't remember any jokes, but he did say, "If I were to write a play, I would write about how the embargo has made people stingy. There is no generosity or sharing anymore. Not even families help each other." He was not smiling, and a group of young men were gathering around us. The minder made a move towards the door and we retreated outside to the empty parking lot with its few beat-up cars.

Sadiq explained that although there was still some state-sponsored theater, the most popular kind was the sort that *I've Seen It With My Own Eyes* typified: pantomime-like physical comedy with humor delivered in broad, easy strokes. "The Second World War lasted only five years compared to eleven years of sanctions, and all of Europe produced theater like this — variety — just to give an outlet to people to vent their hardships and their troubles."

"Before the embargo," he continued, "theater was more serious, more intellectual. Now it has become more popular, with lots of jokes and singing and dancing. There are lots of productions going on, but only some of them have a deeper meaning. People really need to have a good time now and be entertained."

I remembered a particularly entertaining evening in late 2000, when Sadiq had taken me to a popular play at Al-Mansour Theater. At 7:30 the crowd was already getting excited, abuzz with news of actor Majid Nasim, the leading man in the comedy they were about to see, *Foufara* ("The Pretender"). Young couples on dates, women in full abaya out with their families, fashionable young ladies with perfectly coiffed hair, old men with no teeth but expertly pressed dinner jackets, everyone was talking about the latest exploits of the star of the Iraqi stage. It was the middle of the week but the house was full, as it had been almost every night of the play's six-month run.

"Majid Nasim is my hero," said Ali, a young fan out with his girlfriend, Susan. "I've come to see this play five times." His unbridled enthusiasm showed how popular theater was with young Iraqis, but the cultural isolation of the embargo was also obvious in his response to my question, "Who is your favorite actor outside of Iraq?" "Michael Jackson," he answered with a grin.

As I watched happy theater-goers sipping Pepsi and snacking on sweets, it was easy to forget that outside, just a few yards away, were packs of wild dogs howling away in the surrounding parkland as the moonlight illuminated the gigantic "Victory" monument to the Iran–Iraq war, a huge pair of arms holding crossed swords and decorated with the helmets of captured Iranian soldiers; or that the latest floods had ruined the already decrepit sewage system, and that children were still dying of dysentery.

Just as Hollywood films of the thirties provided relief from the Depression, a few hours of escapist comedy at the Al-Mansour Theater did wonders for the psyche. In fact, a night out in Baghdad was not as bleak as one might expect. Despite the intellectual and artistic "brain drain" that had seen so much talent leave the country, the vibrant, state-funded cultural life Baghdad had enjoyed in the oil-rich seventies was slowly being revived. One of the very few positive consequences of the embargo was the fact that Baghdad was free from the usual pressures of globalization. With little internet access, hardly any contact with the outside world, high unemployment, and cheap rents, Baghdad was in many ways an ideal place for artists and writers. While not as high as, say, a doctor's salary, working actors could certainly survive on their average monthly earnings of 200,000 dinar (about $100 U.S.), more than ten times that of a government worker. In fact, the increased popularity of theater had even produced its own star system.

Majid Nasim had been a clothing salesman before he became an actor. "I always knew I wanted to act," the forty-something celebrity told me backstage before the show. "But I didn't get my chance until after the embargo." The ravages of the sanctions helped him out in another unexpected way — he got his big break when he was called up to fill in for an actor who had come down with dysentery.

When asked who his biggest influences were, Nasim cited Egyptian actor Adel Imam, Laurel and Hardy, and "Mr. Ben." Seeing my puzzled expression he mimed driving around in a car and made huge clownish faces.

"Ah, Mr. Bean!" I said.

"Yes, yes, Mr. Bean. Very nice!" Apparently Rowan Atkinson's politically inoffensive and very physical comedy style was a big hit on Iraqi television, appearing regularly on Shebab TV, the station run by Uday Hussein, the president's son.

It was time for the play to begin and Sadiq ushered me into the theater, built by the government in 1980 when the petro-dollars were still flowing freely. As the curtain rose, the sounds of Iraqi pop music filled the stage. The cast began with a rousing song-and-dance number followed by the opening scene, set in a luxurious hotel not unlike the monolithic al-Rashid.

The plot line was an interesting mix of reality and fantasy: two girls, encouraged by their status-seeking mother, dress up in their best outfits and hang out in the lobby of the hotel, hoping to attract the attention of a "rich foreigner" who will provide them with the finer things in life, as well as the basic necessities so sorely lacking in Baghdad: decent food, medicine, housing, and transportation.

In a desperate scheme to improve her daughters' lot the mother, played by well-known actress Amal Taha, enters into a trance and invokes a genie to help her find a "superman" who will arrive on a white horse and carry them away to a palace in the sky. The genie arrives, and the fun begins.

Meanwhile, an attractive-but-dirt-poor young man lands on top of the hotel in a helicopter. Posing as an international wheeler-dealer, he enlists the help of his friend, a penniless musician played by Nasim, who pretends to be his associate. In one hilarious scene he speaks on the telephone in gibberish, pretending to talk about petroleum and pharmaceutical deals in fictitious foreign languages. Although his portrayal was clearly over-the-top farce, it was not that far away from the reality of the year 2000, when hundreds of foreign businessmen hungry for post-embargo contracts had descended on Baghdad.

Predictably, the two girls, posing as rich Baghdadis, meet and fall in love with the two "pretenders." In the end, true identities are revealed, but love prevails. "It is better," says one of the girls in a deliberate poke at the much-loathed sanctions profiteers or "embargo cats," "to love a poor man who is honest than a rich one who is full of lies."

By the end of the play the mood of the crowd was downright jubilant, and I too had temporarily abandoned the feelings of cynicism and despair I so often experienced in embargoed Baghdad. I was seeing life through rose-colored glasses and that song from *Singing in the Rain* kept going through my head: "Make 'em laugh, make 'em laugh."

Buoyed up by the energy of *The Pretender*, I accepted Sadiq's gracious offer to take in the play next door, at a theater originally built as a cinema. But after half an hour of a lackluster morality tale about an evil city con man who tries to fool a village, not to mention a rather unfortunate trip to the ladies' bathroom, I was plunged back into despair. Alas, the play was not engrossing enough to take my mind off the state of Baghdad's sewage system, and we left the theater somewhat deflated.

Dark thoughts were soon interrupted by a beautiful song. Sadiq had launched into one of the hits of Umm Kulthum, who (despite Nasser's best efforts) was the only person ever to succeed in uniting the Arab world. As we walked towards Sadiq's battered old Buick my mood lifted. I forgot about the howling mongrels and sewage smells and giant arms. I looked at the full moon and listened to the words of the song. As long as there were aging actors in cravats singing love songs in Baghdad, I thought, as long as people could still make comedy out of their strange and sad situation, maybe there was hope.

A FEW DAYS LATER SADIQ introduced me to writer and director Muhsen el-Ali, who was preparing for the dress rehearsal of his new play, *Hello Baghdad*, staged at the National Theater. While el-Ali's last production, *World of Smoke,* had dealt with the corruption of petty officials and the smuggler class, as well as the more endemic "corruption of the soul," his new play was about the experience of Iraqi emigrants abroad.

El-Ali was a playwright from the seventies' "serious theater" scene who had managed to subvert the comedic genre with clever use of double meanings. Humorous references to government corruption and smuggling culture crept into his plays in a way that would have been difficult to achieve in, say, a newspaper editorial. For instance, *World of Smoke,* a kind of Iraqi *Carmen,* centers on a young woman who works in a cigarette factory. She is symbolically strangled by her boss's son, a sanctions profiteer. The son is the Don Jose character; the woman, he told me, represents the "true, pure spirit of Iraq."

This all seemed a bit heavy for a popular comedy. "But my humor is dark," the 55-year old playwright told me, between puffs of strong Sumer cigarettes. The subject of his current play was certainly serious: the emigration of many talented young Iraqis, hoping for a better life abroad. When I asked el-Ali to explain the plot line, the humor was not immediately obvious. "Well," he began, "it's about three Iraqi guys who leave in search of work in another country, but once they're there, they encounter only unemployment, despair, and loss of identity."

While the "plight of the emigrant abroad" story is hardly new in North American or European theater, it was relatively novel in Iraq, where, until the Gulf War, residents of the oil-rich country were much more likely to rely on cheap imported labor than to emigrate themselves. And once the play began, I understood what el-Ali had done. In a brilliant twist, he had created scenes that made the audience laugh at and seriously examine the characters' dilemmas at the same time.

For instance, when the Iraqi characters try to leave the country, they are abandoned by their guide and become lost in the desert. A Bedouin who lives in a neighboring state finds them, and although he is still a desert nomad, he has satellite TV, a mobile phone, and internet access, all things that were virtually inaccessible to most Iraqis at the time.

In another scene, the Iraqi characters, who have emigrated to some fictitious Gulf state, meet an African immigrant in a café. Through gestures and facial expressions, they manage to decipher what he is saying in his gibberish language: he comes from "Tangoland," a remote African state that the Iraqis cannot even find on the map. The physical comedy was cleverly executed, but the underlying implication was that both the Iraqis and the African were existing in no-man's lands. Through sign language they learn the African's profession and how much he can earn, reducing the concept of material value to the ridiculous, and at the same time communicating a sense of shared humanity.

After the rehearsal, the mood was upbeat. The cast was just a few days away from opening night and things were going well. *World of Smoke* had enjoyed a nine-month run, so the cast was expecting *Hello Baghdad* to be another hit. El-Ali himself did not appear defeated by the current situation in Iraq, but rather stimulated. "Theater seems somehow more essential to me now than it ever has," he told me. "And there's so much rich, creative material to draw upon from our own lives." He was so inspired that he had written and directed two plays in the last six months.

But with theater's increased popularity, there were now small-scale wars erupting between competing theater companies, as Maki Awad, an actor who owned and operated his own theater in Baghdad, found after the successful opening of his musical comedy *The Dairymaid*. One of his cast members — the donkey, who had been faithfully providing comic relief on a nightly basis — had been stolen. The next day the street was rife with rumors. "Who would steal a donkey?" everyone asked. No one was sure; many just shrugged and said it was a symptom of the sanctions-related crime wave. But given the mania for plays in Baghdad, the popular opinion was that the performing animal had been abducted by a disgruntled member of a rival theater.

The last time I saw el-Ali, in late 2001, I was so inspired by the creative potential in Baghdad's theater scene that I'd discussed an idea for an Arabic/English co-production with him: a musical comedy about journalists and their minders, called *Press Center*. He loved the idea and we both guffawed about scenes with singing and dancing spooks.

At that time, he was working on a new script about Saladin. In it, the great Muslim hero — who reconquered Jerusalem in 1187 and was born in Saddam's hometown of Tikrit — arrives on the scene in 2001. He is a little surprised to find a Jewish state and a full-scale intifada going on. He tries to get into Jerusalem, but is turned back because he doesn't have the right papers. Then he tries to get into a nameless Arab land and is refused entry again for the same reason. In a long conversation with an Arab border guard, he delivers an eloquent soliloquy about stones. He says that the stones thrown by children are really pieces of Arab history and civilization: pieces of the pyramids, pieces of ancient Babylon. Their own culture and history, he says, is the Arabs' best method of self-defense.

BY 2003, IT WAS GOOD OLD SANDBAGS, barbed wire, and armed guards that defended the National Theater. Luckily I ran right into Omran al-Tamimi, a young playwright and acquaintance, who sat smoking with some friends near the entrance. Still tall, slim, and handsome, he recognized me right away.

"Hadani!" he said. "What are you doing here?"

I still had the present he had given me in 2002, a small red velvet box with Koranic inscriptions in gold: "for your protection," he had said. I was glad to see that he too had been protected.

"This theater was burned and looted," Omran explained, "but it survived, unlike all the others. Now we have just this one." It seemed that the theater was open in the daytime but there were no performances, just rehearsals. "It's because of the security situation. We're afraid of so many things now. It's dangerous to go to a mosque for Friday prayers; imagine what it would be like going to the theater at night."

Omran had real emotion in his voice, and spoke spontaneously. This was unusual for me, after all our past conversations with a minder present.

"They destroy our country now," he continued. "The new parties, the Americans, the British ..."

I reminded him that Canada hadn't participated in the invasion.

He paused and smiled. "Yes, we like Canada."

We walked towards the front entrance and saw the sandbags.

"Guards protect the theater from thieves," Omran recounted. "But I tell you, these thieves, they are not from Iraq — they are foreigners." This was a theory I would hear over and again in Baghdad.

"But who are they?" I asked. "Kuwaitis, Syrians?"

"Let's just say they are our neighbors," Omran replied ominously. "They want to break our necks."

"Well, I'm glad to see that you are well," I told him. Later I would find out just how close to danger he had come, when he disappeared for several days only to return with the sad tale of a cousin who had been murdered during a carjacking. Omran would have been in the car too, but a bad cold that had kept him at home.

"And what of Sadiq?" I inquired hopefully. "How is he?"

"Sadiq is fine," smiled Omran. "He is here at the theater."

I was relieved.

"And Muhsen el-Ali?"

"He left for Amman before the invasion," Omran replied. "I have no news of him."

I pictured the soft-spoken Muhsen at a café somewhere in downtown Amman. What place was there for his sophisticated, absurdist Iraqi theater in placid, conservative Jordan? I wondered if he weren't secretly longing to return to this broken-down but addictively inspiring place.

As Omran led me upstairs to look for Sadiq, he asked me discreetly, "Tell me again, was it your mother or your father who was Lebanese?" As usual, there was an awkward pause when I mentioned my maternal connection. Patriarchal continuity is always key in the Arab world.

"So," I said, changing the subject, "Are you writing a play about the invasion?"

"I've written poems," said Omran, "so many poems. But they are at home and only my friends can read them. I'm not writing any plays now."

"But why not?" I was surprised. Recent events seemed like such good dramatic material.

"Let me tell you," he began, "that before, there was only one Saddam. Now there are at least twenty-five. So when we said something before, the regime may have taken offense, but now with all these different groups, I'm afraid to say anything. It could be dangerous for me."

It seemed that rather than liberation, the invasion had brought only the chaos of a power vacuum, and an increase in self-censorship for survival's sake. Ironically, many of the posts in the new Ministry of Culture were occupied by former Iraqi Communists, most of whom had fled Iraq during the CIA-assisted Baathist purges in the early 1970s. Many of the same actors who had been part of the Saddam-era star system were now happily cozying up to the new pooh-bahs. But Omran considered the new ministry bosses "collaborators." "It's even worse than before," he sighed.

"So I'm just sitting in my house now," he continued as we scanned a few empty rooms, messes of wrecked electrical wiring and decrepit furniture, in search of Sadiq. "Writing poems, reading. I don't go outside much."

I noticed one of the theater's elaborate chandeliers was still hanging from its impressive ceiling. Outside, through a picture window, everything looked relatively normal — the traffic island with palm trees, the same old beat-up cars — but for the American tanks and bombed-out air force headquarters next door.

Later I would learn that there were, in fact, a few plays in rehearsal, although their political commentary was veiled at best. One was about a group of unemployed professionals who become tea-sellers in the market. While the harsh new economic realities of "free market" Iraq were explored, there was almost nothing about the war or the resistance. "Why are there no references in the play to the invasion or occupation?" I asked director Haithem Abdul Razzaq.

"Oh, but there are," he insisted, citing a very obtuse connection between the tea sellers in the play, the Boston Tea party, and the American Revolution against British rule.

Sadiq Sayegh, a playwright newly returned from exile to take a post in the Ministry of Culture, offered this explanation: "A lot of the actors and playwrights here are used to very broad-based, physical theater.

Much is suggested through body movement rather than overt language. This is the style of theater they are used to, and it will take a while to change this mentality."

FINALLY, I SAW A FAMILIAR FACE in one of the upstairs offices. It was my old friend Sadiq, sitting at a desk discussing something with a colleague. With his pink shirt and slicked-back hair he looked as suave as ever. He grinned when he saw me.

"Hello, my dear!" he said as we embraced. Everything came tumbling out in a slew of English, German, and Arabic. "War, war ... with bombs — *mein Haus* — bombed — *wie geht's?*"

"*Gut* — good — *al humdillah*," I responded.

"*Keine mukhabarat* [no secret police] now," Sadiq laughed, "*Kein Ali* [my old minder], *kein Problem.*"

He asked me what I was doing in Iraq. Suddenly there was a cacophony outside. "What's that?" I asked Omran. "It's bugles, music," he explained. It might have been a wedding party, or some kind of celebration. Somehow — perhaps via the British military influence — drum-and-bugle bands were a big part of Iraqi life. "It's the sound of freedom!" exclaimed Sadiq, only half-joking.

"*Kif halek inta?*" I asked him: "How are you, anyway?"

"*Kein Arbeit jetz*," he explained, "no work now, for actor, for director."

"It's such a difficult security situation," Omran repeated. "When we have good security, we will have good theater."

"But what about the guards?" I asked. Their Kalashnikovs had looked rather spiffy.

"So what about a car bomb?" Omran replied.

"Have you been getting any threats from the fundamentalists?"

"No," he said firmly. "The Muslims are with us. It's the *terrorists*" — he said the word slowly and deliberately to emphasize the distinction — "we're worried about. Iraq is now a good stage for terrorism. We need to close our borders."

He added playfully, "But we can't close our borders, because then people like you couldn't get in. But," Omran continued in a more serious tone, "a terrorist is dangerous. And the Muslims, Christians,

Jewish here, we don't know the terrorists. We don't know who they are." This unknown fear factor was one of the more terrifying aspects of life in post-invasion Baghdad. It was similar to the old fear that someone was watching you. At least in the old days, you knew it was someone from the regime.

"They blame Saddam," continued Omran, "but I don't think it's him."

"Then who?" I asked.

"We don't know, we just don't know."

I suddenly longed for one of those barbed Iraqi jokes that used to ease the suffering under sanctions. But it seemed that even black humor had taken a turn for the worse. "A joke?" said Omran. He and Sadiq conferred.

"Okay, here's one," said Omran. "American soldiers think that going to Iraq is like going to picnic, right? So, one day, an American soldier is sitting in the street in Baghdad and crying. So someone stops and says, 'why are you, a brave American soldier, crying in the street?' 'Why?' he answers. 'Because I'm going to Falluja!'"

No one laughed, we all just kind of smiled nervous smiles.

"You see," said Omran, "there aren't even any good jokes left. We are in a bad mood now. We don't need jokes. We need electricity, water … Now we are the joke — the big joke. How is it when you see your leader — a big leader like Saddam — abandon you in one night?" He snapped his fingers. "Just like that. How do you feel when you see American tanks in the street? We don't know who our enemy is — who?" he continued dramatically. "We don't know what will happen tomorrow. Maybe tomorrow you won't see this theater."

"Many cowboy here," added Sadiq, smiling. "Like in film."

"Look at our security guards!" said Omran as we walked towards the side door. "They are protecting us. The last good theater we have, in the whole Middle East," he added with great emphasis. "We have to protect that."

I promised to return in the next few days to catch one of the scheduled rehearsals. "Good, I'll have a joke for you then, I promise," Omran replied, rather seriously.

Sadiq walked me outside. "*Meine Princesse*," he said, holding my hand. It was hard to say goodbye. I hoped I really would see them again soon.

Chapter 7: Old Money, New Money

"BAD TRAFFIC," I pointed out.

"Yes," replied the driver. "No law, no president."

Quite, I thought, as we drove by a bend in Jadriyah, a wealthy residential neighborhood where I'd heard someone had been carjacked a week earlier. I was on my way to have lunch with L. The driver he had sent to pick me up was an affable young man who looked as if, under different circumstances, he might have worked as a bouncer in a nightclub. His head was shaved and his English was almost as poor as my Arabic. He was driving a brand new white Mercedes.

We passed by the now-familiar villas, past the old intelligence headquarters and the house that had once belonged to Saddam's half-brother. There were death shrouds on every other block. I wore a self-imposed shroud — a long black linen dress, suitable for lunch with shady businessmen in Baghdad but easily made more Islamic by the simple addition of a shawl and headscarf. One always had to be prepared; if there were now twenty-five "Saddams," there were at least that many "looks." Costumes changed with the company one kept, and in the course of my visit I would keep some very strange company indeed.

We picked up L and headed for lunch at Il Paseo, the chi-chi Italian restaurant in Arasat where the rich and powerful still dined.

"So," I began, "how have you been?" This was the first opportunity I'd had for a real conversation with him since before the invasion.

"Oh, you know," he replied with a half smile. "I'm surviving." The dark circles under his eyes spoke of a harsher truth lurking beneath his *bon vivant* Italian suits and ever-present Cuban cigars. L was something of a legend in Baghdad. Before the war, he had been the main contractor for the lifting of oil under the oil-for-food program. He seemed to know everyone, from the Minister of Petroleum and the top man at the U.N. to key intelligence officials. And he always threw the best parties in town at his villa in Mansour.

I will never forget the time in January of 2002, when we were supposed to meet one evening for dinner. I was up against a *Newsweek* deadline and reluctantly phoned to cancel. "But what will you eat?" asked L. "The hotel restaurant is closed and it's too late to go out. Look — just stay there and I'll have my driver send something round for you."

Some twenty minutes later the driver had appeared, jinni-like in his shiny white Mercedes, bearing a plate full of fresh Atlantic salmon and shrimp. As I devoured the delicious meal that, after weeks of barely palatable chicken escalopes and a steady diet of bread and hummus, felt like manna from heaven, I remember thinking, "Am I really in sanctions-plagued Iraq?" In a country where thousands were dying every month because even basic medical supplies were lacking, here I was eating Atlantic salmon flown in from Scotland less than twenty-four hours earlier. It was an intoxicatingly sinful experience.

"So how did you fare during the invasion?" I asked. "Was your villa alright? Your offices?"

"The house was fine," he replied, "but there was some damage to the office and ... we lost a few staff." He had an extensive entourage of employees.

"Oh, I'm sorry about that. Is Osama alright?" One of L's drivers, Osama had kindly chauffeured me around one afternoon in another white Mercedes after I'd had to fire my official driver, the alcoholic Ferris. The smooth drive, the leather bucket seats, and the pop music (from Uday Hussein's Shebab radio station) had made me feel like a rock star. The contrast with the Ferris experience — swerving dangerously in and out of traffic in an ancient, beat-up Pontiac as he complained about life in Baghdad and his overbearing and overweight wife — was stark.

"Yes, Osama's fine," L assured me.

"So ..." I began, wanting to broach the subject as gingerly as possible, "how did you end up doing business with the Americans? I mean, when I last saw you, you were ... you know ... quite engaged with the former regime." I remembered a lunch where he had told me of his utmost respect for Saddam Hussein. "I'm not a Baathist," he'd said, "but that man knows how to get things done in this country."

"Well," replied L, "it wasn't easy. I was subject to months of scrutiny beforehand. Things looked a little bleak after the invasion, in fact. But eventually they realized that," — L cleared his throat a little — "I was just a businessman. Not involved at all in politics."

Although not officially involved in oil these days, L was actively working in the "security" industry. He was a bit vague, but from what I could gather he was co-ordinating the security at the Baghdad airport. "We were the ones that brought in the Ghurkhas," he told me, referring to the Nepalese mercenaries I had seen at my hotel.

"I'm also thinking of acquiring a few hotel properties in Baghdad," L added casually, as we drove by some flattened buildings on the road to Arasat.

When we arrived at Il Paseo, everything looked pretty much the same: the same waiters in their bow ties, the same weird Austrian ski-chalet décor. But the crowd had changed a bit. The old families seemed to be gone. In their place were American contractors and Polish officers vying for the cleanest-shaven, most Aryan look possible.

IN THE FAMILIAR SUFFOCATING HEAT and weird cultural juxtapositions of the place, I flashed back to the last time I'd dined at Il Paseo, with an Iraqi businessman named Kamal in 2000. A former engineer in his mid-fifties, he had been trained in London, where his daughter and many of his relatives now lived; he had chosen to stay in Iraq, he said, for "business reasons." Besides, it was hard to get out. You needed lots of hard currency and connections and you had to leave all your property behind. And, said Kamal, real-estate prices were on the rise now, what with all the foreign oil executives and U.N. employees coming to town. It was a bad time to sell.

Before we went inside, Kamal had sat in his rusting Buick, counting out dinars. Dog-eared notes of 1,000, 5,000, 10,000 ... It had been over 105 degrees every day for the previous two weeks, and to my heat-addled brain, this quasi-ritualized counting of huge denominations appeared incredible, ridiculous, verging on hysterical, as if all the years of war and suffering, of sanctions and Baathists and bombs, were flashing by in quick, monetary strokes, briefly illuminated by blue and purple likenesses of Saddam Hussein. *Wahat, tneien, kleite ...* He counted in that way Baghdadis seem to have down pat, distracted yet strangely focused, relaxed yet ready for any eventuality, any possible catastrophe. (In those days, if you wanted to be practical and needed to make a quick getaway or retreat to an underground bunker somewhere — say, if the Americans were bombing, or the police were after you, or some rival smugglers were onto you — dollars were the currency of choice. The three hundred percent devaluation of the dinar meant that squirrelling away your fortune in local currency would have required a shopping trolley full of notes. Dollars were much more discreet.)

After a few minutes, Kamal had counted out enough to pay for lunch. He had a good look around, emerged from the Buick and locked the car doors carefully. "Thieves are everywhere," he said, almost casually. "They pay a lot of money for spare parts these days," referring to the black-market price for yet another commodity being blocked at the border.

If I had been a car thief in Baghdad, I would certainly have chosen this area. Here in Arasat-al-Hindaye, you could find brand new Mercedes and even BMWs, usually driven by nouveau-riche sanctions profiteers. A few hubcaps would have fed your family for a month. Back then, Arasat was becoming the Rodeo Drive of Baghdad. Gleaming shop windows boasted 30-inch television sets freshly smuggled from Dubai, and every other store sold European perfumes and silk lingerie. But the legacy of war and sanctions was everywhere: barefoot boys selling cigarettes, potholes the size of craters, barbecued chicken stands on street corners next to raw sewage.

Still glancing at the Buick out of the corner of his eye, Kamal led me into Il Paseo. I had ditched my minder for the day and was a bit worried about security agents, but Kamal put me at ease. "Don't worry," he said in passable English. "Many foreigners, especially U.N. workers, they come here. You could be one of them. Or," he offered graciously, "I could say you are my niece — from London."

While we were ordering, some middle-aged, English-speaking men came in for lunch, their SUVs guarded by lackeys. "Administrators with the oil-for-food program," Kamal whispered. On their combined monthly salaries, I mused, they could have supplied beans, rice, tea, and sugar for a family of five for at least a year. A group of Iraqi notables walked in and took a large table at the back. The women wore designer clothes and had perfectly coiffed hair. The men wore tailored suits.

"Old money or new?" I asked Kamal. After a quick sizing-up he pronounced, "Old. You can tell by the way they carry themselves. Also, the new money would have bodyguards."

Kamal, a trained engineer, was from one of the old families in Baghdad. I wasn't sure how he earned his living at that time, but he hinted that he had made some money in limestone. When sanctions prevented construction materials from getting past the border, there had been a boom in the local market. But Kamal was not flashy about his wealth; he was no arriviste. He drove an old car and lived alone with a ferocious guard dog in a decaying villa not far from Il Paseo. He invited me there after lunch, and seemed to have a great need to talk.

Under the Baathist regime, I was usually suspicious of Iraqis who wanted to talk with me in private, particularly if the conversations had a distinctly anti-regime bent to them. But Kamal seemed genuinely interested in speaking with a foreigner, someone who might ease his intellectual loneliness. After all, there weren't that many people left in Baghdad you could have interesting conversations with. Many writers and intellectuals had fled to Amman or London, and those who were left maintained a guarded silence. The new *nomenklatura* were smugglers and sanctions profiteers whose conversation was rather limited.

When we arrived at the villa, we were greeted by the booming bark of Kamal's dog, who appeared to be part German shepherd and part Bedouin sheepdog, what many Baghdadis call a "wolf-dog." The breeding of such savage guard dogs was enjoying a mini-renaissance in a city where a lack of parts meant canines were more reliable than burglar alarms. The villa was a kind of Babylonian bungalow with smooth concrete walls and a sprawling back garden.

One of the charms of Baghdad is its status as a "horizontal" city, with few ugly high-rises; most inhabitants still live in one-level homes with gardens. The neighborhood, explained Kamal, was full of such homes, many built in the fifties when foreign engineers and contractors came to help construct modern Baghdad. It was now a popular residential area for U.N. workers.

Kamal's living room was cluttered with papers and magazines, mainly back issues of *Time* and the *Economist*. Like much of Baghdad in those days, the villa had a slightly abandoned feel; everything was covered with a thin layer of dust.

After a glass of tea, brewed sweet and strong in the Iraqi style, Kamal wanted to discuss John Pilger's book, *Hidden Agenda*.

"You know what he says," he began, "about 'internal colonialism'? That's really what's happening here in a big way." The sanctions, he said, were definitely to blame for the whole disaster of Iraq in the nineties, but there were "internal as well as external factors" at work. In 1991, he explained, the wealth of Saddam Hussein's "family" — managed by his half-brother Hassan Al-Tikriti — was estimated at $30 billion U.S. "It's all in Swiss bank accounts," Kamal maintained.

But was it true, I wanted to know, what so many Iraqis said about Saddam Hussein — that he was "Son of the U.S.A."?

"Well" began Kamal rather cautiously, "that could very well be true. This is something you should investigate for yourself." Even in conversations in private homes in Baghdad, it seemed, there were limits to what could be revealed.

Kamal did mention that a columnist in the Lebanese newspaper *Al-Hayat* had published an article in early 1998 in which he put forward just such a theory. He had offered up two main facts for consideration: that Saddam had brought the U.S. into the Gulf by means of his invasion of Kuwait, and that he was profiting financially and politically from the sanctions, through the dividends of smuggling and the entrenchment of his power.

"The political dividend," said Kamal, "is also played out in other ways." He mentioned a recent statement made by the president's son, Uday, just before the Iraqi elections of March, 2000: "He basically said that any talk of 'democracy' in Iraq was premature, given the 'extraordinary circumstances' of the sanctions regime. But this is not new; we've grown accustomed to this kind of talk." Kamal cited promises made by the government in 1992 that they would work towards "pluralism, privatization and a free-market economy."

"So far," Kamal concluded with ironic understatement, "not much progress has been made in these areas."

I had just visited the newly opened Baghdad Stock Exchange, where stocks were traded without the benefit of computers and bids were handwritten in felt pen. And yet, at that time it had seemed that everywhere, statism was giving way to the relatively free-market chaos of sanctions profiteering. And what would Baghdad become once the sanctions were lifted? Back then, with the exception of a few pirated videocassettes of Celine Dion concerts, Baghdad was virtually untouched by globalization. I envisaged a near future full of McDonalds and Microsoft. As it turned out, I was not far off, although they would make their way in by invasion rather than sanctions-busting.

"Oh, you can be sure," said Kamal, "that once the sanctions are lifted, the American companies will be first in line at the gate." And then gesturing with his hand and nose, he suggested, "You can already smell the money."

But what of the "internal colonialists" Kamal had mentioned earlier, Baghdad's nouveau riche? Where, besides quasi-Italian restaurants in Arasat, did they hang out?

After a bit of cajoling, Kamal offered to take me to a private "equestrian club" where wealthy and connected Baghdadis went to play. It would be a bit risky, he said, because no foreigners were allowed entry. But if I only spoke to him in Arabic, I could pass myself off as an Iraqi friend.

On the way there in Kamal's battered old Buick, we drove past a real-estate brokerage and a roast-chicken joint with a pseudo-Colonel Sanders Kentucky Fried Chicken logo. Soon we passed an old Ottoman palace, presently inhabited by a Baathist notable, and then a two-story bridge constructed in the early nineties. On the other side of the bridge you could see a few newly built palaces.

"You see," said Kamal, pointing to a pile of uncollected garbage in a middle-class residential neighborhood, "there has been a total disintegration of municipal services since the embargo began. You know, the 'family' [of the president] is not anymore sharing with the people their life. They live in their own palatial enclosures where everything is impeccable." I would remember this when I visited the Americans in their fortified compounds after the invasion.

"Even the traffic police" continued Kamal, losing his cool for a moment as he pointed to a friendly neighborhood policeman, "are connected to 'special security.' It's just like *The New Class*." He was referring to Milovan Djilas's 1957 book that criticized the new communist power elites, from Tito to the Soviets.

Kamal paused in his tirade for a moment when I inquired about a huge sign on the road with a picture of Uday. "Oh, it says," Kamal translated, "'Heartfelt congratulations to Uday Hussein for his great victory for the membership of the national council in its fifth session.'"

"Didn't he win by 96 percent?" I asked Kamal.

"No" he replied with a grin. "It was 96.9."

We drove past Baghdad University, designed by Walter Gropius in the fifties and almost destroyed during the American invasion, and then onto the main road leading to the equestrian club. The air was perfumed with the scent of orange blossoms from the surrounding groves. We stopped to pick a few, and for a moment entered into a kind of amnesia. Here you could forget that there had ever been a war or ten years of crippling sanctions, or that a few miles away children were dying for lack of medicine.

The club, explained Kamal, was created in 1994 and had a very "closed" membership. So how did he get in? I asked.

"Well," he answered sheepishly, "I guess they needed a few of the old families to kind of buy some respectability." I was reminded of the elitist Gazira Sporting Club in Cairo, which survived talk of expropriation after the Nasser-lead coup that overthrew the monarchy in 1952, only to become a bastion of the new elite.

As we pulled in to the club parking lot, Kamal pointed to an old Volkswagen. "You see," he said, "there's some poor people like me here too." I pointed out a brand-new Porsche and he added, "Oh yes, they're very popular here. You know, when Uday was shot [in 1997] he was out driving in his golden Porsche."

As we walked into the terraced gardens of the club, we were greeted by a young man whom Kamal said was a friend of his son's. I smiled and offered a greeting in Arabic. I was clutching a small Sony tape recorder behind my purse.

In the genteel confines of this Iraqi country club, kids dressed in Tommy Hilfiger rollerbladed by while their parents, many dressed in Armani, drove by in golf carts. Kamal and I strolled by a mural of Saddam and his sons Qusay and Uday, all on horseback. "It's the three musketeers," joked Kamal. We walked down to the water's edge, where several yachts were anchored on the banks of the Tigris. "These are the party boats," said Kamal, describing the cruises that took place, complete with fireworks and dancing girls. "Of course, there's less of that now than there used to be," he explained. "But it still goes on."

In the background the flames from an oil refinery were visible. The bingo announcer's voice boomed out numbers and letters in English and Arabic. I wondered what the prize was.

"That refinery used to be owned by Kelloggs," Kamal told me, "before it was nationalized."

In the bulrushes at the river's edge I suddenly spied an old woman dressed in traditional clothes cutting bulrushes with a scythe. I blinked. In the playground nearby, a lone cow chewed quietly as children played on swings.

Moving towards the clubhouse, Kamal said, "This hall was inaugurated on the occasion of Uday's thirtieth birthday, in June of '97, shortly after he was shot. It was a huge extravaganza."

"Do they know who tried to kill him?"

"Oh, there are various theories; some say it was a rival family ..." He was being vague, and I guessed this probably wasn't the most appropriate place for this discussion.

We were interrupted by someone important driving by in a motorcade. We moved to the side of the road to avoid the blur of black Mercedes.

"Who was that?" I asked.

"Oh, a party member or someone. You know," he continued in a low voice, "they say that some top party members have shares in CNN. So when CNN made that fifty-million-dollar deal during the Gulf War, the party members profited two ways. Like Nizar Hamdoon [Iraq's ambassador to the U.N. under Saddam], he's doing deals in the States for sure. They say he even has good personal relations with Clinton."

I remembered a French oil executive who had told me he was disgusted at the "hypocrisy" of the Clinton regime, which condemned Saddam at the same time that Mobil and Exxon executives were having lunch with top bureaucrats at the Iraqi Ministry of Petroleum.

Kamal and I fell silent. We walked by some kids taking pony rides, and a man in hunting gear walking his pointer dog. In the distance I could see a couple of guys in the river on jet-skis. A CD of Lionel Ritchie songs played on, only interrupted by a far-off muezzin's wail calling the faithful to their prayers.

SOME THREE YEARS after my day at the club with Kamal, L scanned the Il Paseo menu, unchanged since the invasion. "The best bet is the spaghetti bolognese," he said decisively. "The schnitzel is a bit dodgy in summer."

I tried to press him delicately for more details of his current business dealings, but he was wary of journalists. He had been "double-crossed" by a prominent *New York Times* correspondent, he told me, who had related the details of a deal that he'd overheard at a dinner party — in the next day's paper. "I lost a cool million because of that. But I got him. I had his visa pulled from the Ministry's list." He'd also told the reporter later, "If you write about me again, I'll kill you." The fateful dinner party had been engineered by a well-known CNN correspondent that L also spoke of disparagingly.

The conversation turned to a mutual acquaintance connected to a Canadian petroleum company.

"That guy is a CIA agent!" exclaimed L with contempt. "I had him deported."

"Really?" I said.

"Yes. They left like dogs. Twenty-four hours to get themselves and their offices out of the country." I noticed L's right temple was throbbing slightly.

"Well, what about those Iraqi-Americans he was connected with?" I flashed back to conversations with a guy from San Diego who always reminded me of Frank in *Blue Velvet*.

"CIA, all of them," pronounced L.

"So you've got some interesting house guests?" I said.

"Yes, some FBI guys and a few 'ambassadors,'" he answered, not missing a beat. When L saw my slightly stunned expression, he smiled as he lit up a Marlboro. "New times call for new associates, my friend."

"Right," I said, lifting my lemonade glass. "Well, here's to old associates."

I was glad that L didn't want to kill me. As long as I was entertaining, I thought, and didn't push him too far, all would be well. After all, he still did have the best parties in town, and was always an impeccable host.

I SENSED THAT L KNEW a lot more than he let on about the workings of the new Iraq. Our conversations always seemed to illuminate what I'd been ruminating on for days. But they were few and far between. In the coming month I would see him only twice. Whenever I called, he would inevitably be just hopping onto a cargo plane to Basra or dealing with the aftermath of mortar shelling at the airport.

Before we left the restaurant, L did mention something serious. "It's about Karim," he said. "I know that you're friends, but ... there's something a little 'off' about him now."

"How do you mean?"

"Well, you know, he's been through a lot over the last few years," continued L, in a not entirely unsympathetic tone. "He hasn't really landed on his feet yet." And then he added in a whisper, "We don't know who he's working for."

In an odd way, L's revelation did make sense. Even though Karim was working for an American-backed NGO, he still had plenty of

Baathist tinged, anti-foreigner invective. Like so many Iraqis of his generation, he was lost in a kind of political and cultural schizophrenia. Ironically, L's loyalties were more straightforward. He was only looking at the bottom line.

By the time L had dropped me off at my hotel, he was in a rather jolly frame of mind. "I'll have my driver come round for you one night this week. We'll have dinner. Great seeing you again."

Chapter 8: Suspicious Minds

ALREADY EXHAUSTED BY A few hours in the September heat, I retired to my room for some air-conditioned respite while L went on to some business. After a little Arabic-subtitled *Dynasty* (it always seemed to be on) in the afternoon as a kind of mental palate cleanser, the phone rang. It was Karim, who had decided to drop by to see me en route from some "important" meeting. In a few minutes he was at my door again.

He looked like the cat who'd swallowed the canary.

"So what did you do this afternoon?" I asked him.

"Well," he began, "I have some good news."

"What is it?"

"I went to the CPA this afternoon," he said excitedly, "to the palace. And they gave us three little villas — just for the institute! It's a former minister's compound," he explained, "but it was looted and burned after the war. There are some squatters living there — but they have houses to go to; we aren't kicking them out," he was quick to add. "They actually have houses outside of Baghdad," he told me, "that they've been renting! So in the end the CPA said we could have the villas!

"There are gardens and even swimming pools," Karim told me breathlessly, "Maybe we'll get some ducks and carp that we'll cook as *mazgouf*," he joked. "The only technicality is that we have to get permission from the commander of the district to remove the squatters." I pictured the evicted squatters making bitter comments about American democracy.

"Do you think this might be a good location for a 'garden of peace'?" I asked hopefully.

"Maybe," said Karim, "The only thing is that it's about five hundred meters from a military base."

Hmmm ... perhaps not. The children's art lessons might be interrupted by mortar fire.

"So," continued Karim, "that was good news. But also, I just love going to the palace. I enjoy sightseeing there. Every time I go I act like I'm lost and try to see more and more of it."

"What's it like?" I asked.

"Well, there's a lot of marble, there's still some Saddam statues. And right in the middle there's a bazaar."

"A bazaar?"

"Yeah, you know, people selling carpets, gold ... Coca-Cola. And, of course, there's lots of Americans. Including me."

"But are you a good American?" I teased him.

Karim took slight offense. "Am I? I don't know. Are you?"

He meant "American" in the same way another Iraqi friend had when he told me once, in an unexpected moment of real hostility, "You North Americans. You don't know what suffering is." I felt that same sudden anger in Karim now. He became serious for a moment and continued, "You will never trust me, will you? I sense that."

"But do you trust me?" I asked back.

He paused for a moment before replying. "No, I never trusted you because you were a journalist."

"But you talked to a lot of journalists," I reminded him. "Remember that English one? You gave him an interview and talked about how respect for Saddam was a cultural issue, that in Iraq it is considered bad form to criticize the leader because he's like the 'sheikh,' the father figure." I had read the interview on the internet, a few months after my last meeting with Karim.

"Oh, yes," he seemed to remember now. "That was for *Travel Intelligence*." The "old" Iraq seemed to be flooding back into both our memories.

"Do you remember when I called you from Barcelona," I ventured, "last year? I was calling from this small, dark room, and the line kept cutting out. Remember? You spoke in a very stilted way — maybe because the lines were tapped?"

"No," insisted Karim. "I was free to say what I wanted. I never cared whether anyone was listening. Look," he said, slightly exasperated, "even when you stayed at my apartment that time — did they ever know? I think they did, but perhaps they never suspected. Some other people might have been executed for housing a foreign journalist. But not me. They couldn't even question me!"

"Why not?"

"Well, let's just say I have my guardian angel."

I felt that same familiar chill I'd experienced when Karim showed me his American passport. "But," I continued gingerly, "you told me, 'They must have had a good reason for denying you the visa' — as if you agreed with them."

"No that's not what I meant." Our conversation was getting dangerous. "You always implied that I wasn't on your side," Karim said accusingly. "The simple fact was that you were not welcome any more in Baghdad. That's all I know."

"Am I now?" I asked.

"Well," he replied cagily, "You're already in the country. That's not for me to decide."

IT WAS TIME TO STOP TALKING in such dangerous circles. We decided to pay a visit to the al-Rabat theater in al-Adhamiya, the Sunni neighborhood that would soon become a hotbed of resistance, where the Iraqi Philharmonic was supposed to be rehearsing that evening. I convinced Karim to make a pit stop in Jadriyah, where he was bunking at a cousin's villa, to pick up his cello.

"Look," said Karim once we were on our way, pointing out the car window at a familiar-looking building. "That's the old American Interests section."

I remembered it well. It was manned by a lone Polish ex-Marine, a charming old-world gentleman who signed death certificates and occasionally took correspondents to dinner, among other activities. Located at the back of the Polish embassy, it had been a tiny American eyehole on the surrounding Iraqi world.

I began filming through the car window. As we passed by the former "intelligence headquarters," I became slightly unnerved. "Are these tinted windows?" I asked. "Can anyone see me filming?"

"Relax," he replied, "it's different now. Even if they can see you, it's okay."

Later I would learn just how untrue this was.

We passed by Uday's old palace, the neo-Ottoman Sindbad, now occupied by American soldiers. It was bordered by small groves of slightly singed pine trees. "Everything was looted," explained Karim, "even the sinks, the safes, the money, the furniture, the sheets in the bedrooms."

"What does that sign in front say?"

"It says 'American troops are here. Don't come close or we'll shoot.'"

I put my camera down.

We arrived at Karim's cousin's place to find that his cello was locked away for safe keeping in a room for which he had no key. So we made our way towards the theater in al-Adhamiya without the cello. En route we passed the former headquarters of the *fedayeen* militia, a wreck now populated by squatters, and then passed the Le Corbusier-designed sports stadium, which had also been looted, even down to the seats. Nearby was the old Ministry of the Interior, which had not fared well either. But behind it was the Ministry of Oil, which still stood relatively unscathed.

At the old al-Rabat theater, a once venerable institution built in the late sixties, we were greeted by yet another post-apocalyptic scene. On what was left of the sidewalk, two musicians clung to the large iron gate, which was locked with heavy chains. They were conversing through the bars with some shirtless squatters, clearly the patriarchs of a few families who had occupied the theater. An old man in his undershirt was shaking his head and waving his index finger. The musicians gestured back frantically.

"There won't be any rehearsal tonight," said Karim. "The theater's been closed."

We decided to visit Babeesh, a restaurant in Arasat where I'd spent many an evening in the company of smugglers and U.N. employees, who had been the only people in Baghdad who could afford the prices. "You know, Karim," I said as we drove through the city. "It's strange.

I keep feeling like I should have a minder with me." It was an odd sensation, not having one. Rather like a phantom appendage that I kept reaching for.

"I'm your minder," said Karim.

AS HE SPOKE, TRAFFIC GROUND to a stop and six American tanks rolled by. Something was going on this evening. But as we passed by some landmarks — the Palestine Hotel, where American forces fired on and killed two of the many international journalists still holed up there; Firdos Square, where the infamous statue of Saddam had been brought down and replaced by a whimsical statue called the Goddess of Liberty; and the Alwiyah Club, founded as a British Officers' club in 1926 and now the favorite hangout of returning Iraqi exiles — the golden dusk bathed everything in an ethereal light.

Soon we were approaching Arasat, which had been a favorite neighborhood of the well-heeled. As we pulled up to Babeesh, the once-vibrant street appeared eerily deserted. This was a contrast to the last time I'd been here in late 2001, when a few unforgettable scenes had been locked into my memory. A man dressed as Mickey Mouse had handed out orange balloons to children in front of a supper club shaped like a psychedelic Chinese pagoda. A flock of pink flamingos had cruised by with its minder, the pagoda owner, who was trying to attract customers.

"So where's the nightlife now?" I asked Karim.

"There is none," he scoffed. "Unless you go to a friend's house for a private function and stay overnight." Curfew was lifted at 4 a.m., just in time for *fajr* prayers.

The entrance to Babeesh was graced by a triumvirate of stone lions spouting water, with electric green eyes that glowed in the dark. I had tried out some black humor here once on a Baathist notable, pointing to a lion and saying, "Look, *mukhabarat!*" Fortunately he had laughed. The joke hadn't been too far from the truth.

As the roar of a Black Hawk helicopter filled the sky, Karim and I strolled in to find the restaurant empty and in darkness. We sat at a table near the window, and eventually a waiter arrived and went off to crank up the generator. Finally the lights flashed on and the smooth voice of Julio Iglesias began to sing "Bamboleo."

The décor looked the same — a kind of heavy Italianate style with some oriental touches — but the restaurant had seen better days. As I would find out, the smugglers were keeping a low profile, the U.N. workers had all vanished, and the new CPA elite were too scared to eat here.

Soon the maître d', a small, mustachioed man, came to greet us.

"Hello!" I said. "Do you remember me?"

"Yes, of course," he replied with a nervous laugh.

"Do you know what that helicopter was about?"

"Mr. Rumsfeld is in town," he explained. "But yes, it is normal, very normal. We see helicopters every day, no problem with us."

"Is Wania here?" I inquired, asking after my old pal, the resident lounge singer and pianist.

"No," came the rather stone-faced reply.

"Where is he?" I asked.

"Wania has left Iraq." It seemed that Wania, a Christian Chaldean, had gone to San Diego to live with his son, an optometrist. But the maître d', who was Wania's nephew, didn't have his forwarding address; they'd had a little altercation just after the invasion and were no longer on speaking terms. Later I would discover that Wania's brother, the maître d's father, had played French horn in the Iraqi National Symphony alongside Karim.

As I looked around the empty restaurant, I thought of all the evenings I'd spent here with Wania, a one-time star of Baghdad's bustling seventies jazz scene, an era when cabarets were open well into the wee hours of the night. A brilliant and entertaining performer, he'd played solo at Babeesh. Limited in the embargo years to playing wedding parties for wealthy smugglers, Wania was always glad to see me and try out his more extended repertoire, everything from weird, phonetically pronounced English-language versions of Elvis songs to Latin lounge and French chanson.

Sometimes Wania's music was strangely moving. Once, when my actor friend Sadiq had taken me to Babeesh after the theater one night, Wania had sung Aznavour's "Yesterday When I was Young."

With the invasion looming and so much suffering already behind him, the lyrics were particularly poignant. The song suddenly became one of fervent nostalgia for a better time.

Another evening, I'd come here with Karim and an unwelcome guest, my minder, Ali. Wania asked me to sing "La Vie en Rose" with him, and poor Ali nearly went apoplectic. Already suffering from a nervous tic — a condition my presence seemed to exacerbate — Ali was beside himself. He got up from his chair and lunged towards the piano where I was singing with Wania. "Sit down," he'd hissed at me. "This is not allowed!"

Of course I'd hissed back at him and kept on singing, after which he'd stormed out of the restaurant in a great huff. The next morning at the Press Center, news of my "singing violation" was the main gossip amongst the minders. It seemed there really was a law — enforced by roaming "restaurant police" — prohibiting women from singing in nightclubs on weekdays.

"So, how's business?" I asked the maître d'.

"It's bad now. All the good families, the ones with money, they've left. We have not so many customers."

As I admired the still impressive collection of Lebanese, French, and American wines on display, the maître d' asked Karim for a quick word outside. I watched them through the window, gesturing and talking, the hulking Karim with his arm around the tiny maître d' at one point.

When they came back in I asked Karim if anything was wrong. "No, no problem," he replied.

But after a few drinks, Karim told me an amazing story that was part Kafka and part John le Carré. Apparently a few days after that fateful "La Vie en Rose" evening, some men had arrived claiming to be advertising salesmen for a newspaper. They were hoping, they said, that Babeesh would advertise with them. But the maître d' suspected they were really undercover *mukhabarat* from the Press Center who had come to check up on the restaurant. He found them later rifling through the accounts book in an upstairs office. Caught in the act, they accused him of having harbored a spy, namely me.

"But that's ridiculous," I said to Karim. "A spy for whom?"

"It doesn't matter," he replied, with no hint of irony. "They just suspected you — that's enough."

I turned to the maître d' and said, smiling, "Do you really think I'm a spy?"

He looked bashful, shrugged sheepishly and said something to Karim in Arabic.

"Well, they couldn't tell," Karim explained. "But they were scared. Even Wania was scared. You know you went to his house with me and spoke with him. This was not allowed. You can't have this freedom." I noted his use of the present tense. "You have to go by the rules of the country."

I imagined running into Wania in San Diego one day. Would he still shake my hand? Would he still want to sing old ranchera songs with me?

"Are you scared of me now?" I asked the maître d'.

"No," he giggled, "no fear now, no fear." Kazem al-Saher's "War is Over" was playing in the background.

"Well, you know," I said in my own defense, "I've been coming here since 1997 because it's a good restaurant."

There was an awkward silence.

"So," I continued, "If you could choose, would you prefer the old days to now? Are things better or worse now?"

"I would choose the future," he replied.

A clever and hopeful answer, I thought. Now, happily, there were no minders or "restaurant police" at Babeesh, but there was no live music either, and the maître d' kept looking out the window. As it grew dark, we hurried to finish our lamb kebabs. We were all alone in the restaurant, and with the windows open onto the darkened street, I felt like illuminated game on display.

When I saw L the next day, he would be shocked to learn that I had dined at Babeesh. "It's not a safe area any more," he would warn me. I realized that the maître d' had not been looking out the window for cops, but rather for robbers.

WE FELL INTO A KIND OF exhausted silence as we made our way back to the hotel. Karim came to my room for a drink. But it was an hour and a half before curfew, so our visit would have to be brief.

Still stunned by the Babeesh secret-police story, I said to Karim, "Can you believe that? I mean, why would they be so suspicious of me just for singing?"

"Well," said Karim rather cryptically, "I'm sure they had their reasons."

"I mean what did they think, that I was some sort of secret agent?" I scoffed.

"Maybe," said Karim quietly.

I was deeply hurt by Karim's accusation, especially after all the Saddamist labels that had been thrust upon me in North America merely for writing about the plight of Iraqi civilians. I was learning that, with the possible exception of "passing" in certain situations, looking like a local was a lose–lose situation in Iraq. Both sides suspected you: Westerners thought you lacked "objectivity" (although if your name were Friedman and you wrote about the Middle East you were safer from accusations of bias), while Iraqis, despite the lip service they paid to pan-Arabism, were often more suspicious of those they perceived as fellow Middle-Easterners — and possible "double agents" — than they were of Westerners.

But mostly I was wounded by Karim's suspicions because I had believed we were friends. We parted that evening wary of one another, and with the feeling that we had seriously misunderstood our connection.

An altarboy at a Chaldean Midnight Mass, Christmas Eve 1998

Chapter 9: Our Lady of the Flowers

THE NEXT DAY WAS SUNDAY. Feeling the need for some sort of benediction after my strange encounter with Karim, I decided to go to Mass. The Greek ambassador, whom I had met through L, had also invited me to meet with the Greek patriarch in Baghdad. His secretary had written down directions in Arabic for the Greek Orthodox church in Karradah. But my driver, Ali, a Shia from a tough neighborhood in the north of Baghdad, hadn't a clue how to find it. As a side benefit, though, I did get a lovely tour of the city's churches.

Iraq's 750,000 Christians include Protestants, Catholics, Nestorians, and followers of several varieties of the Orthodox faith, but the majority are Chaldeans, members of the ancient Nestorian church who pledged their allegiance to Rome in the 16th century. The Chaldean church, like some other autonomous Eastern Catholic churches, is under the jurisdiction of its own patriarch and retains its own distinctive theological, liturgical, and canonical traditions.

First Ali went to the main Chaldean church, the same one where I had attended Midnight Mass in 1998, days after Desert Fox. The Mass had been spectacular, with all the ritual pomp and circumstance: incense, incantations, and the unforgettable sight of the priest walking towards the altar with what looked like a bowl of fire. Apparently this was a throwback to the rituals of ancient Babylon, of which the Chaldean community in Baghdad were direct inheritors. Perhaps, I thought now as I gazed at a statue of the Virgin in the courtyard, it was time for a goddess-worshipping revival; surely the gods of war must be getting tired.

"*Kenisa hon?* [is the church here?]" asked a bewildered Ali.

"*La, la, rom orthodox* [No, no, Greek orthodox]" I said, and pointed again to the directions. I began thinking about all the Christmases I had spent in Baghdad — four in seven years — and remembered the weird-looking Rudolph and Santa statues set up every year in the lobby of the al-Rashid, always accompanied by 1970s Motown Christmas carols. "Santa Claus is Coming to Town" often took on a sinister tone ("He knows if you've been bad or good") as it chirped out from behind portraits of Saddam Hussein. One time right after Desert Fox, I had even bought a tree for the Press Center, a gesture that seemed to warm the hearts of even the most hardened minders.

We drove through a residential neighborhood with garbage on the side of road and graffiti that read DOWN AMERICA. Soon we came to a familiar Armenian church, Our Lady of the Flowers, not too far from the Petra Hotel. I'd come here once before in late 2001, seeking solace from the sheer pressure of life in Iraq. I'd hoped to at least light a candle in front of the Virgin and say a prayer, but I'd found the doors locked shut. A man with dark glasses and a double-breasted suit had come towards me. "You can't go in," he'd explained. "There's a funeral going on."

I'd been accompanied by Khaled, a young street kid who shined shoes in front of the Petra. He was a Shia, a refugee from the south whose family had moved to Baghdad after their village was destroyed during the Gulf War. He'd been disappointed too. He thought the church looked "pretty" from the outside and was hoping for a glimpse inside. Khaled bore a large scar on his forehead, from where his mother had slashed him with a knife after he'd lost one of the family's last remaining lambs. Everyone said she'd gone crazy, he told me, after she'd lost her husband and her house during the war. Soon afterwards, Khaled had run away from home. He'd been living rough — like thousands of other Baghdad street children — ever since. He looked about twelve years old, because of dwarfing from malnutrition, but was actually sixteen.

Khaled was part of a band of a dozen or so kids — some of them orphans, many of them the primary breadwinners in their often fatherless families — who worked in and around the hotel. And despite the tragedies he'd endured, he retained an essential sweetness that sometimes shone through his world-weary eyes. I remembered walking back to the Petra, past open sewers and feral cats and once-grand but now crumbling villas, and starting to sing Gounod's "Ave Maria," slowly, quietly. Khaled held my hand and hummed along as we walked together. God, I'd thought then, how long can Iraq go on like this?

On that same visit in 2001, I'd attended Mass at St. Teresa's Church in Karradah. I remember seeing a woman kneeling in prayer. Making the sign of the cross, she offered up silent benedictions as the priest led a prayer for the peace and prosperity of his congregation, their country, and their president, Saddam Hussein. With its candles, icons, and crucifixes, the church's interior looked like any other in the Catholic world. But in Baathist Baghdad, the power of God could never try to rival that of the president. And George W. Bush's recent inclusion of Iraq in "the axis of evil" had put renewed pressure on Iraq's Christian community, already caught in the delicate juncture between East and West.

Most people associate Iraq with Islam. But the land is steeped in Biblical history: it was the birthplace of Abraham, the supposed site of the Garden of Eden, and a place where the apostle Saint Thomas sojourned, en route between Jerusalem and India. Iraq's Christian community has always enjoyed a relatively important place in Iraqi society, exemplified by once highly visible Christian figures such as Saddam's former deputy prime minister and right-hand man, Tariq Aziz.

But since the embargo had begun in 1991, Iraqi Christians had been slowly disappearing. Many used family connections to emigrate to Detroit, which has the largest Chaldean community outside Iraq. While most left for the usual economic reasons, others were concerned that Iraq's secular society was becoming increasingly Islamized. As rural migrants from the predominantly Muslim south flooded into the cities, urban cosmopolitanism was yielding to fundamentalism. In Baghdad, more and more women didn't leave home without donning an abaya or at least hijab, and streets in many neighborhoods were empty of women after sunset. The hardships of the embargo had made Iraqis of all faiths more religious, but the Christians stood out in an increasingly visible Muslim majority.

The fall-out from September 11, 2001, had put even greater pressure on Christians. Global tensions and the "with us or against us" mentality, which was prevailing on all sides, had eroded the usually benign boundaries between Christians and Muslims. When I talked to the Chaldean patriarch, His Beatitude Rafael Bedawen, in his modest Baghdad office in late 2001, he admitted that "Iraqi Christians, we are sometimes accused of being agents of the West. Although," he added drily, "when the bombs fall they are not especially for Christians or for Muslims; they're for everyone."

And yet, the patriarch insisted, Iraqi Christians strongly identify themselves as "Iraqis first and then as Christians." They felt abandoned, he said, by the "Christian" nations that were persecuting them. "No country in the Western world can call themselves Christian. They do not act according to the Christian principles of peace and justice." After the invasion, many Iraqi Christians would again feel abandoned by the Americans when the CPA appointed only Muslim men (and three women) to the Interim Governing Council, many of whom espoused the introduction of the traditional Muslim legal code of *shariah*.

"Those who point the finger at Iraq should not forget Hiroshima and Vietnam," the patriarch continued. "They should not forget that they are starving a whole generation of children here." His views did not stop him from having good relations with Christians in America — not only Chaldeans, mind you, but even Episcopalians. In fact, a delegation of Episcopalian bishops had been set to arrive in Baghdad shortly before September 11. Since that day, the delegation's visit had been postponed indefinitely.

Archbishop Kessab, whom I visited on that same trip in his Basra parish, also welcomed contact with American Christian groups. In fact, he had celebrated Christmas Day with some Christian anti-sanctions advocates who came to express their "solidarity" with the Iraqi people. "The fact that they spent Christmas with us means they have not forgotten us. There are some who care about what's going on here.

"We love our enemies," continued Archbishop Kessab. "During Mass on Christmas Day I delivered a special message to Mr. Bush, saying that we are both men of faith and that we are praying for our leader and for him. We are praying that he will come to know that sanctions come from a place that is evil."

Although there were only a thousand Christian families left in Basra in 2001, compared to three thousand before the Iran–Iraq war began in 1980, he said that Christians got along well as a minority in Basra. "We are living here like brothers with Muslims," the Archbishop assured me, pointing out that at least seventy percent of the people who benefited from his parish's free pharmacy and daycare center were Muslim.

During the ravages of the embargo, it was not uncommon to hear such stories about Christians who literally helped keep their Muslim neighbors alive. As Christians had the monopoly on the lucrative liquor trade and benefited from substantial hard-currency "cousin-aid" via the Detroit diaspora, they were often in a position to do so. But after the invasion, many of these same Christians would become targets of fundamentalist violence. In August 2004, six churches were bombed in a single day, killing ten Christians and injuring another fifty; further bombs and attacks in October and November 2004 added to the misery. Since then, more than forty thousand Iraqi Christians have fled their homeland.

BUT BACK IN SEPTEMBER 2003, such sectarian violence had not yet erupted into the open. As we pulled up to another church, this one called the Virgin Mary Chaldean Church, I saw a shrine in the courtyard where some women and children were lighting candles and praying. A Shia woman in a long black abaya begged hopefully at the churchyard gate; as security worsened, many Shias, who also venerate Mary, were now joining their Christian countrymen in praying to her for peace. It was almost time for Mass and soon the sun would set. No one seemed to know where the church we were looking for was, so I decided to stay at this one.

I told Ali to wait for me and went inside. Mass was just beginning so I slipped into a back pew next to an old woman dressed in black. Three ornate chandeliers hung from the ceiling and fans kept the heat at bay. As the liturgy proceeded in Arabic and Chaldean — an ancient language close to Aramaic, the language spoken by Christ — I stared at the golden madonna and child over the altar. In his long white-and-gold robe, the priest looked old and frail, but his voice was still strong.

Little girls in frilly dresses wandered distractedly in the aisles. Soon I noticed a tall, pale, red-headed man in the pew next to mine. He did not join in with the congregation as they sang in response to the priest's calls, but stood ramrod straight, staring in front of him. His name turned out to be Wenton, and he was an Episcopalian from Montgomery, Alabama.

"I came with a friend that I work with on a construction job," he told me after Mass. He was a contractor for the American military. "It's an interesting service," he said politely. "Unfortunately, I can't speak Arabic." He had taken communion though, he said.

AFTER MASS, MANY WOMEN stopped at a special shrine inside the church, touching it, kneeling before it, praying fervently in front of it. "*Shlama ilalkh Maryam mletha na*," they recited in Chaldean: "Hail, Mary, full of Grace." Their faces were young, old, pretty, and plain, but their eyes all had a look of profound weariness, as if they'd grown tired of waiting for miracles.

I spoke with some of the women in the courtyard.

"Is it easy to be a Christian now?" I asked.

An older woman with a friendly face and long grey hair told me, "Some are afraid to come to church now because of the crime. More people came to Mass before."

"Yes, it's very dangerous in the street now," agreed her friend. "But there is no problem between Muslims and Christians here."

A younger woman, maybe 35, with thick auburn hair spoke up. "My name is Linda Naim Yusef," she told me. Linda was dressed in a velour leopard-print outfit. "Now, you know, there are only two classes," she said: "poor and middle class. And we, the middle class, we're just living day by day. Our income is barely enough to survive. It's hard for us to provide for our children. All these new things they see in the market — electronic gadgets and computers — are expensive. They need many things, but we can't afford them."

She paused for a moment to touch her rosary. "You know, under Saddam, times were better for Iraqis. The Iraqi Christian girl could go out on the streets to the church with her head held high. Now it is not safe. We can't even go out to visit our friends and relatives."

I knew that under Saddam's secular Baathist state, Christians and other religious minorities had enjoyed a sense of protection. But the situation that Linda was describing was not one of religious intolerance so much as a lack of security bordering on anarchy.

When I brought out my video camera to film some of the church's facade, a small crowd gathered in front of me. They knew I was a Canadian journalist and somehow assumed that I was filming directly for Canadian television. People began to approach the camera and make heartfelt appeals to their friends and relatives in Canada.

A woman and her young daughter came forward, took my tiny microphone and said, "I send special regards to Father Edward and to Sister Nabil in Montreal. And my very best regards to Iraqi Christians in Canada ... and Detroit."

Another lady said, "Hello to Sarab in Toronto and condolences for your wife." Then she said, to no one in particular, "We miss them so much, but they never called us. And hello to our uncle."

Her sister began to speak. "We are sending regards to friends in Toronto. We are all well. There is still no telephone but they are working on it. And Uncle George, we did everything we could when your mum died." She looked as though she might burst into tears. I began to feel the same way.

A middle-aged woman named Shonia came to me and complained, "My dad died a month ago — none of my relatives in Canada helped me. No one contacted me." I had morphed into a kind of itinerant Canadian consul.

An old man came forward in an agitated state and said, "I want to speak to my son. I want to speak to him." He told me his name was Hanna Toma, then took the microphone and said, "I miss my son and haven't heard from him in six months. He is in Toronto. Please, Millad, please write to me."

Later the man asked me how he could apply for a visa to go see his son. I explained that there was no embassy in Baghdad, and suggested that he go to Amman. Of course he just shrugged his shoulders in despair; there was no way he could afford the thousands of dollars such a trip would entail. He couldn't even afford to telephone Canada. The old man thrust a piece of paper into my hand with his son's e-mail address and phone number on it. "Please call him for me," he begged.

"Please." The e-mail address was a variation of "snoop doggydog," with indecipherable punctuation and numerals.

Later, back in Canada, I tried to ring the phone number. It turned out to be a Chaldean church in North York, but there was never any answer, except for one time when a woman answered in Arabic and then hung up. Finally one night, after weeks of unsuccessful ringing, another woman answered and passed me directly to Father Johannes, who introduced himself as the Chaldean bishop in Canada. I explained who I was and why I was calling. After some language difficulties he finally said, "Yes, Millad. I think he is a member of our basketball team." Father Johannes assured me he would tell Millad to call his elderly father in Baghdad the next time they met. Then he said, almost as if he were conducting Mass over the phone, "And please, please, we must all pray for peace and tranquility in Iraq, through the intercession of Our Lady."

Chapter 10: Guns at the al-Gaylani

FROM SUNDAY TO FRIDAY, from one holy day to another, there was much to contemplate. On Monday the Canal Hotel — still in ruins after the huge blast that ripped it apart in August and killed 22 people, including the U.N.'s top envoy, Sergio de Mello — was hit for a second time, injuring nineteen people and killing two. I discovered this when I tried to drive there that afternoon, only to be turned away. A few days later the hotel where NBC TV lodged was bombed and one person died. On the same day Aquila al-Hashimi, one of three women appointed to the IGC and a former Baathist notable, died from her wounds in hospital; she had been ambushed on her way to work some days earlier.

That Friday I slept late and found myself rushing to prepare for my meeting with Sharmeem. A former Ministry of Information visa clerk, Sharmeem had offered to take me to the al-Gaylani mosque for Friday prayers. Worship was segregated, so a woman translator was essential. I took a cold shower in my ancient bathroom and hurriedly changed into my Islamic-peasant-from-Falluja-on-a-particularly-pious-day costume. I also brought along my white abaya — purchased in 1994 in Jerusalem before a visit to the Dome of the Rock mosque — as a backup.

I arrived in the lobby to find Sharmeem, a handsome, fifty-something Turkmen, dressed in a faux Chanel suit and heels. We were visions of each other's studied projections.

"Hadani!" she exclaimed. "You look so … authentic."

"Thank you," I said, not entirely convinced her tone was complimentary. "You look nice, too."

Though she professed a certain religiosity, Sharmeem was obviously from the old school of liberated Baathist women state employees. However, her husband, who now worked for the *Washington Post* as a translator, had insisted on coming to check me out before allowing her to work with me. She spoke enthusiastically about our outing, as if she were working for the Iraqi Ministry of Tourism. "Very good," she clucked, "The al-Gaylani is an important historical mosque."

On the way there, Sharmeem decided to take me to the Friday book market in the old part of the city. On a winding street named after the Iraqi poet al Mutanabbi, the market had once been a testament to Baghdad's thriving literary scene (a popular Arabic proverb goes, "Egyptians write, Lebanese publish, Iraqis read"), where Baghdad's writers and academics met to buy and sell books of every description. In the bad old days of the embargo, it was not uncommon to see tearful writers selling off their entire collections of Shakespeare, Rimbaud, or Walt Whitman to buy basics like food and medicine. Now the biggest sellers appeared to be Shia religious texts, computer magazines, and pornography. Amid back issues of *Architectural Digest* and *Time* magazine, I found an array of international girlie magazines, from *Playboy* to Jordanian smut. A few yards away, a man sold prayer books alongside portraits of the Ayatollah Sistani and images of Imam Ali.

Next to volumes about the Ayatollah Khomeini I was surprised to see one with a giant Star of David on its cover. The salesman explained that the book was a discussion and comparison of the Torah and the Koran. Most of his stock, he explained, were books that had been banned under the old regime. Now they were selling like hotcakes: "There is more freedom, but there is also much conflict in society. People are becoming more religious now — it is a form of security." Faith was one of Iraq's few growth industries (security was another).

I noticed there were fewer women in the crowded market than the last time I'd been there. As Sharmeem and I retreated to the car and began our journey to Friday prayers, I started reminiscing about the al-Gaylani. An 18th-century mosque named for Abdul Kadir al-Gaylani, a Muslim saint revered by Shias, Sunnis, and Sufis, it was an old haunt of mine. I had spent many a Friday afternoon there, speaking with worshippers and clerics about everything from sanctions to Koranic texts. In 1998, just days after Desert Fox, I'd spent Christmas Day praying with the women there and being received warmly by their families afterwards for tea. I'd once spent almost two hours discussing Islam in Iraq with the mosque's spiritual leader, Sheikh al-Samarrai, whose impressive robes and turban gave him great presence. "In Islam there is no compulsion," he had told me. "True devotion comes from the heart, not from external pressure. This is not Iran."

I had met all kinds of women here, not just religious hajjis (believers who have made the pilgrimage to Mecca) but educated, "modern" women — engineers, doctors, lawyers — who had started to pray again after the Gulf War. "It gives us strength," they told me. "It helps us to survive."

But the other reason that so many people came to the mosque was that, like many others, it had become a center for food distribution under sanctions, and remained so after the invasion. With its cool balconies and incense-perfumed air, it was also a refuge, both literally and metaphysically.

On a visit here in December 2000, I'd entered the mosque about 45 minutes before the Friday afternoon prayer, dressed in a black abaya that Ali, my minder, had lent me (it belonged to his mother). After a brief talk with the sheikh and some extended haggling with a few mosque "minders," I was able to access the inner sanctum of the refuge — the women's prayer area. Here I was taken in by a kind old hajji with a tattooed chin. I put away my camera and pulled my abaya closer, as the hajji extended part of her prayer mat to me. "I am a journalist from Canada," I told her, "and a Muslim."

"Welcome, my child," she said, helping me tuck in my flailing hijab with great dexterity. She introduced me to her friends, who smiled warmly, holding their hands to their hearts, before the prayer began. I stood and prayed with these women, shoulder to shoulder, then prostrated myself beside them.

I listened with the others to the imam's sermon. He spoke of the "jihad" (literally, "striving") of the Iraqi people as a basic struggle for survival, and prayed for the lifting of the embargo. At some points he sounded as if he were choking back tears; at other times he was almost too angry to speak. Some of the women wept as they listened. What were they thinking of? Sons and husbands who had died in the war, or who were still imprisoned as POWs in Iran? Children for whom they could not provide?

As I watched the faces of the women at prayer, some with their small children beside them, I also felt the strength and solidarity they shared here. Their prayer brought them together as much as their pain. There is no spiritual crisis here, I thought. Only a material one.

After the prayer, the sheikh reluctantly agreed to let me photograph and interview the women, who were queuing up for the daily rations of soup and yogurt. As soon as I approached one woman, I was swarmed by groups of skinny, dirty-faced kids asking for money. Many of the women I spoke to were young, some barely out of their teens, but they already bore the signs of hardship and malnutrition: pallor, large dark circles under the eyes, hollow cheeks. I asked them about their lives before and after the embargo, but many had trouble remembering what it had been like in the 1980s. Most of them had still been kids; I realized I was speaking with a generation of Iraqi women who had come of age knowing only war and sanctions.

Most recalled that sewage and electricity systems and medical care had once been better, and there had been more food, but other details were vague. Their pre-embargo memories were already fading like old photographs. I asked one woman, named Maryam, how her life had been different before the embargo and she gave me a blank look. Her friends encouraged her to answer, but all she could say was, "Um ... We had a television then, I remember." Maryam smiled sheepishly and then stared at the mosque's stone wall as if in a mild state of shock.

When I mentioned the women to the sheikh he replied, "They are only thinking of Paradise now."

SINCE THE INVASION Sheikh al-Samarrai, tainted by his Baathist connections, had been replaced. But as I would discover, the al-Gaylani mosque remained one of the last public arenas where women could meet and express their views, albeit in an atmosphere of ever-declining security.

As we drove to the mosque past wrecked buildings and bombed houses, Sharmeem lamented the burning of the Baghdad library right after the invasion. Before entering, we adjusted our hair and clothing to the correct standards of modesty. While we did so, Sharmeem reminded me that the al-Shaab mosque in the north of Baghdad had been bombed the Friday before.

"Do you think it's safe here?" I asked.

"Oh, it will be fine," she reassured me. It was hard to tell whether she was trying to convince me or herself. Sharmeem still seemed locked into a time when party membership made you safe from the madding crowd.

As we passed the "mosque security" — two exhausted-looking men in ragged clothing clutching ancient Kalashnikovs — I concealed my small video camera underneath my abaya. As we walked across the stone courtyard towards the women's area, three American Apache helicopters flew overhead, like dark insects against the bright blue of the sky. Two small boys danced together in the open area, pointing upwards and grinning, while their mothers sat in quiet contemplation in the shaded area, beneath majestic stone archways.

We sat down next to a friendly woman with several small children. While the kids climbed over me and their mother offered us glasses of strong mint tea, Sharmeem explained that I was a visitor from Canada. The children began introducing themselves. The oldest girl, Khadidjah, told me she was studying geography, history, and English, and that she wanted to be an engineer when she grew up. Her mother politely shushed her as the sheikh's sermon began.

The imam told the story of the early Muslims who had had to defend themselves against the Meccans, and of how the Prophet Mohammed encouraged his followers to find strength in unity. He then spoke of how the "Zionists" were attacking Iraqi women in their homes (although from what the women told me later, it seemed they were having a harder time dealing with Iraqi men). I focused on a little girl, too young for the hijab, who leaned against an archway in a starched pinafore party dress. She seemed a little bored.

Suddenly an old woman with a weathered face began shouting and gesturing with her arms, opening her hands skyward and screaming, "Look what they've done to us Iraqis, what they've done to the Iraqi people! Our children are dying, their blood is spilled! Let God be the witness! They have ruined everything! We had everything before, now we have nothing!"

A young girl in the courtyard of the al-Gaylani mosque just after Friday prayers on Christmas Day 1998, a few days after the Desert Fox bombing campaign

As I bowed and prayed with the women, I reflected on her genuine, spontaneous expression of grief and rage. Very possibly, this was her only venue to vent such emotion.

After prayers, two little girls began making the rounds selling fans made from date palm fronds and small toys for the children. A group of women gathered around me and all began to talk at once. A woman about my age approached me and introduced herself. "We miss so many things that we had before the Americans came," she said. "I'm trained as a civil engineer, you know, but there is no work now." She had been an engineer for the Iraqi Ministry of Defense. "And the security situation is terrible. There are armed gangs who want to kill and steal, to break into your house. Before at least I worked in freedom. Now we are afraid to walk in the streets. There is no freedom for women in Iraq."

She recounted how she had fended off a car-jacker just the other day, thanks to her trusty Kalashnikov, and how one of her friends had been wounded recently trying to fight off a gang of men who had broken into her home and assaulted her. "We don't know what will happen tomorrow," she said. "We hate the Americans and we hold them responsible for such a situation."

"What about Iraqi men?" I asked her. "Don't you hold them responsible too?"

"They are all unemployed now," she shrugged. "They are nervous and angry."

Then a woman named Shama approached me. She was the sister of the mother I had sat next to at prayer. She was eight months pregnant, she told me, and already had one child, an 18-month-old girl. She began to cry as she told me her story.

"Two weeks ago," she said quietly, "I told my husband I was leaving him because he beat me. The next day, he came and kidnapped my daughter. He told me he was going to take her to the north and sell her! I don't know where he is. He may be in Kut, his hometown, south of Baghdad, but I can't afford to travel there — it is so far away. I could go if I had money and help — with all my heart I'd go." She began to sob again. "Nobody is helping me these days, nobody." She put her hand over her face and turned away.

Her older sister with the children came to comfort her. "She's afraid that her husband might find her and hurt her if she talks any more," she explained.

Then a third sister, Messadi, came forward and told me her problem. "You see," she began, " I am infertile and ... This is a problem. My husband will divorce me if I don't produce any children."

Just as Mesadi was going to continue, one of the mosque security guards came running towards us, telling us we had to leave at once. There had been a bomb threat and the mosque was to be evacuated. Later I would learn that the guards had actually caught a man with a small bomb in his bag, minutes before it was set to explode.

"Why don't you come and visit us in our home?" suggested the older sister. "We can discuss all this at leisure." As we walked towards the exit, Sharmeem took down their address and we agreed to visit them the next day.

THE FOLLOWING MORNING I set out to find the three sisters. They lived in Karkh, the neighborhood where Saddam Hussein had spent his youth. Despite heavy bombing during the invasion, the spirit of this tough, working-class neighborhood had not been broken. I'd asked Ali, my driver, whether it was a safe area to visit. He had squinted slightly and said, "We'll see. I'll know when we get there."

As we neared the address, Ali stopped to ask directions of an old man sitting on the sidewalk in front of a silversmith shop. He gave some vague instructions and we continued driving slowly through the narrow, potholed streets. Many buildings had been flattened by bombing, although a solitary green patch did appear miraculously in the midst of the concrete chaos. Ali slowed again and checked the address with some middle-aged men wearing long white *jabalas*. An old toothless woman dressed in a black abaya emerged from the sidelines and gave her two cents' worth. Eventually we found the sisters' house.

It was an old stone house that looked at least a hundred years old. I knocked on its rusted copper door and a smiling Shama came to greet us. She ushered Sharmeem and me into the two-room dwelling that seemed to be home to three generations and almost a dozen people.

The grey bareness of its concrete floors and walls was punctuated by an aging refrigerator decorated with plastic flowers, two wooden couches with a few cushions, and a ceiling fan. I noticed an embroidered depiction of a garden pinned to the wall. A single fluorescent light was evidence of some electricity.

I was introduced to various family members and then given a brief tour of the place: a tiny kitchen where a pot of chai was boiling; a stone stairwell leading to the roof; a minuscule bathroom with a single drain to serve all needs; a bedroom with an old Singer sewing machine pressed up against a wire-mesh window; and a storeroom with bags of flour, rice, and salt that was also home to a live chicken. These were the main parameters of the sisters' daily lives. Compared with this cramped space, the al-Gaylani mosque must have been a paradise.

A man appeared to check things out. He was introduced to me as the husband of Maryam, the sister with all the children, and I to him as a "Canadian Muslim journalist doing a story on Iraqi women." Out of respect for her age and experience, I decided to begin my interview with the elderly mother. She wore a long black abaya and appeared to be in her early seventies. Her face bore the weight of experience and I felt honored to speak with her.

She told me that her name was Camila Ali Kamal. I was shocked to learn that she was only fifty-five years old and that she had been married off to her cousin at age eight. Her husband was a retired mechanic, she explained, and she had eight children — four boy and four girls — although eight others had died in childbirth or childhood.

"My boys have no work," she complained. "Only one has a job, and he only makes 1,500 dinars [about $2 U.S.] a day. It's just not enough for all the mouths we have to feed. We are poor and we've been living in this one house for over nineteen years. It's too small for such a big family."

"During the invasion," continued Camila, "it was really bad. A lot of attacks happened in this neighborhood." It seemed the area had also been a *fedayeen* stronghold. "All my family came here. I tried to protect them, but it was stressful. Now I am sick with diabetes. It is not easy to get the right medicine — and it's expensive. If I have 500 dinars I give it to my son to go to the pharmacy and get it for me."

"Are things getting better or worse for Iraqi women?" I asked her.

"She thinks things will improve," Sharmeem translated.

"Really?" I asked. Perhaps Camila was just expressing that familiar old Iraqi stoicism.

"How is her life different from her daughters' lives?" I asked. "Were things harder for her or her daughters?"

"I hope my daughters' husbands will treat them better," she replied. "My husband was always very good and kind — he's a hajji and he reads the Koran every night. My life was better than my daughters' lives. My husband understood me very well and he gave me everything I wanted. But with my three daughters, it's different. Well, one [Maryam's husband] is fine. But Mesadi's husband, well, something happened to him during the war, now he's changed. And the third one," she continued, referring to Shama's wife-beating, child-stealing husband, "well, he's very bad, I'm afraid."

Apparently Shama's husband, who ran a small cold drinks' stand, had returned from Kut the previous evening, without his eighteen-month-old daughter, whom he had left with his brother. He was now living across the street and continuing to threaten Shama, saying that he would put their child in an orphanage unless she went back to him. There was really nothing that Shama could do; there was no state, no law, no police she could trust, no recourse.

"Do you think things were better under Saddam?" I asked Camila. I remembered the old Iraqi Women's Union (IWU), an official Baathist organ but nonetheless a powerful organization with chapters in every town and village in the country. The IWU women I'd met were strong proponents of women's rights, lobbying to liberalize divorce laws and prevent domestic violence and rape. They were tough negotiators, intimidating even the macho male minders at the Press Center; "They frighten me," my minder Ali once confessed after translating a long interview with some of the IWU executive. Now Iraq was on a backward course, with the Interim Governing Council well on its way to reverting to religious law in matters of divorce, inheritance, and property rights. One could only imagine what might happen if the powerful Shia clerics came to power via direct elections.

"Yes," Camila replied, "things were better under Saddam. You know, Saddam grew up here and he gave me a piece of land once on Palestine Street." It was hard to tell if she meant the government had given her the land or that Saddam, the boy from the 'hood, had done so personally. "I sold that land and survived on it for a while, so I can't say anything bad about him."

Suddenly there was the thud of guns firing and what sounded like a low-flying helicopter.

"What was that?" I cried, somewhat taken aback.

"This neighborhood has a lot of gun sales," Sharmeem told me. "Some people here sell guns, and they fire them off to show that they work."

Oh, is that all? I thought. Just a little Kalashnikov demonstration. Nothing to worry about then.

I tried to continue with the interview. I learned that Camila was originally from a rural area near Basra. "My father died when I was young, my mother remarried, and they sent me to marry my cousin in Baghdad," she said matter-of-factly.

But trouble was brewing with the daughters, who had become suspicious when I'd inquired about the gunfire. Perhaps their husbands or brothers were involved in the local gun trade, and they thought we'd been sent by the Americans to check up on them. When I asked Shama about her husband, she replied, "These are private problems. How can you help me? How are you going to solve our problems? You are a journalist, not a social worker."

The sound of a fighter jet overhead filled the tiny room.

"Why are you asking all these questions?" continued Mesadi. She grabbed the microphone from Sharmeem and spoke in a loud, formal voice. "We had freedom under Saddam and we have freedom now. We were fine then, we are fine now. We are strong. We are Iraqi."

"Please, Hadani," said Sharmeem," we have to go now!" Things were getting tense.

Out of the blue, a bearded photographer appeared to take my

picture. I filmed him photographing me. "Can I get a copy?" I asked, at which the young, intense-looking man simply smiled and shrugged. This was no souvenir-making photographer. He had a more sinister purpose.

Sharmeem was practically dragging me out now as I tried to leave as politely as possible, saying goodbye and thank you to Camila and her daughters. She practically pushed me into the car and we drove off. As we cruised through the narrow streets, I noticed rows of shops that included shawarma stands, shoe stores, vegetable markets, and gun boutiques. Kalashnikovs hung precariously close to eggplants and zucchinis, AK-47s next to black death shrouds.

As we left Karkh, we passed an old portrait of Saddam holding a basket of fruit. His face had been erased, but the rest of his body and the oranges were still in fine form. Nearby, a bearded man walked down the street in plastic shoes, a new-looking Kalashnikov strung over his shoulder, a pregnant woman following a few steps behind.

Chapter 11: Press Conferences

MY PLANS TO LOOK FOR my old friend Ahlam always seemed to be interrupted by some dramatic news event. One day, as I was about to seek her out, I learned that Paul Bremer and a newly appointed minister on the Iraqi Governing Council would be holding a press conference at the Sindbad Hotel. I was keen to see the CPA "commander" (his actual title was "Ambassador") in action, and to find out whether he really did wear combat boots. I was also interested to get a first-hand look at the new Minister of Public Works, a Kurdish woman named Nesreen Mustafa Siddiq Berwari. I only knew her name because it had been carefully spelled out to the waiting news media by a clean-cut American in a navy blue suit. He enunciated each syllable with a marked drawl, until the Arabic-speakers in the press gallery corrected his pronunciation.

I was curious to see what a post-invasion press conference would look like. Who would be there? Would it be in the same theater as before, when most conferences happened on an upper floor of the Ministry of Information? I remembered how we would all be ushered in to the same Spartan room with a hundred or so seats and harsh fluorescent lighting. Usually CNN would have the first row, with ABC not far behind them. All the Iraqi journalists working for the wire services would sit as close to them as possible, always dressed in flak jackets. Lone Canadian writer chicks got to sit wherever there was space.

Once assembled, we would all wait while assorted "protocol" flunkies made careful scans of the room. Finally the day's government bigwigs — always in military dress — arrived and addressed us, mainly with Baathist platitudes. Sometimes they would spout statistics, such as the latest infant-mortality rates or even, as in 2000, the election results. They rarely said anything interesting or even relevant, but that was not the point. The point was the ritual of the whole event, and getting a five-second sound bite on to CNN that night.

On one occasion, a question of mine actually made it onto Iraqi TV. It was December 1997, and the day's guest was deputy prime minister Tariq Aziz. I asked him about access to the palaces, which was a hot topic then; the U.S. and the U.N. weapons inspectors had accused the Iraqis of storing arms and missiles there, but the Iraqis objected to the palaces being searched on the grounds that it would violate their sovereignty, comparing it to a search of the White House. I introduced myself as a journalist reporting for the *New York Times* and asked something like, "Does this whole issue boil down to one of national dignity?" He ignored the question and instead insulted the *Times*; his reply ended with a terse, "We will never allow them access."

In any event, the question and answer ended up being broadcast nationally on Iraqi state television, and from that day on, I was a celebrity among the chambermaids and elevator guards at the al-Rashid. As it turned out, only a few days later, the Ministry would arrange a tour of the palaces for a few select journalists. And a few days after that, I would be called into the office of the portly Sadoun, a heavy — in every sense of the word — at the Ministry of Information.

Sadoun had a beef with one of my *Times* articles. To my surprise, it turned out the offending article was the one about the growing humanitarian crisis in Iraq. In it I painted a grim picture of life for average Iraqis, including interviews with a struggling middle-class café owner in Mansour and a malnourished twelve-year-old boy in Saddam City, the desperately poor working-class area of Baghdad (now renamed Sadr City, after the martyred Shia Ayatollah Mohammed Sadek Sadr, father of young firebrand Moqtada al Sadr). I also included UNICEF statistics on infant mortality, and it was this part of the article that had Sadoun all riled up. Ironically, the article had only been brought to Sadoun's attention by well-meaning American peaceniks who had carried photocopies in by hand from the States.

In his tiny office, Sadoun appeared a bloated giant. "What is this?" he hissed at me, pointing to the article with a pudgy finger.

"What's the problem?" I asked. I was genuinely puzzled by his anger.

"Here you say 'According to UNICEF — which relies largely on Iraqi-provided statistics — the infant mortality rates have doubled in the last six years.'" He glared at me and narrowed his dark, bushy eyebrows. "You are trying to discredit us — and UNICEF. They are an independent organization and their statistics are accurate!"

I pointed out that the article showed American readers the reality of life under the embargo, but Sadoun was unmoved. The truth of the matter was that UNICEF probably *did* rely on Ministry of Health statistics, as they did in many other countries. If anything, in Iraq, where the civil service was slowly being eroded by economic collapse, their statistics were *under*estimates. The resources to record accurately every death of a child under five — even the ones that made it to hospitals — simply weren't there. But Sadoun and his colleagues at the Ministry of Information didn't recognize a good PR opportunity when they were presented with one. Instead of thanking me for broaching a subject that was rarely mentioned by Western media, Sadoun chose to insult me.

"Well," he pronounced, "we can't expect accuracy from a mere amateur. After all, this is only the Sunday edition of the *New York Times*." As I stared back at him in mild shock, a slow rage began to build. It wasn't just his ignorant, arrogant, sexist paternalism; it was also the knowledge that hundreds of thousands of babies *were* actually dying, and that this increasingly distant and corrupt regime could cynically manipulate these sad statistics. Political point-scoring was more important than the actual needs of all those poor mothers and infants, who couldn't afford the private health care allotted to party apparatchiks.

Suddenly, after five weeks of dealing with the likes of Sadoun every day, I exploded. I called him a bad name in English that he understood. "How dare you speak to me about accuracy, you *&^%$#! You used to be the editor of *al-Thawra*!" *Al-Thawra* was one of Iraq's state-run, *Pravda*-like papers and was not exactly famed for its factual reportage.

"Yes, it's true. You have a point there," he admitted.

He offered me a Marlboro as a mild kind of peace offering, but I refused. By now I had worked myself up into a self-righteous lather. I was ready to take on the entire overweight middle-aged male population of the Press Center — including the Americans. Forty-eight hours later, I was unceremoniously expelled from the country.

And so, as I scanned the banquet room of the Sindbad Hotel, which had been procured for the Bremer press conference, I was most surprised to catch sight of none other than Sadoun! He looked slightly slimmer and perhaps more subdued than in his Press Center glory days, but he still glared at me from across the room. Later I would find out that he had taken a job with CBS.

Compared to the old days, the Bremer conference was so low-key it was almost a letdown. Security was lax, and I had been able to enter without the requisite media badge (often just a laminated business card). There was only a half-hearted attempt at frisking for weapons. In the erstwhile dining room that had been commandeered for the occasion, a group of twenty-odd journalists had gathered, including representatives of CNN and Al Jazeera. Besides Sadoun there were other familiar faces: many of the same Iraqi wire-service reporters were present, but also, rather amazingly, were some of the old minders from the Press Center. Later I would discover that they too were now working for the American media.

After a twenty-minute delay, Ambassador Bremer strode in with Berwari, an attractive young Kurdish woman. He was in fact wearing combat boots and a blue business suit. She was wearing a kind of modest, professional outfit that wouldn't have been out of place in, say, a mall in Washington, D.C.

Berwari gave a brief speech in Arabic and then in English. "It's an historic moment for me to be here," she said, not without emotion, "because I am here as an Iraqi taking charge of Iraqi citizens' affairs and day-to-day services. We've been dreaming of this moment for a long time — to reach the population with water, improved sanitation, to create jobs through the implementation of projects." Bremer looked on approvingly. "And we will be doing this in close coordination with the municipal councils that have been created across the region and also the involvement of the communities. We want to involve the people of Iraq in planning projects and managing their own affairs." It sounded naive then, but not a fraction as much as it does today, a mere year and a half later.

Bremer stepped in with a kind "thanks-but-I'll-take-it-from-here" nod.

"Thank you, Madam Minister," he began. "... Thank you very

much for the kind hospitality you've shown." Hospitality? I wondered. As in, thank you for letting us invade your country? "We had," he continued, smiling for the cameras, "in diplomatic terms, what we would call an extended and frank discussion. What that really means is that the minister — as she has just indicated — has a big to-do list. In fact, we all have a big to-do list, in returning Iraq to sovereignty and to economic and political viability."

Bremer looked like a man who loved to make to-do lists. I could imagine him making them in bed at night. To do: 1) immediately disband Iraqi army so that hundreds of thousands of armed men will wander the country, unemployed and angry; 2) pick compliant Iraqis with anti-regime pasts and shady business histories to front the governing council; 3) make sure you give them zero power; 4) if they try to protest, offer even bigger kickbacks for them and their cronies or, if all else fails, replace them; 5) ignore pesky resistance forces, even if they bomb your fortress; 6) pack an extra toothbrush for Armageddon.

"The President of the United States announced last night a major initiative— more than $20 billion for the reconstruction of Iraq. This is one of the largest non-military budget requests in American history," he related with a certain pride, "and is a clear, dramatic illustration that the American people are going to finish the job we started when we liberated Iraq some four months ago. And it is a clear step along the path to Iraqi sovereignty."

Bremer continued to explain his "clear path" plan, as if it were some cure-all herbal medicine designed to rid Iraq of intestinal parasites. Apparently there were seven steps to Iraqi sovereignty, and three had already been taken. "The first step," he said, slowly morphing into Minister Bremer at his tiny pulpit full of camera mikes, "was the appointment of the governing council on July 13 — a group of twenty-five brave men and women working to create a new Iraq. The second step was the appointment in August of a preparatory committee to prepare a constitutional conference to write Iraq's constitution. The third step — taken last Tuesday — was when the minister and her twenty-four colleagues were appointed as cabinet members of the Iraqi Governing Council ...

"The steps ahead are also clear. First of all there will be a constitutional conference convened on the basis of the recommendations of the preparatory committee ..."

There were several more steps, and countless part-steps, but by this point he had lost at least half the room, and that was just the English-speaking half. We all perked up for the ominous-sounding Final Step, when the CPA — "as is foreseen in both international law and in the relevant U.N. resolutions" — would "hand full sovereignty back to that Iraqi government." By the time he mentioned international law, even Madam Minister didn't look too convinced. But Bremer left before anyone could ask any questions, with a smile and a nod to the assembled media throng.

I would attend other press conferences during the course of my stay in Baghdad. And as the situation went from bad to disastrous, there would be a progressively worsening case of American denial. As attacks by resistance forces increased in number, CPA and Pentagon officials would speak of the "improving security situation." Eventually these staged events would take on the same air of farce that "Comical Ali" — former Iraqi Minister of Information Mohammed al-Sahaf — had so perfected in the days leading up to the fall of Baghdad. His impassioned denials of an American military presence in the city could only be matched by the Americans' continued insistence that the new Iraq was a freedom-lover's paradise.

A LOT OF OTHER THINGS in the new Iraq were beginning to resemble their predecessors. In the chaos after Saddam's sudden fall, dozens of new newspapers had appeared, many with only a vague grasp of journalistic ethics, and the CPA had taken to banning the ones that spouted anti-American sentiments. And a press conference at Ahmad Chalabi's headquarters had given me a bad case of déja vu all over again.

Unlike Sharif Ali, the pretender to the Iraqi Hashemite throne, Chalabi — the leader of the Iraqi National Council and a long-time Pentagon favorite — seemed cocksure about his own coronation. He didn't rent his villas, he just took them over. Three months later, allegations of corruption and espionage would destroy his standing with the Americans. But the day I attended the press conference, it was the media that was in the hot seat — specifically, two of the most popular Arabic satellite channels in the region: Al Arabiya and Al Jazeera.

The latter, of course, had long been a bugaboo for everyone from corrupt Arab dictatorships who didn't enjoy media scrutiny to right-wing Zionist groups who accused it of anti-Semitism (even though it was the first Arabic television station to broadcast interviews with Israeli politicians). But today, both stations were under fire for "inciting violence" against the Interim Governing Council (IGC), presumably by their criticism of its ineffectual, cronyist members. They were also accused of having "advance knowledge" of resistance attacks, on the evidence that their camera crews showed up to cover the bloodshed. Had anything really changed? Even the name for the new U.S.-backed newspaper/coalition mouthpiece, *Al-Huriah* ("Freedom"), had once been the name of the old regime's state-run publishing house.

One difference was that the IGC couldn't deport journalists any more. In fact, they couldn't do much at all except bluster; they certainly couldn't stop the satellite transmissions. The worst punishment they meted out was a two-week ban on both stations covering IGC "news," whatever that meant. Of course, both Al Arabiya and Al Jazeera were present, filming the entire press conference. A CNN correspondent in the crowd dutifully brought up the issue of media censorship and freedom of the press, and afterwards I approached Chalabi's spokesperson, opening with a line that I thought might win his sympathy: "I'm from Canada and we've had some issues with Al Jazeera too." Things went well until I asked him, "When do you think Iraq will have an independent national broadcaster?" At the moment, there was only the U.S.-run Iraqi Media Network, which ran rose-colored reports. "Soon, soon," he replied, brushing me off and heading out with his gun-toting henchmen.

BUT THE ULTIMATE press conference was one that featured Ambassador Bremer with a very special guest: U.S. Secretary of State Colin Powell, on his first visit to post-invasion Iraq. Security was much tighter than it had been at the Sindbad, where I had simply walked in with a smile and a nod. Today, Bremer and Co. were speaking from the imposing pulpit of the Baghdad Conference Center, a gleaming complex built by Saddam in the early nineties that the CPA had taken over. It was a modern American palace whose dirty little Baathist past had been covered up with shiny new Coke machines.

Located deep in the heart of the "green zone" — the CPA heartland — the conference center was not easily accessible. It was surrounded by barbed wire and concrete barricades. Negotiating the series of checkpoints arranged along its length, I felt like a rat in a maze. Once inside the impressive lobby, we were clearly in American territory. We walked upstairs to the press center/holding tank for journalists. Security was tight, and after being searched and walked through a metal detector, we had to vacate the conference room for a bomb sweep. As a group of about a hundred mainly Iraqi media workers milled outside and sniffer dogs did their job, I took in a sea of faces. Many of the familiar players from CNN and other agencies were still there.

Back inside, we all cooled our heels for another half hour, while Pentagon types scanned the crowd for potential assassins, and giant television screens blared *Seinfeld* re-runs. I met with a young couple, both Iranian-American reporters who worked as stringers for the CBC. They in turn introduced me to Robert Fisk, the celebrated reporter for the London *Independent*, whom I knew only by reputation. He was an impressive blend of anarchist and social butterfly as he whizzed around the room, a bundle of nervous energy, offering rapid-fire observations about the whole situation. "I think," he said with a wry smile, "the Americans should learn from the history of Roman civilization. They made all the slaves citizens. The Americans should do the same with Iraqis, then they'll all move to the U.S. and join the army to get a free education!"

"No," laughed the young Iranian-American, "I think that an Arabic-language Fox is the real solution."

Soon a tough-looking, Australian-accented general took the podium and told us all to shut up. He laid down some basic ground rules for the conference. "Ladies and gentlemen," he began, "this area" — he gestured around the circumference of the podium — "is no-man's-land. No one comes up here. Cameramen are only allowed thirty seconds to come down the side for a shot — and they must not walk in between the journalists. Journalists, you must press the red buttons in front of you and give your names and organizations." I was secretly hoping they'd let Robert ask a question.

A few minutes later, they turned off *Seinfeld* and the monitors displayed the triumphant entrance of Ambassador Bremer and the secretary of state, who oversaw Operation Desert Storm in the first Gulf War. After a brief introduction, Powell began a short speech.

"I am deeply impressed by what I saw here," he declared (his visit had been less than 72 hours). "All the hard work is paying off." He made it sound as if U.S. forces had been out plowing fields rather than invading a country. "We are building democracy," he claimed, "... so we can move forward with the writing of the constitution, leading to free elections and a democratic leadership."

"We are not occupiers," Powell continued. "We have come under a legal term having to do with occupation under international law, but we came as liberators. We have liberated a number of countries, and we do not own one square foot of any of those countries, except where we bury our dead." Or where we build our oil pipelines or install our military bases, I thought.

After extending "greetings to all Iraqis" and restating the "president's pledge to give $20 billion for reconstruction" (I wondered which half would go to Bechtel and which to Halliburton), he continued along the "liberation" track. "I was impressed by the spirit I saw here, at the city councils, about education, the role of women ... There's a vibrancy that I attribute to the winds of freedom blowing through here." Vibrancy was one way of describing the situation; hours earlier, an improvised explosive device had ripped through an 82nd Airborne Division convoy west of Baghdad in Falluja, killing one soldier and wounding three others.

An earnest young Iraqi from the Iraqi Media Network — a TV channel that hardly anyone watched, and whose correspondents received no security protection even though they regularly received death threats — pushed his red button. "Today you met with members of the governing council," he said. "What was their message to you?"

"Well," answered Powell, almost smiling, "first of all, gratitude for what we've done to liberate Iraq and for giving them a new chance. Gratitude for what our soldiers are doing. It's really quite astounding how much has happened in the last few weeks!" Indeed, I thought, as Powell went on to promise the establishment of an independent judiciary as well as the return of basic services such as electricity, sewage treatment, and health care to "pre-war levels." Having witnessed some of those horrendously low pre-war levels first-hand, I marvelled at how the U.S. invasion had managed to lower them even further.

Next up was a tricky question about the deaths of Iraqis in detention and compensation for "checkpoint deaths" — usually of innocent Iraqis who had the misfortune not to hear or understand the "stop" command in English. Bremer breezed through it by speaking vaguely of certain incidents that "are still under investigation by our military" and mentioning that, "We have paid families in the past where it was appropriate."

Some brave soul whose name I didn't catch asked, "Will Powell have the opportunity to meet anyone who is unhappy with the U.S. presence?"

I had a vision of the secretary of state having chai with a disgruntled Iraqi resistance fighter on Rashid street. After a long chat about American values and a heartfelt promise that their intentions had been good all along — even during the decades when they'd supplied Saddam with chemical weapons, even when they'd encouraged the Shia uprising in 1991 and then helped in its brutal repression, even during those twelve long years of sanctions when they'd crushed the Iraqi economy — the resistance fighter would finally see the light. "I get it now!" he'd cry, throwing down his gun in the middle of the chai house. Then Powell would offer the fighter a job in the new Iraqi police force, where he'd risk being killed as a collaborator or accidentally shot by U.S. soldiers (just a day earlier, angry demonstrators in Falluja had protested the deaths of nine Iraqi security personnel, blamed on an "accidental friendly-fire incident by U.S. forces"), at a salary that wouldn't even pay for his family's basic needs. But he'd be grateful, because secretly he had always longed to move to Idaho and start his own private militia, and he figured that one day he could apply for U.S.

citizenship. Then Powell and the ex-resistance fighter, now the best of friends, would link arms and sing "My Way" before heading off to one of the cinemas on Sadoun Street to watch an old John Wayne flick.

As hundreds of journalists waited for a response, Powell didn't miss a beat. He sidestepped the question by speaking of newly formed PTA committees as a concrete example of "democracy in action." (Parent to teacher: "What should I do, Mr. Hamid? I'm worried that my daughter might get abducted on her way to school, but there's no one to accompany her, as I'm working three jobs to make ends meet and my wife died during the invasion when our house was bombed." Teacher: "Don't worry, Mr. Jabar. Take one of these newly de-Baathifized textbooks — a special edition in red, white, and blue!")

"Good news like this," concluded Powell, "is simply not as newsworthy as the bad stuff."

When asked about the thorny issue of Iraqi elections, Powell replied, "You can't just say, 'You're a government. Go. You have full authority.' You have to build the capacity to govern ... The worst thing that could happen is for us to push this process too quickly ... and see it fail." He ended by promising that the United States had no desire to stay in Iraq "any longer than necessary."

And then the secretary of state was whisked away to his bullet-proof vehicle, before Robert Fisk ever had a chance to press his red button.

Chapter 12: Fortress America

EVERY MINUTE HAD BEEN SO INTENSE, it was hard to believe that it was only two weeks since I'd flown in with Hank, the "mayor" of Baghdad. I'd been meaning to go and see him, and after borrowing a phone from a kindly contractor at my hotel, I managed to get an appointment. Hank's office was in the palace — that is, Saddam's former Republican Palace, now appropriated as headquarters of the CPA. My driver, Ali, took me over the bridge that led to the "green zone," also known as the "American security area," if that wasn't already an oxymoron. As we approached Saddam's old haunt, razor-wired for almost half a mile, it occurred to me that the new American version of the palace was almost as inaccessible as its previous incarnation.

Ali had to let me off about fifty yards from the main entrance, known as "assassin's gate," where all kinds of heavy artillery seemed to be pointed directly at us. I said goodbye to Ali, trying to remain cool despite all the stories of trigger-happy Marines at checkpoints that were now invading my thoughts. I would have to make my own way back to the hotel of happy Ghurkhas.

I walked slowly towards the main gate. There was nothing and no one in the fifty-yard space between me and the U.S. soldiers. I forced a big smile and said "Hullo" with the most American-sounding vowels I could muster. A blond, blue-eyed kid who couldn't have been over twenty said, "What are you doing here?" His stare was almost as relentless as one of the old Baathist officials.

"Umm ... I'm here to see Hank," I said.

"Hank who?" he replied with clipped, military precision and an unmistakable Southern drawl.

"Hank Bassford," I said, assuming that he would know right away who I meant.

"Who's he?"

"Ah ... the regional director of the CPA in Baghdad." I guessed that all those stories about infighting between the Pentagon and the state department were probably true.

"Well, whoever he his, we don't know anything about you. Where are you from?"

I handed over my Canadian passport.

"You Iraqi?" he asked me suspiciously, pronouncing it *Ay-rak-ee*.

"No," I said, "I'm Canadian."

"Yeah, but I mean, you look, well ... You don't look Canadian. What's your background?"

"Mohawk and French," I replied, thinking these to be the more prudent ancestral links to emphasize. "What's yours?"

"Uh ... I'm from Mississippi," he drawled, slightly taken aback. "Well, is this Hank expecting you?"

"He is."

"Well he's supposed to send an escort down to see you. And there's nobody here."

I felt for a moment the virtual bareness of my unprotected back, and perhaps some of what lone soldiers on patrol might feel. I wasn't sure which was more frightening: the fear that someone might take a pot shot or throw a grenade any moment at these troops, or their gunners pointing at me from tanks.

"Well, I have his phone number," I offered, "Can't we just call him?"

"No, ma'am," came the reply. "We don't have any telephones."

Later I would discover that most soldiers, unlike their commanding officers, had virtually no telephone access, even to call home. In this they were not alone. In the new Iraq, the real aristocrats were those with magical MCI phones — the ones that allowed free calls to anywhere in the world.

Just as I was beginning to have visions of the airport gulag, an anxious-looking woman in a hijab came by and started speaking to the soldiers. She glanced at me and then continued talking to them. "I'm looking for a Canadian," she said.

"That's me!" I piped up, "I'm the Canadian."

"You?" she said, slightly perplexed. Then she smiled. "Hi, I'm Nadia, Hank's assistant. Sorry to keep you waiting."

The kid from Mississippi let me through.

As it turned out, Nadia was a real sweetheart. Half French and half Iraqi, she was trilingual and had been working for the CPA for only a month. Like millions of others, she and her Iraqi husband had suffered through the invasion, but she was now very happy to be working at such a well-paid job. She was an enthusiastic tour guide.

"What's that building over there?" I asked, surveying the bombed-out ruins next door to the palace.

"That was the Ministry of Planning," she said. It didn't look like it would be used to plan anything for quite a while.

We approached an imposing archway from which every trace of Saddam had been carefully erased, but there was still an old Iraqi flag painted on it. Beyond was a sprawling estate that took in several palaces with their gardens and paved driveways, most of them now used to house troops, security guards and tanks.

I explained to Nadia that I'd been in Iraq before, but that I'd never had a chance to see any of the palaces. "Yes, it was kind of exciting for me the first time as well," she beamed.

We walked towards a waiting SUV, which took us the five hundred yards to the palace where Hank had his office. Nadia led me through a series of long marble hallways with ornate ceiling fixtures and chandeliers. Much of the old Louis XVI style furniture so favored in the Gulf had survived intact. But the place was vast and maze-like. The sense of disorientation was heightened by the odd juxtapositions of soldiers camped out in ballroom-like spaces, with exhausted Marines sprawled out on cots on marble floors, and uniformed bureaucrats working away in rooms that looked as if they'd been designed for far more interesting tasks than filing papers.

I thought of the tale from the *1,001 Nights*, about the prince who finds a magical palace filled with many rooms. Each room contained some unusual thing, like dancing cats or enchanted vases of perfume. But the lovely princesses who inhabit the palace tell him that there is one door he must never open. Of course, he cannot resist, and one day he succumbs to temptation, letting loose an evil genie. Suddenly everything goes black and the palace disappears, leaving only smoke and the smell of sulphur. What bad genie, I wondered, had these cowboys let loose?

Soon we arrived at Hank's office, which looked like it could have belonged to an English colonial administrator. Hank smiled but eyed my camera equipment warily.

"With all that gear you look a lot like a journalist," he said. "Are you sure you're not a journalist? We don't like them around here." He was still half smiling.

"Oh, you know," I said, as casually as possible, "I'm trying to document as much as possible for the project."

This seemed to put him at ease. Or who knows? Perhaps he'd been on to me the whole time. But given the current state of American intelligence, I rather doubted that.

Hank was with an Australian colleague, whom he introduced to me as Major Rob Shortridge. Major Shortridge was an affable sort and, considering the setting, I was impressed by the relative lack of stuffiness. Unlike previous regimes, there was very little in the way of ceremony.

As I sat in Hank's office, explaining my "garden of peace" concept, I transcended the absurdity of the whole scenario through pure magical thinking. Maybe this could actually work, I thought, as the two men exchanged glances, took notes and occasionally raised eyebrows.

After my ten-minute spiel, Major Shortridge smiled at me.

"You know, I think she should talk to Bushra."

"Good idea," chimed in Hank.

"Who's Bushra?" I asked.

"She's in charge of Baghdad parklands," explained Shortridge. "And she works out of an office at the Baghdad Zoo."

Hank and Shortridge then gave me a few names of people to contact. Unfortunately they all had MCI phones and I didn't, which meant it would be far easier to contact them from Canada. But Shortridge did introduce me to a certain plucky woman named Sergeant X. She was a bundle of energy, had short, cropped hair like a military Audrey Hepburn gamine and carried a small white puppy around the office.

She looked less like an officer than an extra from *Best in Show*. But Sergeant X knew a few things about Iraq.

"My unit's in charge of getting the municipal garbage disposal up and running again," she said. And, quite amazingly, they had! I was impressed; the system hadn't really been working properly since the Gulf War. The sergeant had also been meeting with women from different neighborhoods in Baghdad, tough working-class areas like Karkh and Sadr City. Of course, she told me, the only way she'd been able to meet with women was to get their husbands' permission first. "It's also really important to tell people that you're married. Then the women don't think that you're out to steal their husbands. And I get a lot more respect when I tell them I'm a grandmother." She must have been a young one, I thought. Who did Pilates.

When I told her about my garden-of-peace project, she immediately responded "Great idea!" The sergeant was beyond perky; she was energized. In a civilian incarnation I'm sure she would have been one of those soccer moms who organized the local PTA, volunteered with the boy scouts and became the top producer at her real-estate office. I pictured her with her team out in the streets of Baghdad, getting that garbage picked up now and on time! Hopefully there weren't any unexploded grenades lying in her way.

As she played with her puppy — an Iraqi street dog she'd adopted — she told me about "working groups" she'd organized with women in different neighborhoods. One of the things on their "wish lists," as she put it, was green space for gardening. When I expressed some doubt about whether my project might work, given the difficult security situation, she said, "Don't even think about giving up. You can make it work! You can do it! You will succeed!" As she left the room I felt hypnotized by her optimism.

Nadia, who had been with us for most of the conversation, was also impressed. "You American women," she said, including me, "you know how to get things done." I suddenly felt acutely uncomfortable at being associated with the role of Protestant missionary, fixing things that your countrymen had broken, of destruction and salvation all at once. It was a crazy persecutor/rescuer complex. How could you condemn the people who were bombing your homes? Look how clean they'd made the streets of Baghdad!

I glanced at my watch. It was already five o'clock and it would be getting dark soon.

"How are you getting back to your hotel?" asked Hank.

"Well ..." I actually wasn't sure. How would I navigate my way out of this enclave that was so hard to enter?

"Don't worry," said Hank. "You can go home with Nadia." Apparently she and some other Iraqi women employees were escorted home every night by a pistol-packing truck driver — not much in the way of protection from anti-"collaborator" attacks, but better than nothing.

As I walked to the parking lot with Nadia, we passed a bunch of newly trained Iraqi policemen. They looked very much like the old Iraqi police, mustachioed, comfortably paunchy men who gave us dirty looks as we passed. Who are these local girls, their eyes said, working with American men? They must be whores. Brothers killed their sisters for less.

"Don't mind them," Nadia said. "They're just not used to this new reality. There are many of us women working now with the CPA."

Some months later, newly trained Iraqi police would assassinate an American woman named Fern Holland and her Iraqi deputy, Salwa Ourmashi, in charge of setting up CPA-funded women's centers in the south of Iraq.

Chapter 13: He's Not Heavy, He's My Minder

"CAN I SERVE YOU something cold to drink?"

"Yes, thank you."

An awkward pause was broken as Ali got up and disappeared into the kitchen. I took the chance to look around his living room. Like many Iraqi homes, the decor had been arrested somewhere in the early seventies. A red velvet couch was set off by orange velour drapes; ornate vases held silk flowers and a dining table looked like Louis XVI on acid.

I had come to Mansour, a middle-class neighborhood in central Baghdad, to see what had become of my ex-minder. During the Saddam years, visitors were always assigned a minder by the Ministry of Information, and I had been burdened with Ali on several visits. One of his ex-colleagues, a young Kurdish man called Salar who now worked for the *Los Angeles Times*, had given me Ali's address. I was pretty sure that it was Ali who had blacklisted me in 2002, and I had decided to find him and ask him why. But Salar had talked about Ali in a quiet voice, like he was worried about his sanity. "Ali's at home now," he had whispered. "He sits at home."

Originally established by the Caliph Haroun al-Rashid as a perfectly conceived round city, Mansour was now a sprawling, mainly residential area, more suburban Miami than Abbasid. As we cruised down the main commercial boulevard looking for the seafood restaurant that would signal the location of Ali's house, I took in the stores and shopfronts, unchanged except for the electronic and computer goods now on offer. A series of portraits of Saddam still hung festively from streetlights, but with his visage erased. At one intersection, a monument to the former Iraqi president featured a giant portrait on a cement slab. His features had been scratched out and replaced by a giant happy face.

As we searched for Ali's house, memories of our pre-regime-change days together came flooding in. On my last two assignments in Iraq, the director of the Press Center had insisted that Ali be my minder. No amount of polite requests or maneuvering seemed to be able to change this unfortunate circumstance. At least Ali's English was quite good.

I remembered the day in early 2001 when I had asked my friend Ahlam, a hairdresser and single mother whom I'd first met in the beauty salon at the al-Rashid Hotel, to take me to the market. I had explained to Ali that I wanted to do a story on the effect of sanctions, on the price of meat and oranges, to understand how long people's rations lasted and how much things cost.

Ahlam is the same age as me, so then she was thirty-three. But eleven years of sanctions and suffering had made her seem so much older. She had been widowed in the Gulf War when her husband was sent to the frontlines and was one of the thousands of retreating Iraqi soldiers massacred by the Americans on the road to Basra, the "highway of death." Her ten-year-old son, who was slightly stunted and looked about six, had still been in her womb when his father died. He wanted to be a doctor when he grew up, he said, but sometimes his mother couldn't pay her grocery bills. They could only afford to eat meat twice a month.

It hadn't been like that before, of course. Ahlam and her husband had had a house in a middle-class neighborhood, with a color TV and VCR and a huge freezer to store all the meat they wanted. But then gradually, she'd had to sell everything off, bit by bit. The VCR had gone when her 13-year-old daughter needed an operation, the freezer had gone for food. The nice house gave way to a room in a basement with no running water. Her life became someone else's. In Arabic her name means "dream."

She worked then in a beauty salon in Mansour, painting the toenails of smugglers' wives, and living in Dora, a working-class suburb on the road to the country. She wanted to take me there to visit the farmers' market, "where you can get the best deals."

Accompanied by the ever-present Ali, I had set out with Ferris, a driver also supplied by the Ministry of Information, to pick up Ahlam and the kids. Ferris was a thin man with an even thinner moustache, a raging alcoholic who reeked alternately of gin and strong cologne. In his more sober moments, he tried to entrap me with inflammatory comments about the regime in strained English ("Saddam bad man, no? Don't think you?") when he wasn't complaining about his life ("My wife is too fat. I want to leave Iraq"). But like minders, drivers were impossible to ditch once they had been assigned, so we headed off to Ahlam's in mild fear for our lives, as Ferris bobbed and weaved through heavy Baghdad traffic in his badly aging Buick.

Ali was then 35 and unmarried, with a nervous tic, the requisite moustache and a penchant for chain-smoking. He still lived with his mother in the family home in Mansour, a nice boy from what was once a good neighborhood. I felt sorry for him when he wasn't driving me crazy, demanding written permission for everything in triplicate.

We arrived at Ahlam's basement apartment and she and the kids piled in. Ahlam had told me that she wanted to leave Iraq. But she never talked about visas and jobs in Canada when Ali and Ferris were around. That day, we could only speak of the price of rice, and of how she managed to stretch nothing into the last two weeks of each month, when the measly rations would run out.

At the market, several dozen salesmen hawked fresh produce from their stands, calling out the prices of lettuce and bananas in loud sing-song voices. The few women there were swathed in black abayas; the men wore red, village-style kaffiyehs wrapped around their heads. Ali wore a double-breasted sports jacket.

I slowly took in the faces of the merchants, the price of apples, the things unspoken. There was food here, but there was hunger too — the kind of hunger that is made worse by the memory of a time when you ate well. The younger ones had forgotten those days by now; after eleven years of never enough, they had become inured.

We walked into a butcher shop to talk about the cost of meat. Ahlam explained that the rations she received did not include any meat or produce, only flour, rice, beans, oil, tea, and sugar. The butcher was a pleasant man, with a moustache and a beard. He posed for a photograph holding a cleaver in mid-air. Behind him was a portrait of Imam Ali.

As we left the butcher shop, I stopped outside to take a photo of a man selling oranges. I was about to click, when Ali shouted "Stop that!" When I didn't, he screamed at me like I was an errant kindergarten student, "I saw you take that photo and I'll tell the director of the Press Center!"

I was puzzled by his outburst, but not surprised. What was it this time? I wondered. Some military installation in the background?

No. "I saw you take that photo of those dirty, uneducated children standing in front of that mud!" Ali shouted accusingly. I blinked twice before I noticed what he was talking about. The dirty kids, the mud, were so ubiquitous I honestly hadn't noticed. The kids and I exchanged stares for a moment. Then one grinned at me.

The Ministry of Information, it seemed, had some new edict: DO NOT PHOTOGRAPH EXTREME POVERTY. A little bit was okay, but not too much. Some genteel, well-dressed poverty, but never genuine dirt, never real despair. This information might be used against the regime; it would be blamed, went the reasoning, for what was really the fault of the embargo.

So, I had been bad, and we had to quickly return to the car. Ali took out another black Sumer cigarette and puffed away nervously. His tic was getting worse now. And then the unthinkable happened. Almost casually, from the third floor window of a market building, some faceless, nameless person began to throw orange peel and rotten fruit at the minder. And suddenly a sea of faces, half-smiling yet all with that angry orange-peel potential, were looking up, noticing us with new eyes.

"Let's get out of here," said Ali, quickly brushing the fruit off his jacket in disgust and walking faster towards the car. We all piled into the battered Buick, like some weird, dysfunctional family on its way home. Ferris had been drinking again and he weaved in and out of lanes as we approached the highway leading back to Baghdad. Ahlam's son sat on Ali's lap in the front seat, proudly holding a bag of oranges. It was hard to tell from behind, but I was pretty sure I saw him smiling.

NOW, SEATED DEMURELY in Ali's living room, I was wondering how my former minder had adjusted to life after Saddam. Just then, he arrived with two ice-cold cans of Coke on a silver tray.

"Ali!" I gasped in mock shock. "Such an American drink. Where's your sense of nationalism?" I tried out my new Iraqi phrase: *al iraq lil iraqayeen* — "Iraq for Iraqis" — an old nationalist slogan that had recently been resurrected.

"Yes," said Ali, half smiling, "for friends of Iraq." It was hard to tell whose side he was on.

But for a slight paunch, he appeared unchanged. He had greeted me like an old friend when I'd turned up unexpectedly at his front door. This was not without sincerity; in the midst of our love/hate relationship a strange sort of fondness had developed. "I still see you are taking pictures wherever you go," he said, pointing at my tiny video camera. I must have looked a little worried, because he hastened to add, "No, relax, it's fine now, you can take pictures wherever you like."

"So what are you doing now?" I asked him.

"Oh, I still work with journalists, but it's casual. Sometimes friends like you that I used to work with in the past come to find me. I like this work. I always like to see people now who I worked with before, now that's it's more free." There was no sense of irony in his voice at all.

"What kinds of subjects are you suggesting these days?" I inquired, with memories of all those "official" stories that had once been force-fed to us hacks.

"Oh, any subject at all. Life is all stories, you know." His tone managed to be both philosophical and slightly menacing. "You are a journalist, you can make a story out of anything."

"Was your house bombed during the invasion?" I inquired, switching tracks.

"No, thank God. But when the bombing started, when some of the paramilitary forces were deployed in the last few days of the war, not all the American sorties had set targets. In the last few days, they went everywhere — wherever they saw weapons. So whenever you saw some military deployment behind your house, you got scared."

"Our department," continued Ali, referring to his branch of the Ministry of Information, "distributed us amongst the hotels where the journalists were. I was sent to the al-Rashid Hotel — absolutely the worst place. There were almost no journalists there because everyone said it was a target." The al-Rashid had been bombed during the first Gulf War, and a week after my meeting with Ali, and by then occupied by U.S. military personnel, it would become a target of resistance bombing, as it remains today. "I spent several days there," continued Ali, "seeing bombs all around me, until two or three days before the end of the war. Then they [the department] told us to go to the Meridien.

"By April 7, I couldn't even get to the Meridien. All the roads were blocked from Mansour. The Americans were inside Baghdad, they covered all the main streets. So I stayed at home until I saw it all on television. Thank God we had electricity! I saw it all on Iranian TV, what happened in Firdos Square. When the statue went down, only then did I know that the government was gone."

We sat together for a moment, both lost in thought. I was imagining Ali in this very room, watching the Marines and the rent-a-crowd take down the statue of Saddam in Firdos Square via Iranian satellite.

"Well, Ali," I began, "do you think things have changed for the better, or not?"

As if on cue, the power went off and left us in darkness. This was now so common that we carried on oblivious.

"Well, now it's way more dangerous. The security is bad. There are accidents, looting, robbing, killing. It's not safe any more at all."

"Have any of your friends or family been attacked?" I asked.

"Just yesterday, my brother's friend — from a famous sheikh's family — his Mercedes was carjacked on Palestine street at 1 p.m., in front of all the people! They chased him in two BMWs and he was shot everywhere!" Ali gestured frantically to different body parts.

"So this is the price of freedom?" I was watching closely for his reaction.

"I think sooner or later things will be better," he replied. He lit up a Marlboro, which he was now smoking instead of the familiar Sumer cigarettes of old. "It's only been a short while since our new government [the U.S.-appointed Iraqi Governing Council] was formed. When you have some *order*," he intoned, with a familiar, authoritative ring, "ministers, directors of security, it will be better than the last five months." In fact, after our conversation, things would become much worse.

"Remember all those times we went to the theater?" I asked, recalling all the plays that Ali had translated for me, suspicious of subversive motives all the while. "You can listen to my radio pieces on the internet now. In some of them your voice is the one translating!" In free Iraq, former minders could hear themselves on CBC radio broadcasts, as long as they made it safely to the nearest internet café.

"Really?" he replied. "I'd like to hear them." His eyes dropped to the small camera I held in my hands, which was still filming most of our conversation.

"Hadani," he said in a serious tone, "you should be careful with your camera, you know. In some places people will kill for your camera. You might put your life at risk just carrying it — it's very likely in this time." If the robbers didn't get you, I thought, the Marines might. A Reuters cameraman had been shot and killed by trigger-happy troops the week before; the official line was that they had mistaken his camera for a rocket launcher.

"Ali," I asked, "do you think if the Americans leave now, the situation will get worse?"

"Yes, of course. Now we have terrorists in Iraq, so if the Americans leave, terrorists will take over, and there will be many small fights for power. I think now they are a stabilizing force, although," he faltered slightly here, "they are not so successful in certain areas."

"I have a question for you, Ali. You remember how you always said I had a big police file? Do you think I could find my file?"

"Well," said Ali, slightly taken aback, "everything was burned at the ministry — even our files. We couldn't even find our own staff files." He smiled just a little. "Of course, not every piece of paper was taken. But I don't know where the files were kept. We, in our department, kept only the current files when you were there. You know, what your program was, what you saw, where you went."

Ali made the Ministry of Information sound like a tourist bureau. Now a burnt-out shell occupied by looters, it had once been the journalistic equivalent of Dante's nine circles of hell. If things went really well — or sometimes even if they went really wrong — you would make it past the ring of minders and onto the seventh floor of the building where the number-two guy in the ministry — a grotesque caricature of a bloated bureaucrat, named Uday — would receive you. Glancing distractedly at three 1970s-era television sets blaring different Iraqi TV programs, his right hand was always occupied with his prayer beads, while his left hand was always ready to receive baksheesh, preferably in crisp American $100 bills. Ministry "fees" varied wildly, depending on the current crisis level, but you could always count on shelling out a minimum of $100 a day in basic bribes. Rumor had it that after the invasion, Uday had been one of the first to ask for a job from American media outlets. But now he was playing it safe, biding his time at home.

Ali seemed lost in some other kind of nostalgia for the place. "I'd like to go back there," he sighed, "for the memories."

"You know some of your colleagues said that they thought I was a spy because I spoke many different languages," Salar had offered up this nugget, saying I was suspect because I spoke French, German, and Spanish.

"Ah ... many people spoke languages," Ali said dismissively. "But you, yes ... There were rumors about you."

"Did you think I was a spy?"

"No, no," he replied, "but I heard things — like everyone did."

"But who did you think I was working for?"

"Sometimes," said Ali, " I even suspected that you were spying for the Iraqis."

"Spying on you?" I said, somewhat bewildered.

"Yes, because of your friends at the foreign ministry." How bizarre, I thought. I wasn't even aware that I had friends in the ministry. What had Ali written about me in his reports, I wondered.

"Look," he continued. "I want to tell you something. But I don't want it all on the camera." I turned it off. "Some people wrote things and they were blacklisted. Sometimes there were misunderstandings ... but other people made decisions, not me." This was a classic "former" Baathist response. In fact, a colleague from *Newsweek* had told me that the day I left Iraq in January of 2002, Ali had told him, "Hadani will never be allowed back into this country."

And then a crazy thought entered my brain. Perhaps I could hire Ali now, as a translator. Perhaps that might be a way to discover the truth. But Ali had other plans.

"Thanks for thinking of me, Hadani, but I'm already engaged." He had, in fact, been snatched up by some British broadsheet journalists.

"Well, let me know if you have any spare time, Ali." I could hardly believe I was saying this, but after all, his English was pretty good.

"Yes, I will," he assured me. "Nice to see you again."

At the end of my trip I would see Ali again, waiting with other former minders in the lobby of the Palestine Hotel. He would question me in his old familiar way about which hotel I was staying in, and I would lie to him. But for now, I took one last look at the small, mustachioed man with the nervous tic, the nice boy from Mansour with the secret-police eyes. I shook his hand and said, "Nice seeing you, Ali."

Chapter 14: Baghdad by Night

I HAD ONLY BEEN IN BAGHDAD two weeks and I was already starting to lose it. The constant gunfire, the night-time roar of tanks, the armed mercenaries at breakfast, not to mention the weird muzak in the hotel lobby, were all wearing me down. I was starting to feel sympathetic towards Karim and his delicate mental state. Living in constant fear of abduction or assault was a new experience for me and other women in Baghdad. Sometimes it seemed like a conspiracy to keep women inside after dark. So, with the frightening statistics — four hundred women raped or abducted in Baghdad within the first four months of the invasion — pushed to the far reaches of my brain, I decided to go to a party.

Parties had always been key to mental and emotional survival in Iraq. Just as there was always some tragedy to mourn, there was always something to celebrate as well: a wedding, a birth, a holiday, even an occasional gathering of friends was an opportunity to dance, socialize, and generally have a good time. In fact, I would always complain upon returning to rainy Vancouver that my social life had been much better in Baghdad.

Besides the miraculous Desert Fox dance party at the al-Rashid, there had been other, equally unforgettable nights out. In 1997, when I first went to Iraq for the *New York Times*, the Hotel Babylon housed what was one of Baghdad's few remaining nightclubs. It was a Thursday night when I first entered the subterranean disco and, at 11:00 p.m., despite the omnipresent threat of bombing, things were just starting to heat up. The band, composed of an oud player, a drummer, and an electric keyboardist, began to play an old Umm Kulthum song. The strobe light spun and the lights were lowered. Slowly, a young woman with peroxide-blond hair and a leopard-print dress strolled out onto the floor and began a dance that was half Salome and half Sweet Charity.

The crowd, made up of wealthy businessmen, Arab sheikhs, "embargo cats," and bemused U.N. employees, kept the rhythm with enthusiastic clapping. Gradually, a few brave men made their way to the dance floor, where they were joined by some more leopard-print lovelies.

The rhythm changed and the melody morphed into what might be described as "techno-Arab" or "oriental themes on a drum machine." The girls, who looked about sixteen, did a weird, skittish move that could be a time-warped, mutant form of Iraqi breakdancing, as middle-aged men danced around them with a leering kind of machismo. Soon the tune changed to what sounded suspiciously like an Arabic version of "the Macarena." Meanwhile, an older woman sold plastic-flower wreaths for 4,000 dinars (a civil servant's monthly income) and a photographer circulated, snapping photos of men sitting together, smiling and smoking.

All this was a tinny, cheapened version of what had once been a vibrant scene. The exodus of renowned artists, writers, and musicians had resulted in the worst kind of cultural impoverishment. Once an intellectual and artistic center for the region, Baghdad's cultural death rattle could be heard in places like the Babylon. Nearby were pharmacies whose near-empty shelves were lined with medicines that only the wealthy could afford. These were the dog days of the embargo.

I talked to a French aid worker named François who remembered Baghdad in the 1980s. "It was very different, you know, before the embargo," he told me. How so?

"The whores were foreigners, *never* Iraqis," he deadpanned. "Really, it's quite shocking. It used to be something quite exceptional." The choice, it seemed, between earning a few dollars a month at a more legitimate job and getting upwards of thirty dollars a night was not a difficult one. "Many of these girls are supporting their entire families," explained François, pointing towards the dancing teenagers.

The nationality of dancing girls was not the only thing that had changed. In the eighties, Baghdad had had a great nightlife, even with the Iran–Iraq war raging. Its many discos, bars, and casinos were frequented by hedonists from surrounding Gulf states, not to mention many prominent members of the international press corps. But by late

1997, the city, a phantom of its former self, could only offer places like the Babylon disco, skeletal remains of what had once been a relatively Rubenesque scene.

But Michael, a visiting German photojournalist, insisted that there was still a rich underground scene in Baghdad. "The other night I was at this amazing party," he confided. "It started with fireworks on the banks of the Tigris and ended with go-go dancers in cages." And who was there? "Mainly children of the elite, rich kids, a couple of diplomats," he said vaguely. He wouldn't name names; he wanted to be invited back the following weekend.

For Baghdad's poorer classes, there was less variety. Former family haunts such as Baghdad Island (a run-down amusement park) and the city zoo (bereft of most of its animals since sanctions began) had now become illicit meeting places for covert copulation. You could go to the movies, but there wasn't much on offer except Bollywood musicals and violent kung-fu flicks. The one exception was a series of French films being shown at Baghdad's Center *culturel français*. There M. Martinez, the unabashed aesthete who ran the center, bravely screened films such as *Le Dernier Metro*, amid posters of Alain Delon and Brigitte Bardot.

After one screening there I met Madame Feris, a francophile former fashion designer who had worked at *la Maison de la mode Iraqienne*: the Iraqi House of Fashion. She wistfully recalled the days when she'd accompanied la Maison on a European tour where they presented a fashion show in Paris and stayed at the Hôtel Georges V. "But these days in Baghdad," she cautioned, "it's dangerous to take a taxi at night." Most women she knew now carried guns in their evening bags, she said.

For those who could afford it, a lavish wedding reception at a five-star hotel was great entertainment. For others, there were simpler celebrations: dancing and singing through the streets or merrymaking in cars and buses. One evening I remember a small two-door car, covered with shattered windows and rust, rattling down Rashid Street with a wedding party of six crammed inside. Hanging out the back window was a trumpeter blowing out a triumphant tune on a battered old bugle.

I thought of the party I'd attended at the Sabean Club in the spring of 2000. It was the night I arrived in Baghdad for my *Wallpaper** assignment on Iraqi architecture — a great vehicle, I would discover, for understanding Iraqi political history. Be it the Abbasid university, Ottoman villas, British-inspired 1920s buildings, the brutalist chic favored by Saddam or nouveau-riche smugglers' dens from the 1990s, Baghdad architecture said it all, in silence.

The Sabeans are an Iraqi religious sect who, while neither officially Christians nor Jews, are followers of John the Baptist. The main attraction of their club was that alcohol could be purchased and consumed on the premises, a rarity since public drinking was banned in 1993, as a crime-reduction method in increasingly desperate times.

The club itself was fairly typical of post-revolutionary sixties' architecture: a square quadrangle with the omnipresent portrait of Saddam Hussein gracing the entrance. The president had as many guises as Lord Krishna, including a Tyrolian outfit and another that included a Panama hat and a (presumably) Cuban cigar. I sat with my minder, Ala, and the club's president and his family. The president's beautiful 19-year-old daughter, who was soon to depart for Germany where her Iraqi fiancée lived, sat beside him. Her name was Ishtar and she looked like a film star. Everyone drank whisky on the rocks and ate salted pistachios. Soon plates of kebab and bowls of hummus and salad arrived. On a makeshift stage, a well-known singer crooned traditional love songs as couples got up to dance.

Among the club's respectable middle-aged married couples, several pairs of handsome young men dressed in tight jeans were shaking their shoulders and moving their hands and hips in a serpentine arabesque. I sensed a mild disturbance as the president left our table and went over to the same-sex couples. After a few friendly but stern words from the benevolent patriarch, the male couples dispersed, some holding hands as they left the dance floor. I assumed the worst.

But after a quick introduction to the renowned Iraqi poet Abdul Razzaq Abdul Wahid, who was sitting at the adjoining table with his family, I wasn't sure what was going on. Abdul Razzaq had been well known in the sixties, when his international friendships included an acquaintance with the late Allen Ginsberg. "No, no, it's not what you think," he assured me. "This is not about homophobia. Those boys are only dancing together because they have no sisters and they are too shy to ask a girl to dance."

A few minutes later, another boy–boy couple got up to dance. After a brief exchange of words between one of the boys and a man dancing beside them with his wife, some fisticuffs were exchanged. In no time the scrap became a violent free-for-all with friends and family members on both sides joining in. The dance floor was littered with blood and broken glass.

"Just ignore it," said Ala, trying desperately to look unruffled. "It will all be over soon." The club president and some security men moved the scuffle off the dance floor. The band continued to play and some more married couples got up to dance. Beneath the sounds of oriental drums and keyboards, I could hear screams and police sirens.

NOW, OF COURSE, THE SOUND of violence threatened to drown out the love songs; it was much louder, much less contained. What would a night out be like in post-invasion Baghdad? I wondered.

One thing was certain. As a woman in the new Iraq, the ritual of discarding the maternity clothes / peasant look for a genuine party dress was a real thrill, if not an outright act of defiance. So when some Greek journalists at my hotel told me there was a soirée at the Greek ambassador's residence, I was ready to roll.

There is something about driving around an occupied city oppressed by unbearable heat and despair that will age you beyond your years, so I took great pains to try and revive my exhausted self. I chose a pink dress with straps, high heels, and my all-purpose Uzbeki shawl/cover up as a replacement for my overworked daytime hijab. I emerged from my room transformed. After a gut-wrenching journey with a driver who had no idea where the address was (we had to stop several times in the dark to quiz armed guards — kids with guns — for directions), I arrived to find that no one else was there. I had the wrong night.

The ambassador, a charming man, was pleasantly surprised to see me and tried his best to persuade me to stay the night "for security reasons." But when I politely declined his offer, he was a good sport about it all and, half an hour before the 11:00 p.m. curfew, accompanied me back across town with his driver in an SUV, armed with a pistol and a global-positioning device.

We were stopped at an American military checkpoint by a young man with a Southern twang. He was immensely polite as he inquired after the driver's "weapons card" and apologized by rote for any inconvenience he might have caused. It was a military meets McDonalds drive-through experience.

The streets were dark and deserted, except for the odd sight of kids playing soccer on the empty roads; they only stopped to let tanks pass by. My heart now a little aflutter, I sang Leonard Cohen songs with the ambassador all the way across town — a kind of darker version of Rodgers and Hammerstein's "Whenever I Feel Afraid" refrain:

> The stories of the street are mine
> The Spanish voices laugh
> The Cadillacs go creeping down
> Through the night and the poison gas
> I lean from my window sill
> In this old hotel I chose.
> Yes, one hand on my suicide
> And one hand on the rose.

> I know you've heard it's over now
> And war must surely come,
> The cities they are broke in half
> And the middle men are gone.
> But let me ask you one more time
> O children of the dust,
> These hunters who are shrieking now
> Do they speak for us?

> And where do all these highways go
> Now that we are free?
> Why are the armies marching still
> That were coming home to me?

It worked. Cohen's songs seemed the perfect soundtrack for these dark Baghdad nights. I arrived back at my hotel relieved but strangely exhilarated — at least, much more than I would have been had I stayed in for another night of American B movies subtitled in Arabic.

The next evening I returned to the Greek ambassador's house. This time I found a party in full swing, complete with champagne and canapés served by Iraqi waiters and beautiful Greek girls who worked for an Athens-based NGO. L was there as well, with a Greek woman named Aphrodite; in fact his cook had provided the elaborate Italian smorgasbord that awaited us in the dining room. After days of hotel food, this was a little bit of heaven. But it was the kind of paradise that made me think of the Hashashins who would drug new recruits, take them to lavish palaces and then, once hooked on the lifestyle, force them into a life of crime. I could get used to this, I thought, but at what price?

"What's wrong, Hadani?" asked the Greek ambassador, offering me a fan made out of palm fronds. "You look a little worried." As he fanned me, I told the ambassador about my musings on the nature of change in Iraq.

"But of course," he said. "Here it's just a case of *changer la femme*. It's the same as before. Life is always the same. For the last 25,000 years Baghdad has remained the same. It's all a game of power, love, and money." It was comforting to hear the dulcet tones of a wise old Greek, observing the new Romans from the sidelines.

Actress Shadah Salem in costume on the set of an Iraqi TV show filmed at Baghdad's Abbasid Palace, 2000

Chapter 15: Dancing in the Dark

THE NEXT DAY I RESOLVED to find Ahlam, my beautician friend. With a half-remembered address in Mansour, I was able to locate her old salon. Her colleagues recognized me and told me where I could find her. It turned out that, after scrimping and saving for years, Ahlam had finally been able to buy her own business and now had a shop just a few minutes away. The bad news, I would discover, was that she had purchased the business a mere three months before the American invasion. Now she was mortgaged to the hilt, with only a handful of customers. Many women dared not leave home even for essentials such as groceries and gasoline. Beauty was not a priority for the moment.

Ahlam's salon had always been a kind of litmus test to gauge how things were going for Iraqi women. In the past I had used the female-only environment to great advantage. Because there were never any women minders, all I had to do was tell Ali that I was "going to the beauty parlor" and he would leave me on my own for hours at a time. Minder-free, I would get real stories, minus the usual platitudes. Here I had met with women like Susan, a 43-year-old mother of a 17-year-old girl, who, in 2001, confided that her daughter's life was "like a prison" compared with her own youth, saying that she had no future, poor education, and that even at that time, it was unsafe for her to go out with her friends in the evenings. An embargo-induced crime wave and increasing poverty had already defined class lines much more sharply. Nice girls from good neighborhoods did not venture out at night for fear of robbers.

I had also learned a lot about the state of things from Ahlam herself. She suffered from ovarian cysts, and worried that they would result in one of the cancers that seemed to have multiplied since the British and Americans had used weapons armed with depleted uranium in the Gulf War. Besides the financial struggles imposed by single motherhood,

Ahlam also had to contend with her daughter's ear problems, which required expensive surgery. Public hospitals were hopeless, and the private clinics dealt only in hard currency, usually U.S. dollars.

Iraqi women once enjoyed one of the highest statuses in the Arab world. In the 1980s, they comprised seventy percent of civil servants and played a strong role in public life. But since the Gulf War, their situation had declined dramatically. By the late 1990s, an alarming number of women had turned to prostitution as a means of economic survival, something unheard of a decade earlier.

Just getting by required great stamina and I was constantly impressed by the resilience of the women I met. During my visit in 2000, I talked to Shadah Salem, a famous Iraqi actress in her mid-forties who was filming a TV series in Baghdad's Abbasid palace. The show, called *The Wisdom of the Arabs*, was a mildly burlesque take on the *1,001 Nights*. Madame Salem was playing the "storyteller" or "keeper of knowledge," a role that seemed appropriate given the ongoing exodus of scientists, intellectuals, and artists to foreign lands. Salem was one of the few who had chosen to stay.

She was currently starring, she told me, in a play called *Paradise Opens Its Doors*, written and directed by the Iraqi playwright Muhsen el-Ali. It told the story of a woman whose husband returns after fifteen years as a POW in Iran to find a country in economic ruin and a wife who does not recognize him. In 1999, Salem had starred in Falah Shakir's *100 Years of Love*, about a woman with children who remarries out of financial necessity when her husband goes missing in action in Iran, only to be faced with an impossible choice when he returns a decade later.

"The plays concern a very real dilemma," Salem told me, as many Iraqi women have had similar experiences. She said that she was constantly receiving letters from fans expressing their problems and asking for assistance. "Just this morning, before we started filming, the woman who works here as a cleaner came to me and told me how moved she'd been to see me in *Paradise Opens Its Doors*. There were tears in her eyes." The cleaning lady was a widow with five children whose husband had died in Iran, and whose brother had died in Kuwait.

Although Madame Salem admitted that "Iraqi society can be fairly conservative" and "actresses do not expose their bodies here as much as in Hollywood," she saw this as an advantage. "Here there are many good roles for women my age. Brains count more than looks." And with that she was off to the shoot: "I have to go on. It's very important for me — now more than ever — to keep working."

But if things were bad in Baghdad, they were far worse in Basra. When I visited in 2001, this southern port, once the wealthiest city in Iraq, was a jewel scarred by two decades of warfare. In the working-class neighborhood of Jamhuriyah, in the home of a woman named Iqbal Fartous, I was given tea in a concrete-floored room, bare but for a single red rug and a picture of Imam Ali. Fartous had lost her four-year-old son Haidar in January of 1999, when a bomb killed seventeen people here. British and American air raids had been on going since the end of the first Gulf War and had increased since Desert Fox, in late 1998. In deference to her loss, she had since been referred to as Um Haidar, "Mother of Haidar." She was an elementary school teacher and told me that when the air-raid sirens interrupted her kindergarten class, she had them sing the Arabic alphabet song to drown out the noise.

Um Haidar was a tall, handsome woman who spoke almost perfect English. Outside her door some kids played on a makeshift ferris wheel of rusted iron bars, oblivious to the filth below them. We went up onto the roof to speak, away from the chaos of the house Um Haidar shared with two other families.

She remembered the morning of January 25, 1999, with great clarity. "We were just finishing breakfast," she told me, "when we heard a big boom that shook the whole house. I was in the kitchen at the time and all the cups and dishes fell out of the cupboards and onto the floor. Everything was shaking. Then, I remembered that my two boys [then aged two and four] were outside playing in the street. I ran outside and saw that the sky was dark and full of smoke. The whole neighborhood was out on the street and everyone seemed to have panic in their eyes. I went to look for my children and saw a small mound of earth mixed with blood and missile parts. There were my sons, Mustafa and Haidar. I called their names but only Mustafa responded."

Haidar, her older son, was lying face-down in a pool of blood; Mustafa's face was bloodied, but his eyes were open and responsive. A doctor broke the news that Haidar was dead. "But I already knew," she said. "When I first saw him lying there I knew."

Mustafa survived but had to undergo a series of operations on his hands (he lost two fingers) and to remove shrapnel from his liver. "His body," said his mother, "is still full of missile parts." Mustafa, then five years old, played nearby. He was restless, fidgeting and sometimes screaming while we talked. "He's very nervous," said his mother. "He can't sleep at night; he's always having nightmares."

Life before sanctions had been good, she said. "We had a proper sewage system in this neighborhood, clean drinking water. We had a Japanese car, good furniture ..." Her voice dropped off as she remembered a time that seemed like another life. Now the school had "no water, no books, no lights, no electricity, no blackboards, and no pencils." But she saw her job as vital. "I have to fight with the parents sometimes, to convince them to keep their children in school. One father tried to keep his little girl away so she could sell things in the market. I said to him, 'What kind of future will she have?'" The father had replied that soon she would be married anyway.

Um Haidar's faith in Islam had helped her survive the hard times, she told me. She had begun wearing hijab in the mid-'90s and she prayed and fasted with great devotion. "Before the embargo," she explained, "I used to dress in Western clothes. But now this," she said, pointing to her voluminous black abaya, "is my protection."

She wanted me to deliver a message to American women. "What quarrel does your government have with our children?" she asked. "Stop the bombing, stop the sanctions, because they are destroying the lives of innocents." But she did not share the opinion of some of her neighbors, who questioned why she befriended American activists who had come to visit her. "I know that many Americans are kind, good people who care about what is happening to us here," she said. "They must."

FAR FROM LIBERATION, the U.S. invasion had only brought increasing economic woe, violence, and fundamentalism. The only woman on the

U.S.-appointed governing council, Aquila al-Hashimi, had been assassinated, and the "feminist" rhetoric espoused by Cherie Blair and Laura Bush to help justify the invasion of Afghanistan had been conveniently ignored in the case of Iraq. By the fall of 2003, it was not impossible to travel south from Baghdad to other towns and cities, but it was even more dangerous than it had been in 2001. Armed robbery and murder on the highway were now commonplace, and being a female traveler was much more risky and complicated than it had been on previous visits. But luckily, I was still able to visit with Ahlam at her beauty parlor.

When I found her, she was in the midst of doing a woman's hair. The familiar Baathist-era décor — bare floors and stark fluorescent lighting, a slightly clinical feel — greeted me. The only difference was that the familiar portrait of Saddam, which had presided over the tubs of peroxide in Ahlam's old salon, was now gone.

Ahlam and I embraced. "You want me cut your hair?" she asked.

Why not, I thought? If Iraq was having a makeover, I might as well too. And I looked forward to spending a few hours at Ahlam's salon, catching up on what had transpired in the year and a half since I'd last seen her. But she seemed unusually quiet. In this land where writing had been invented, she seemed exhausted by stories, as if overwhelmed by the tragedy of her country and her own life. So I tried to break the ice by telling her about my visit with Ali the day before.

"Do you think it was dangerous for me to have seen him?" I asked.

"No" she replied matter-of-factly. "He has no more power."

"But you were afraid of him before, weren't you?" I remembered Ahlam's pat responses to Ali's translated questions.

"No," she said with a hint of bravado. "Not now or before."

"Remember Karim?" I ventured. "Do you think he was *mukhabarat*?"

"I don't think so," Ahlam replied, as she mixed some hair color in a plastic bowl.

"You know, everybody used to be followed by intelligence men — even my parents," said another customer who spoke good English. It seemed that her parents had worked for the U.N. at the Canal Hotel, until it was blown up a month earlier. "Every Monday the *mukhabarat* asked them about all the foreigners there. They told them to write reports on them. They were forced to do this, but they usually wrote about what they ate at lunch, things like that — you know, like 'Mr. X from Pakistan had a deviled-egg sandwich at noon.'"

I wondered how much totally useless information had been collected over decades of Iraqi spying.

Meanwhile, Ahlam's daughter sat watching an Iraqi pop video on TV. Now a fully developed 13-year-old, she spent her days at the salon because her mother said it was too dangerous for her to walk to school. The primitively shot video was about a poor student who loved a girl in his class; in the end, the rich guy he worked for got the girl. In between scenes of dancing and clapping, the hero despaired at his fate and at the lack of water and electricity in his rundown apartment building. This was a very Baghdadi, social-realism version of *Top of the Pops*.

"How are Iraqi men now?" I asked. " Better or worse than before?"

"They are the same — Iraqi men never change," replied Ahlam's sister Maryam, who also worked at the salon.

"Do you like Iraqi men?"

"Yes, my husband is Iraqi," she replied, "but I have no problem with him. He lived in Cyprus so he is more open-minded than most men here, who have very traditional ideas about women. Here men want to give orders to the women, there's not much freedom for women. The Iraqi man is simple, not complicated. He just wants to be in charge."

"What do you think Western men are like compared to Iraqi men?" I asked.

"They are different," said the sister. "They have a different religion. The Iraqi men take care of the women more than foreign ones."

"If you had a choice would you live in America?"

"Yes," she conceded, "it's better than Iraq, unfortunately. The American men make it like this."

"So, you prefer Iraqi men to American ones?"

"Yes," she replied. "He is like the water, like the earth, like the sky. He is from Iraq — he will never change. But I like ..." she struggled with the name slightly, "Pruce Wills."

"Bruce Willis?" I guessed, slightly incredulous at the overwhelming reach of American pop culture.

"Yes, him ... I like because he is not angel, he is devil. I like!" she smiled.

During subsequent visits to the salon, I would meet other women: a young mother who had been eight months' pregnant at the time of the invasion and who had given birth to a premature, sickly baby who had problems breathing properly; a widow and single mother who, like Ahlam, struggled to provide for her children and had been reduced to acting as an ad-hoc taxi driver for her friends; and a photographer whom I'd first met in 1997, when she had worked for the Iraqi press agency, but who now sat cowering at home in fear for her life, because several of her relatives had been abducted in revenge killings or hostage-takings for ransom. Without exception, everyone agreed it had been much better before the invasion.

"We just want the Americans to leave," said Ahlam. "We are so tired of all of this."

Of course, no one wanted the Americans to leave before the security situation had improved: a good definition of "quagmire" if ever there was one. And it was security that was very much on my mind as dusk fell and I realized that the only thing that separated us — five women in a salon — from the random violence of the street was an unlocked door. But so far, thankfully, Ahlam assured me that no one had tried to rob or assault her in the shop (in 2005, armed Islamist groups would begin targeting hair salons and barber shops because of their "sinful" Western styles). She had, however, been caught in American/resistance-fighter crossfire on her way to and from the salon more than once.

But right now, there were more important things to worry about. As a minor argument erupted between Ahlam's sister and daughter about the best shade of pink for a bridesmaid's dress, I learned there was a wedding going on the next day. This was cause for some excitement, as hardly anyone could afford to get married these days, and weddings had once been the mainstay of the salon's business. Ahlam insisted that I attend.

THE BRIDE-TO-BE WAS NADIA, Ahlam's old colleague from the salon at the al-Rashid Hotel. She still worked there, and it was there that she'd met her husband-to-be, a German television journalist. The religious ceremony was at the Virgin Mary Church in Karradah. Unfortunately I missed it completely, owing to its uncharacteristic punctuality. The invitation said 5:00 p.m., and when I arrived at 5:15, after horrific traffic snarls caused by American roadblocks, it was already over. "Security concerns," a fellow guest explained.

But the wedding reception, in the BBQ Garden of the Palestine Hotel, was just getting started, undeterred by the mortar fire of the night before. The Palestine was a towering fortress designed in a kind of Baathist modernism, with brown circular motifs on every balcony that made it look like Spiderman's lair. It was now home to many CPA officials, contractors, U.S. Marines, and assorted foreign hacks. To enter the barbed-wire-encased hotel, one had to first pass a series of military checkpoints manned by Iraqi security staff and flanked by American tanks. At one checkpoint, two of the guards greeted me by name. I was unnerved for a moment, until I recognized them; they were the same guys that had guarded the Ministry of Information. They were happy, they told me, as their new salary was four times what they used to earn.

As I walked towards the hotel entrance, a potent version of "Besame Mucho" wafted through the night air from the party. A few yards from the main door, I noticed some congealed blood on the curb. I walked through the lobby, past crowds of soldiers, bored-looking contractors and drivers with prayer beads, into a scene that was Fellini meets Kafka. Amidst wandering militiamen, feral cats, and deadly lounge muzak, a strange wedding party was unfolding.

Lively Iraqi *chobi* music, punctuated intermittently by Celine Dion songs, pierced the hundred-degree heat, while the newlyweds — whose romance had been cemented in Nuremberg, where Nadia had fled during the invasion — sat enthroned in gilt-edged chairs on a red oriental carpet. Some fifty yards away, American Marines cooled off in a kidney-shaped swimming pool, while CNN prepared its latest broadcast in a nearby compound. In the BBQ Garden, a sprawling green space that framed most of the hotel's ground level, trees and flowers gave the place the feel of a coy Eden, some time well after the Fall, still feigning innocence.

Bridesmaids dance at a wedding reception in Baghdad at the Palestine Hotel,
September 2003

Ahlam, who was there with her two children, greeted me warmly and introduced me to some of the bridesmaids. Dressed in bright pink and green dresses, they milled about among the guests like aging Cinderellas, their features wrinkled by twenty years of war and hardship. They asked me to join them in their *chobi* dance on a makeshift stage, presided over by a lounge singer and DJ who wore a bolero and reminded me of a Babylonian Waylon Jennings. Soon the newlyweds arrived on the floor and slow-danced to a song from *Flashdance* as a few television cameramen began to film them. Little girls dressed like fairy princesses ran around giddily with baskets of flowers, while sharpshooters remained on high alert on the roof above them. The DJ began to play "La Vida Loca."

A woman with incredibly bouffant blond hair introduced me to her two daughters, dressed in starched lace pinafores. "This is Magda," she said, pointing to the younger one. "My husband named her after Hitler's daughter," she explained. "He is an admirer." I guessed she was really referring to Goebbels, but it still seemed like a weird thing to tell a stranger. "Are you married or single?" she inquired.

"Single," I replied.

"Good," she said. "You are free. I am not." There was an awkward pause before she added, "Never marry an Iraqi man. They are too controlling."

Before we could delve further into the topic, we were interrupted by cameramen crowding around the towering wedding cake to capture images of the newlyweds feeding each other slices. Soon after, a huge buffet feast was served, including a wide array of barbecued meats and plates piled high with rice and vegetables.

As I sat with Ahlam and her children watching the scene, I remembered the last Iraqi wedding I'd attended.

IT WAS NEW YEAR'S EVE, 1998, in Baghdad, and I was with Karim, a mustachioed, middle-aged minder. The wedding was in the hall of the Iraqi Union of Geologists, rented for the occasion. We were greeted at the door by a portrait of Saddam Hussein, this one showing him dressed as a serious academic in a navy-blue suit. We wandered into the hall, the music of the wedding band blaring from inside like a beast with a rather ferocious feedback growl.

The scene inside was vaguely post-apocalyptic. It was less than ten days since the Desert Fox bombing campaign, but Iraqis continued to try and live their normal lives as best they could, going to the market for food in the afternoons, returning in the early evening to wait out the night-time air raids. There were even a few weddings going on as cruise missiles lit up the sky. But tonight the feeling was somehow more desperate. On the eve of the ninth year of sanctions, the young couple perched on a makeshift stage in throne-like chairs seemed dwarfed by the giant multilayered wedding cake in front of them, as if their lives were being squashed by circumstances beyond their control.

The bride was named Inas. Her dress, a lacy confection of silk and taffeta, was rented for the evening. That night, she and her young husband, a twenty-four-year-old goldsmith named Hussain Ahmed Ali, would retire to their suite at the Hotel Babel. The very next day, they would begin their married life in a three-room house together with ten of Hussain's family members. Inas' dark, kohl-rimmed eyes were full of silent expectation as she related her hopes for the future. She had just turned eighteen.

"I want to have a big family," she said shyly. "And I want my children to have the important things in life — a good home, a good education."

There was something heartbreakingly poignant about her simple dreams of domestic bliss in a land where many mothers were so malnourished that they had no breast milk to give their babies, and where university students had to sell family heirlooms to afford basic textbooks. The women guests, many in traditional black hijab, chatted together in small groups. Beyond their smiles, there was a look of vacancy, of exhaustion. There was a conspicuous absence of food and drink, and I guessed that Hussain, who earned about twenty dollars a month, had had little of his savings left after renting the hall and paying the band.

The singer, a dark man with a lined face, sang a *makam*, a traditional love song. "I'm afraid I will lose you," he sang. "I'm afraid you will disappear / But no matter, if you leave me / I will always love you." A group of teenage boys danced together, their arms around each others' shoulders. A few girls sat nearby, pretending not to notice them.

I met two women, friends of the groom. Hanan, 23, was an unmarried student, and Abir, 27, was a married hairdresser with two children. They laughed when I asked them, "Which is better, married or single life?" Hanan, timid yet hopeful that she might meet someone at the wedding, said, "Married." Abir, who had got married in 1990, nine months before the Gulf War, said, "Single."

"Look," Abir told me matter-of-factly, "I would never recommend marriage to anyone now. It's a terrible time to get married. Raising children under this embargo is really difficult. First, there's the cost of their education, and then, when they get sick, there's no medicine. *La* [no]," she concluded with a disapproving cluck of the tongue, "it's better to stay single. You know, there's a saying in Arabic: 'If love comes through the door, it goes out through the window.' Love is not enough. You need money, you need property."

Her own husband, she explained, was off on a "buying trip" to Syria. "He's into import/export" she said, which made me suspect that he was one of the new crop of "embargo cats," the smugglers who had sprung up in the early 1990s. By her own admission, her life had "turned upside down" since her marriage. Then, her husband was a civil servant and they owned their own home in Baghdad. After the war and the sanctions, everything changed. Now they lived in a dingy rented flat with no furniture, and she had only "two good dresses left."

Our conversation was interrupted by the piercing ululations of the women. It was time for the traditional carrying of the groom. Hussain's friends, who had been dancing together all evening, hoisted the groom up on their shoulders and paraded him around. Back on the stage, the beautiful Inas looked like a miniature doll overwhelmed by this boisterous male dance. Nearby her mother-in-law, covered in a black abaya, was crying. It was hard to tell whether the tears were of joy or sadness. "I hope God helps them and that they are happy in life," she told me.

I WAS JOLTED BACK to the Palestine hotel wedding when the electricity went off in the middle of a song. But the bridesmaids continued to dance, their hips and arms swaying in serpentine movements. How long, I wondered, could they keep this up?

Chapter 16: Tales of the *Tariqa*

THERE WERE SEVERAL WAYS to survive Baghdad: in armed compounds, at diplomatic cocktail parties, in fervent prayer at mosques and churches or, if one were in search of something more transcendent, by joining a Sufi spiritual group or *tariqa*. The mystical Islamic tradition had an important history in Iraq and its esoteric nature had long intrigued me.

While joining a *tariqa* was not high on the list of most journalists, I had sought out the main Baghdad dervish group at the suggestion of an Italian reporter I'd met at the al-Rashid, thinking it might make a good "color" story to offset the newsier items I was doing for the *New York Times*. But since it wasn't on the Press Center's top-ten list of journo activities (number one being the official state press conference, number two officially staged rallies, etc.), I had gone on my own, ditching my minder for the evening on the grounds that I was dining out with some friends.

And so I found myself one night in November 1997 in a leafy residential suburb of Baghdad, being served tea by a smiling devotee of Sheikh Mohammed, the *tariqa*'s rather jolly-looking and roly-poly spiritual leader. As members of his dervish order counted their prayer beads in a circle around him, the sheikh explained, "Today we have been fasting for the embargo to end." The sheikh's substantial girth seemed to belie the day's sacrifice, but in fact he had not eaten anything since dawn and it was now just past sunset. He sipped the hot tea and said, "God is all knowing." The sheikh offered a unique perspective on the sufferings endured under the U.N. sanctions: "They make us stronger, spiritually," he told me. "And even if Mr. Clinton decides to bomb us," he added dramatically, for this was an imminent possibility, "this will only hasten our path towards Allah."

If the sheikh seemed unconcerned by the threat of American military intervention, it was possibly because in a few hours he would be sticking needles, daggers, and swords into his head. For this was the meeting place of the Tariqa Aliyyah Qadiiriyyah Casnazaniyyah, a dervish order whose adherents believe that the miracles of the prophets can be re-created under special circumstances. At the height of their Sufic trance, entered into after a careful ceremony of prayers and chants, they pierce their flesh with sharp objects. Their sincere submission to God, they say, prevents them from being hurt. "Surrender to Allah is the greatest of protections," Sheikh Muhammad explained. Whether it could protect them from stealth bombers or the sanctions-related shortages of food and medicine was doubtful, but their faith certainly gave them a psychological edge on their fellow citizens. The strength and confidence arising from their beliefs appeared to help them through the hassles of daily life under the embargo. On a more practical level, the *tariqa* ran a soup kitchen that fed its own members as well as hungry neighbors. "We are open to everyone," said Sheikh Muhammad. "Men, women, foreigners, Jews, Christians, Muslims ... even journalists," he smiled. "We are all children of the same God: *wa la ilaha illallah.*"

Tonight the group was an interesting mix of taxi drivers, rural migrants, and educated professionals. The men and women practiced their *zikr* — or spiritual exercise — in separate rooms. Earlier, the women, dressed modestly and covering their heads with scarves, had greeted me downstairs. They had their own sheikha, who led them in their *zikr*. But I was allowed to sit — properly covered in hijab, of course — in this room full of men so that the sheikh could tell me the good news. "Miracles can happen," he exclaimed. "What Jesus or Mohammed did, we can do too — if we surrender to Allah."

"You are like my daughter," said one of the sheikh's disciples, a wiry old man about half the leader's size with a white beard who hailed from Peshawar, the border area between Pakistan and Afghanistan. "Even though you are from America, and your people are causing this embargo, you are welcome here." When he found out I was leaving the country in a week, the old man even offered to pay my hotel bill so that I could stay longer. "Iraq has many sides," he said enigmatically. "You must stay and see them." Certainly the scene that night was different from anything I'd seen so far in Iraq.

Slowly the Sufis began their prayers. The rhythmic chanting of *wa la illaha illallah* was both soothing and hypnotic. Soon they started to sway their heads back and forth in elegant synchrony. The room — its walls covered with Islamic calligraphy and pictures of Mecca, the bare floor warmed by carpets and one tiny gas heater — began to be transformed. It was no longer just a room in a Baghdad suburb in the middle of a cold, deprived winter. It was somehow now a universal space where anything might be possible. Even my presence seemed miraculous: a woman from "America" in a crowd of chanting Iraqi taxi drivers.

The Sufis began to take out their swords and head towards the central outdoor courtyard. Slowly they gathered in a circle around the sheikh, who sat front and center on a throne-like arrangement of cushions. The women remained behind the men at the edges of the circle, chanting and swaying. Eventually two young men entered the circle and began to eat pieces of glass, with no apparent bleeding or other injury. Next, one of them took a long sharp sword and delicately pushed it diagonally from his left cheek down through the lower right side of his jaw. Again, he emerged apparently unscathed. Several similar demonstrations of "acts of faith" — as the sheikh would call them — followed, accompanied by increasingly frenzied prayer and chanting.

I stood with the women just outside the circle, mesmerized. No wonder, I thought, the Sufis were persecuted; such rituals were beyond the purview of Baathist apparatchiks, and very much beyond their control.

After the ritual was over, the sheikh invited my driver, Ferris, and I to join him for supper. We couldn't refuse without being terribly impolite, so we accepted. We were received by the sheikh and his assistant in a small, carpet-lined room on the mosque's ground floor. To Ferris's obvious delight, plates of roast chicken, rice, and kebab were brought before us, followed by groaning trays of sweets and pots of chai. I could barely eat anything — the ritual I had just witnessed seemed to have put me off my food — but the skinny Ferris was voracious.

I was beginning to feel concerned about the late hour and our drive back to the hotel, but after the chai, we received another offer we couldn't refuse. The sheikh invited us to become members of the *tariqa*. Saying no at this point would have been terribly bad form, and besides, I thought, under the circumstances I could use all the protection I could get. The ceremony was relatively low-key, merely involving a recitation similar to the Muslim recitation of faith, in which the believer accepts God and his Prophets, and accepts that through faith and surrender one can attain the realm of the miraculous. This seemed a particularly easy thing to accept at the time. Within a few short minutes, my driver and I had become bona fide members of the Tariqa Aliyyah Qadiiriyyah Casnazaniyyah. Soon we said our goodbyes, expressing gratitude for the sheikh's hospitality and promising to visit again. In the corridor leading to the mosque exit, some small children played with toy guns and a girl with hungry eyes begged for money.

I WONDERED HOW MY old Sufi friends had fared since that night in 1997. I was never able to make contact with them on subsequent trips because such displays of spiritual devotion were frowned upon by the old regime, in spite of the rumor that Saddam's son Qusay and vice-president Ezzat Ibrahim al-Douri were members of the *tariqa*. And despite the fact that during the difficult years of the embargo, many Iraqis were turning not only to established religions but also to esoteric practices as a psychological coping mechanism.

Iraq has a long Sufi tradition and in many ways, Baghdad is the heart of Sufi Islam. The three main schools of Sufi Islam — Suharwardi, Qadri, and Naqshbandi — emerged from the city and spread to other parts of the world. Although Sufis do not like to be bracketed with any particular sect, all three schools belong to the Sunni tradition. And yet many Sufis say that Imam Ali, who became the inspiration for Shia Islam, was the first *darwish*. At the *tariqa*, Sunnis and Shias worshipped together, as they did at the shrine of Abdul Qadr al-Gaylani (at the al-Gaylani mosque). Gaylani was the founder of the Qadri school, the largest of the Sufi orders, with an estimated two million adherents in Iraq and eighty million worldwide. The most famous Sufi woman saint, the eighth-century dancer/musician-turned-dervish poet and mystic Rabia, was born in Basra.

With their disavowal of worldly power and hypocrisy, Sufis have an equally long tradition of rubbing authorities the wrong way. Al-Husayn ibn Mansur al-Hallaj, famous for his phrase *"ana al-haqq"* — "I am the Absolute Truth" (often rendered as "I am God") — and known as the "Martyr of Love," was executed in 922 in Baghdad as a result of his teachings. And, as I would discover, in post-invasion Baghdad the Kurdish-influenced Tariqa Aliyyah Qadiiriyyah Casnazaniyyah was practicing its own delicate balancing act.

A young man named Ehab who worked for the security firm Custer Battles — curious about my quest to find this seemingly obscure Sufi *tariqa* — volunteered to accompany me and translate. As we set off, I chatted with Ehab about what it was like to be a young person in Iraq. His father had been a diplomat for the old regime and he appeared to be a "good boy" from a "nice family." Impeccably mannered and well-spoken, he seemed the cream of the Baathist crop, the flower of Iraqi youth. So what was he doing, I wondered, working for a company that guarded the airport gulag where Tariq Aziz awaited his fate?

"Well," said Ehab, "I'm a young man, but my opinion is that Iraqi people can adapt to anything. I mean, it's hard that another country invades yours, but ... you know ... you get used to it. For 35 years, we just accepted whatever Saddam said. We were obliged to agree, so when the Americans came we got used to it. You see, if there's no one controlling us we can't do anything. We got used to being controlled and directed, so now that's normal for us."

We passed by the long, sad line of former Iraqi army men waiting for their pay, just a few yards away from the entrance to the once flourishing Baghdad music and ballet school.

"Here, look, they pay the salaries for the army. You should see how it is, it's awful: men come here at four in the morning and stand all day in the hot sun. But people just accept it — they take the risk of standing here in the sun, just to get some small amount of money." Ehab seemed to wear the humiliation of such a scene on his young face.

"I'm 23, you know, and personally, I'm not used to being controlled. My father is very educated. He treats me like an adult. Plus, I lived abroad in Switzerland and London — my father was a diplomat as I said, so I got used to living in a different way."

"What is your father doing now?" I asked.

"Well, he is retired and living in the UAE [the United Arab Emirates, where Comical Ali had also decamped]. He was the first secretary at the Iraqi embassy in Switzerland and ummm ..." Ehab's voice cracked slightly here, "he used to work with Barzan — Saddam's half-brother." Barzan was a notoriously corrupt and violent member of the Hussein clan. "That's why he retired," Ehab explained. "He didn't want to work with him."

"Was it an offer he couldn't refuse?" I asked.

"Well, yes, you know how things were before."

"So how did you get this job?" I asked.

"Well, I just graduated from university last year, and then after the invasion I started working for the CPA. And I met someone there from Custer Battles and they offered me a job."

We were just passing by CPA headquarters, so I asked him, "What do you think about the Americans being here, at Saddam's old fortress?"

"Well," replied Ehab thoughtfully, "I don't know what to say ... When the Americans came here, that was the first time I got to see it from the inside." He smiled at the irony.

Ehab, who had studied languages at college in London, confided that he hoped one day to become a diplomat like his father.

"But when," I asked, "do you think there will be a government to be a diplomat for?"

"I heard they want to hire people soon," he replied optimistically. I mentioned a contact who might be able to help him, but he replied, "Don't worry, my father is a big man here." His tone made me think that Baathist connections still counted for something.

"So what do you do for fun at night?" I inquired, switching to a less political subject.

"Nothing, really," he replied rather forlornly, "Just maybe take a spin in the car before curfew — that's it, really."

A few minutes later, we got stopped by the Iraqi police, curious about the girl in the back with the video camera. But after I shouted in English and waved my Canadian passport they let us go.

"You know," said Ehab, "if it had been just Iraqis in the car, they would have threatened us and asked for a bribe." In some ways, he said, having "Americans" around offered a paradoxical sort of protection from fellow Iraqis.

SOON WE ARRIVED IN HAY AL-SAFARAT, part of al-Amariyah, where we drove past the Chinese embassy, which had been bombed by the Americans and then looted by the Iraqis. The neighborhood was also home to other embassies and featured large, often vacant lots, relieved by occasional tracts of greenery. Barbed-wire fences surrounded elegant villas on palm-lined streets. It may have once been an upper-middle-class neighborhood, but holes in the roads and cracks in the aging villas were signs that it had seen better days.

We pulled up to the entrance of the compound of the *tariqa* and were greeted by a friendly armed guard. After a mild interrogation we were ushered into the central courtyard area, where the *zikr* was now underway. The evening *zikrs*, I would discover, were a thing of the past; security concerns meant that the rituals had to take place during daylight hours. And the jolly Sheikh Mohammed, it seemed, had fled to Sulemaniyah out of security concerns.

The sheikh (although he insisted that I call him only "friend" or "brother") now leading the group was a slender man with delicate, almost feminine features. As the *zikr* began, a group of maybe three dozen men stood in a circle, with the sheikh at the center. Invoking the name of Allah, the men bowed their heads and then stood upright again, oblivious to the sounds of cars honking and cocks crowing in the distance. A man clothed entirely in white robes sat at the center of the circle at the sheikh's feet and soon the familiar rhythmic chanting began. Accompanied by loud, insistent drumming, the group began to chant *Allah-hu, Alla-hu*, swaying their heads from side to side in unison. Slowly, three men standing next to each other began to loosen their long hair, and in a typically Kurdish manner, let it sway in wild abandon.

I noticed some small children in the circle as well, including one little girl who seemed lost in a trance. Three women — two in white hijab, one entirely in black — stood on the sidelines, swaying and even crying as they prayed. Soon the sheikh began to walk around the circle of worshippers, praying over them and offering spiritual support. Finally everyone knelt down and the loud chanting retreated again to quiet, inward prayer. The men with the long hair discreetly tied it back up to the nape of their necks.

After the *zikr* was completed, I was welcomed by an older black man, dressed entirely in white, who smiled and thanked me for coming. Then I was introduced to the slender, youthful-looking sheikh. He seemed to remember me vaguely from 1997, but clearer in his mind was the memory of my companion — not Ferris the driver, but a colleague who had accompanied me on my first attempt to find the *tariqa*, when we had got lost and arrived at the end of the *zikr*.

"Yes," said the sheikh. "You were with the man from ..." he smiled a spiritual smile and grinned "CNN." Of course, I remembered now, I'd come the first time with Peter Arnett, a most unlikely candidate for conversion. "Yes, CNN," repeated the sheikh, like it was a kind of televisual mantra. One could only imagine how things might have changed if America's chief conduit for news from Iraq had been suddenly flooded with Sufi converts.

The sheikh obliged my request for a formal, sit-down interview, but before I'd pressed the record button, he told me off-camera, "You know, things are very difficult for us now. They were hard before, we were watched all the time. But now, with this occupation, our members are afraid to travel here for the *zikr* ... It's the crime ... the American tanks in the streets ... It's very difficult, God give us strength." Later I would discover that, just as there had been "plants" in the *tariqa* from the old regime, now there were plants from many different groups and parties. The Sufi doctrine was open and flexible enough to accept many disparate types, and this left it open to suspicion from various factions.

On camera, sitting by the mosque where the men were now performing their sunset prayer, the sheikh spoke of formal spiritual matters. "Our *zikr*," he began, "is the spiritual reality of Islam — the *hakekat*. This *tariqa* came down from God to the Prophet. The *tariqa* survived through a series of great men. We feel happiness in our heart doing *zikr* and we wish this happiness everywhere and for everyone." The Sufis' message seemed harmless enough, but when we retired to an upper floor of the mosque as the outdoor light grew dim, the sheikh would reveal some surprising facts.

"When I first visited in 1997," I said, "it was difficult for me to even come here. How was the situation for you?"

"We were suffering under that regime," he replied. "I was afraid of everyone, I did not know who to trust. There was no freedom." I asked for some specifics on how the *tariqa* had been persecuted, but his answer was vague and careful.

"I'm not a political man," he replied. "We are just worshipping Allah. We are far from all the trouble of the world; we are on the spiritual side of things. Our future is after death, because we believe we will face Allah in paradise. Our way is not political and we have no problem with anyone. We love all and we wish mercy for all."

"But just now you told me you were under the constraints of occupation, and that it was hard for people to come here for *zikr*."

"We have no problem with the coalition forces," the sheikh was quick to respond. "The problem is with the lack of security. Many people come here from far away, and there is a problem with transportation — it is not safe. We come here every Monday and Thursday to pray and worship God. And all the difficulties we enjoy, because we are in the service of our God. If there is a curfew — okay, we follow it, we follow the rules." Considering the options and the *tariqa*'s past experience, this seemed a pragmatic approach.

"Are there more people now in the *tariqa* than before?" I asked.

"In difficult circumstances," replied the sheikh rather cryptically, "man seeks refuge with God — his only refuge. In difficult circumstances, man starts to understand that this world will all disappear one day into the world of the spirit."

"Have more people joined since the invasion?" I inquired.

"We keep no records of people who have joined," said the sheikh. "It's just a spiritual experience between man and God. We are not an organization or a party." Indeed, the Sufis' kingdom was elsewhere. I thought of Jesus before the Romans.

"So things were difficult under Saddam, and are difficult now. But what was it like doing *zikr* during the invasion?" I asked.

"During the war we were in prison," the sheikh responded calmly. "Because they accused us of being agents of America and Britain, we were put in jail. Some of us were released before the fall of Baghdad and some afterwards." Later I would learn that in the days leading up to the invasion, the Sufis had been sent to the notorious Abu Ghraib prison, and that some had been executed.

"Did they put the whole *tariqa* in jail or just the leaders?"

"Both," replied the sheikh.

"Because you were Sufis or because of the Kurdish connection?" I asked, knowing that the sheikh and many of his followers were Kurds.

"No, not because of that. We are connected to a sheikh who is Kurdish, but he receives everyone, including foreigners. Because of this he was under suspicion. For us there is no difference between Kurdish and Arab. We are from everywhere — even Canada," he smiled.

"Would you even welcome an American?" I asked.

"Yes, of course, welcome, welcome."

"Did you do *zikr* in jail?"

"Yes, we practiced prayer in our hearts. We were always hoping that God would intercede in our case."

"And when you were released from prison, how did you feel?"

"It was an act of God," replied the sheikh, in the same calm manner he would employ throughout our interview.

"What order do you belong to?" I asked, wondering just how to classify the Casnazaniyyah.

"We are like nobody, but some are like us."

"Well, are you close to the Naqshbandi?" Some Iraqi friends had told me this.

"We are close to God," was the sheikh's reply. I was beginning to see how these inscrutable responses might frustrate a Baathist — or an American — interrogator.

"But was your order founded by an Iraqi sheikh?"

"It was founded by a *Muslim* sheikh, for all people — just like Islam, just like the Prophet's message."

I wanted to ask the sheikh more questions, but it was getting dark and we all had to get back home safely. "I am happy to see you again in

Iraq," he told me as we parted. "Please come to join our *zikr* anytime." I felt a sudden admiration for the sheikh's profound calm amid such danger and chaos.

As he showed me out, the sheikh's assistant and translator, a young man in his early thirties named Wael, told me an incredible story about his own decision to join the *tariqa*. His mother, he related, had been cured of terminal cancer after drinking some holy water given to her by Sheikh Mohammed. He also introduced me to a man with his young daughter, who claimed that the girl had been cured of a fatal wasting disease after the sheikh appeared to her in a dream. It was impossible to tell if these stories were true, but the Sufis' faith was certainly real enough. And it seemed almost more pragmatic to put one's faith in such miraculous healing experiences than to rely on Iraq's crumbling public-health system, devastated by two decades of war and sanctions.

As we parted, Wael offered me some "sacred" dates. "Eat these," he said, "and you will be healed." I shared the dates with Ehab and my driver Ali, but saved one for Robert Fisk, the famed *Independent* journalist whom I had arranged to meet for dinner that night. I recounted my Sufi tale to Robert and offered him a holy date. In return, he offered me something that might only in the madness of post-invasion Iraq have been considered a sign of affection: an invitation to join him the next morning for a tour of Abu Ghraib prison. I accepted at once.

Sarhan Daoud watches the coffins of his only sons, Ahmed and Ali, being carried out of the Baghdad morgue, September 2003

Chapter 17: A Prison and Two Morgues

THE NEXT MORNING I ROSE EARLY to prepare for our visit to Abu Ghraib. It was one of Saddam's most notorious prisons, and it had been appropriated by U.S. forces right after the invasion. The abuse scandal that would hit Washington was still eight months away, but there were already signs that all was not well. Mortar attacks on the prison were commonplace and there was much concern among Iraqis whose relatives had the misfortune of being detained there.

Under Saddam's rule, Abu Ghraib had been off-limits to journalists. I was more accustomed to interviewing returning Iraqi POWs, who would describe in detail their years of imprisonment and torture in Iranian jails such as the underground desert prison of Arak-Mahbous. Some of these stories had happy endings. I interviewed a man in 1997 who had come home after 17 years in jail to find his wife still waiting for him in the same apartment; he was older and thinner and his country was on the brink of economic collapse, but true love had prevailed. An army captain I met in December of 1998 had been released from an Iranian prison two days before the start of Desert Fox. He described sitting in his bathtub in his Baghdad home shaving off his long beard while cruise missiles lit up the night sky. At first he thought it was the Iranians on the attack again; only later did he learn that the new enemy was Uncle Sam. Other returning POWs were not so warmly welcomed; soldiers whom the regime feared had been indoctrinated against them by the Iranians were incarcerated again upon their return to Iraq. Some even ended up in Abu Ghraib.

Although a visit to an infamous prison was not exactly a cheerful prospect, I was looking forward to the outing, perhaps because I would be part of a "team," however briefly. Robert Fisk worked with Haidar, an amiable out-of-work engineer in his early thirties who acted as his translator, and Mohammed, a young Shia driver whose family ran a car business. Besides their official duties, they played the roles of "straight man" and "rapt audience" as Robert entertained us with jokes, poetic recitals, impersonations, and show tunes. His manic joker personality was an interesting contrast to the serious Middle Eastern correspondent persona of his writing; after years of covering the region's bloodiest conflicts, perhaps it was simply a psychological coping strategy.

And so, as we drove west towards Abu Ghraib — on the same road that led to the "Sunni triangle" of Ramadi and Falluja — our spirits were surprisingly high. Robert recited Yeats' "Pilgrim Soul" and a British poem from the First World War, but when asked for another show tune declined with mock severity: "I'm sorry, I can't sing that, we're on our way to prison." An appropriate ditty, he suggested, would be "*Ana bahabek ya Saddam*" — the old "I love Saddam" chant, a favorite at Baathist rallies, which he joked should now be *Ana bahabek ya Bush and Bremer*. Then he delighted us with an imitation of Mohammed al-Sahaf ("Comical Ali"), but wouldn't do Tony Blair: "I don't listen to him enough, he's so boring." He kept the game going with a spot-on imitation of an old Baathist *mukhabarat* pretending to interrogate Mohammed: "When we come, we speak to you as a brother, and you will tell the truth as a brother or we will beat you! And if you tell the truth we will beat you! So tell the truth!"

I offered my best imitation of a Marine at a checkpoint and then a lost Texan tourist: "Is this the right bus for the Abu Ghraib tour, y'all?"

"Is that tourism or terrorism you're after, ma'am?" Robert drawled back.

We were now driving down a lonely stretch of hostile highway, where car bombs and mortar attacks were not uncommon. This was the traditional Sunni area of Kahndari, known both for the local hospitality and as the site of one of the area's biggest graveyards. But at 8:00 a.m. it was almost empty, with only the occasional glimpse of humanity: an old man with a sack of flour on his back walking along the shoulder of the road, a woman in a black abaya waiting for someone, something. As we neared the prison, a sense of foreboding began to intrude.

I chatted briefly with Robert about his frightening experience in Pakistan, near the Afghan border, shortly after the American invasion in 2001. I'd read his chilling account of how, when his car had broken down on a dusty highway in the mountains, he had been swarmed and almost killed by a group of angry Afghan refugees whose villages had just been bombed by U.S. warplanes. The refugees had no idea who he was: one of them had asked, "Is that George Bush?" shortly before the attack. Even if someone had explained that Robert was the Great Defender of the Arab and Muslim Cause in the Liberal English Newspaper Tradition, it wouldn't have made any difference. He was a white man in a nice car in the wrong place at the wrong time. That's the trouble with wars: no one ever stops to ask who you are.

But today if we were stopped by a group of angry Iraqis, I mused, we might be alright. Haidar had already scolded me for looking "too Iraqi" in the baggy clothes and hijab that Robert had suggested I wear. Perhaps Robert was thinking of modesty or even "street cred" (only a few months later, most Western journalists would adopt Iraqi disguises as a matter of course), while Haidar was thinking that it was safer to look "Western" for the Americans. In fact, my outfit and general "look" would arouse much suspicion among the American soldiers at Abu Ghraib. As we approached the main gate and stopped to ask a small boy at a market stall for directions, Robert cautioned me, "These people are not terribly pro-Western so be careful with the camera." Local girls did not usually carry video equipment, and many of the townspeople's close relatives were currently being detained at Abu Ghraib.

Except for the sign in English saying "PRISONER INFORMATION NOT RELEASED. THERE IS CURRENTLY NO VISITATION AUTHORIZED," the prison entrance was little changed from the bad old Baathist days. We were ushered in by a young U.S. soldier who instructed us to stop the car and wait. He seemed to know that an assortment of international media would be arriving that day. He was polite, even courteous, as we chatted with him while he waited for a signal to let us through. He was from Ohio, he told us, and was 21 years old.

"When was the last time you spoke to your mother?" Robert asked him.

"Well, let's see ... maybe five months ago," he replied. Robert offered him his Thuraya phone, and a few minutes later he was talking to his mother in Dayton. "I'm all right," he told her. "Yeah, I got those shirts, but could you send some more CDs? We're going crazy listening to the same old music here all the time." Life at Abu Ghraib was no picnic for the soldiers: the local populace was hostile, there was nothing to do and nowhere to go, and there was mortar fire to contend with at least four nights a week.

Soon we were waved through to a kind of gravel parking lot, where an assortment of sleepy-looking international media were waiting: CNN, ZDF, AFP, and a few other minor acronyms. A portly general came over to greet us and escort us to an area nearby, where a canopy of camouflage and some plastic chairs had been set up. There were even sugar cookies and pink lemonade. As a group of us converged around the sweets, I noticed a familiar face: Mr. Ziad, the one-time head of the Press Center who had once expelled me from Iraq. He smiled sheepishly when I greeted him and told me in German he was now working as a translator for ZDF. Here we were again in a familiar scene: obedient lambs being herded through another photo op.

A middle-aged blond general named Janis Karpinski would be our guide to the New and Improved Abu Ghraib Prison. A brigadier-general appointed by Donald Rumsfeld in early 2003 and the highest-ranking military woman in Iraq, Karpinski would be suspended by the Pentagon after the abuse scandal broke. Although she ran Abu Ghraib and oversaw the entire prison system in Iraq, she would plead ignorance of any wrongful activities and insist that she was a scapegoat for higher-ups.

"We welcome you to our central detention facility — a work in progress," began the handsome general. Her accent was vaguely midwestern, her tone earnest. "We'll end up at the death chamber, where you can do one-on-one interviews with some of the staff. And by the way, thanks for coming out here today. It gives us an opportunity to show you how much progress is being made in this country. This is an opportunity to show you what Coalition forces and Iraqis working with us can do for this country. Feel free to ask questions, even of the soldiers running the facility." I almost expected her to sing "The Star Spangled Banner."

"A few months ago," General Karpinski said proudly, "you would have seen only large piles of rubble here. The facility was looted after

Saddam opened the doors and let the prison population out on the streets of Baghdad. We have several different locations here. There are 240 prisoners on the ground. We have the capacity for 600 but we're moving them in incrementally. We also have Camp Gancy — a quick response for criminals — a blueprint for a hasty-confinement facility, with concertina wire and guard towers. We have about 800 there. We have a very small population of security detainees — the ones that are left over are in Camp Bucca or Umm Qasr [the Gulf port in southern Iraq]."

Robert started the question period with a good one. "General Karpinski, how do you define 'criminal'?"

"Well, sometimes we get confused, too," responded the general. "Here 'criminal' refers to Iraqi-on-Iraqi crime — rape, theft, curfew violations. The rest are 'security detainees.' But here there are less than a dozen." I wondered how a curfew violation might count as an Iraqi-on-Iraqi crime, and thought of all the stories I'd heard of innocent taxi drivers caught in checkpoint mayhem, fathers ratted on by neighbors who wanted to steal their houses, students wrongfully imprisoned for months for no other crime than being Palestinian. Just how loose was their definition of a "security detainee"?

Robert continued with his genteel yet pointed line of questioning. "Do you talk to them, General, the criminals and the detainees?"

"Yes, we do, we talk to them, we ask if they are relaxed, comfortable and have everything they need ... Several days ago the MPs [military police] went out to Camp Gancy and they called off a list of thirty names and said 'Get on the bus 'cause you're being released.' And then they called out a list of twenty who weren't being released, but were being taken into the main Abu Ghraib facility. Once the criminals came inside they said, 'This is very nice! How much do we have to pay to stay here?'" I wondered if this was gallows humor, but the general's tone was totally devoid of irony.

"What about the recent riot where a prisoner was shot?" Robert asked.

"I'm not aware of that incident," replied the general, who quickly conferred with some of her colleagues. "Yes, I wasn't here then, but Captain Armstrong said the prisoners used tent poles and rushed the guards, who had to resort to force." Deadly force, unfortunately. We

U.S. General Janis Karpinski lowers the hanging platform in the old
"death chamber" at Abu Ghraib prison, September 2003

would later be told that the Americans were training Iraqi police in, among other techniques, the use of "non-lethal force" in crowd control.

"What facilities do you have for women prisoners?" I asked the general.

"We have a facility in Baghdad which is a combined juvenile and women's facility. Under Saddam, it was a horrible place. There was routine rape and assault." We would later learn that some of the same staff who had worked at Abu Ghraib under Saddam were still there under the Americans.

"How are you dealing with the 'honor crime' issue now?" I asked. Before the invasion, women and girls guilty of such "crimes" — usually related to premarital sex or dating or marrying someone the family patriarch did not approve of — were often kept in prison under the guise of "protective custody."

"The women prisoners now are different than the ones before," replied the general. "Some are guilty of murder, some are there because they're guilty of adultery and they are there for their own protection." In effect, she admitted, "protective custody" was still being practiced. There was no time to ask about the number of men imprisoned for domestic violence, but I was not surprised when, a few months later, the IGC repealed Iraq's secular laws pertaining to women's rights, replacing them with the regressive *shariah* or Islamic law.

Asked about the process of "screening" prisoners, the general explained that they came in to a "processing facility. Within 72 hours they have an additional interview. If they are determined to be security detainees they are given a military interview, say within 14 days, or 30 days. But they are informed every step of the way why they are being detained." In English, I wondered? "In all of these cases," continued the general, "rather than tell families 'Your son is here or there,' we waited until the system had settled itself. People were being moved around as different facilities opened up. There were no telephone lines, which also made things difficult. And the CPA processor spells names as he understands them from the Arabic. In some cases, translators have helped with spelling issues — but it's not a clear process." To think a man's life could be ruined by a stray double consonant typed by a military clerk from New Jersey.

Then it was time for a little visual presentation. The general held up a color-coded map of Iraq and pointed to a dozen or so prisons. "The blue blocks indicate the prisons under construction by the 31st of December [2003] or under contract, and the ones in black are open prisons or confinement facilities."

"Are you holding any foreigners here, general?" asked Robert.

"Well, prisoners often come in without papers and if they tell us they are Iraqi ... Well, it's difficult to ..." The general drifted off, not finishing her sentence. Eventually she admitted there were six security detainees "claiming to be Americans and two from the U.K." They were in the process, she said, of "verifying information and conducting interviews."

"Are you present at these interviews?" asked Robert.

The general confirmed that "military police are not in the room when interrogations take place" and that, in fact, they couldn't even hear the interviews. The implication behind Robert's question was that torture or forced confessions would have been easier without the presence of MPs.

"Were you ever in Guantánamo, General?" Robert asked, always polite but unrelenting.

"Yes, but it's a different scene in Iraq," replied the general, guessing where he was heading. "There was a war here, and we have security detainees, foreign nationals, etc. — unlike Guantánamo, where prisoners were taken out of the country and into a new place." (Later, Karpinski would admit that military police under orders from those above her talked of "Gitmoizing" Abu Ghraib, Gitmo being slang for Guantánamo — of making it into a tougher facility in terms of treatment and interrogation of prisoners.)

I was beginning to feel a little sorry for the general. She looked like a good gal. In another time or place she might have been someone's favorite gym teacher or the CEO of a small company. In fact, in a *St. Petersburg Times* profile of Karpinski published a few months later, I would learn that, "in her civilian life, Karpinksi is a consultant who runs grueling executive training programs for those hoping to scale the corporate ladder. The courses, which put participants under various kinds of stress, are 'not a lot of fun ... but are a true test of the toughness of an individual's mettle.'"

It was time to begin the prison tour. To kick things off, we were shown some of the prisoners' artwork, although it wasn't clear if it was all from former inmates. The portraits of Saddam were most likely from before the invasion and the inoffensive Tower of Babel and Arab stallions could have been from either era. The depiction of Marsh Arabs in a boat was iffy but the English sign saying "Bomb Shelter" in magic marker was definitely new, as were the rows of army cots spread out beside it.

But it was hard to distract the attention of the international press corps for long. Soon someone asked whether the old practice of prison guards taking bribes from inmates was continuing. "We will not allow that to happen," the general replied. "It used to be that inmates had to bribe guards for food, showers, clean clothes, even early release. But things are changing, they're moving away from the old ways," she proclaimed optimistically. "They'll make mistakes, they'll fall down, but we'll pick them up and show them the way. Now jails are 75 percent controlled and run by Iraqis." As we walked down a dimly lit corridor of the prison, half a dozen Iraqi workers hammered and welded the doors of new jail cells that would soon hold hundreds of their fellow countrymen.

"They replaced the flooring here, which was looted," the general told us proudly, as if there really hadn't been an invasion but rather a kind of national redecorating scheme. "The kitchen and bakery are under construction. The baker is proud of the kitchen. He knows that he's a participant in this whole process and he wants to do it the *right* way." Amazing, I thought, how the liberal language of inclusion was being used to justify an illegal occupation. Who cares about Geneva conventions, as long as the pita bread tastes good?

We continued our walk down the corridor. "Some people say that some of those small rooms in the hallway there were used for medical experiments and torture. But," the general gestured dramatically, pointing towards a new wing of the prison, "there is light at the end of the tunnel — literally. The new medical facility, which is a success story in itself."

As we walked down the dark hallway, we peered into tiny cells with minuscule windows bleeding points of light. An Iraqi teenager repaired a loose hinge on one of the cell doors, oblivious to the cameras in his face.

Soon we arrived in the refurbished wing, where the latest equipment and medical supplies spoke of a brave new world. But the chief medical officer, Doctor Majid, was very much part of the bad old Baathist universe. He had held the same position under the old regime, and his Orwellian double-speak skills remained flawless. As he showed us some of the new medical equipment, I asked the doctor, "What were the most common illnesses you treated then, and now what are they?"

"Well, it used to be tuberculosis. We would have a few hundred cases at any given time. But now we have a good schedule for treatment. We have only 23 inmates with active TB." Twenty-three out of 240 was almost ten percent.

"Now the most common complaints are flu, dysentery ..."

"What is the main concern of prisoners here?" someone asked.

"Well, the diet is hard," replied the doctor, admitting that it consisted mainly of army-regulation "instant meals" with no fresh produce. "And meeting with families is another concern. But the prisoners say they've never been treated so well."

"Do you treat any prisoners here for psychiatric disorders?" I asked.

"No," he answered in an odd non sequitur, "Most are well-known looters."

The doctor went on to describe the terrible conditions at Abu Ghraib under the old regime, for which he was a well-placed civil servant. "There was a lot of torture before," he explained, "and inmates had to pay money for good beds, for visits ..."

"Were inmates tortured every day?" I asked.

"No, no," replied the doctor with a certain authority. "Not that often, maybe twice a week."

"Were you allowed to treat them?" another journalist asked.

"Well, they never told me they'd been tortured, of course, they'd just say, 'Here are some sick inmates, please treat them.'"

"What was the most common form of torture?" I asked.

"Breaking legs was quite common," replied the doctor nonchalantly.

As we were shown yet another cell, I wondered if my old friend Subhy Haddad had been imprisoned here. A charming Turkmen gentleman in his sixties who was once a member of the Communist Party and later one of the highest-paid Iraqi journalists, Subhy had been the long-time Baghdad Arabic BBC correspondent. He was jailed for two years in the early nineties after jealous colleagues at the Press Center accused him of being a foreign agent. The British-Iranian journalist Farhad Barzoft, charged with "espionage" after he took soil samples from a chemical-weapons testing site, had also been imprisoned here, and executed. Luckily Subhy had been released during a political amnesty.

"You should have seen this old cell block before," continued the general. "It was dismal, dirty. Each one of these cells that will hold twelve in bunks used to house one hundred men. It was literally standing room only, and there were no bunks or mattresses."

"Which company has the contract for prison reconstruction here?" I asked.

"El Air, from Baghdad" I was told. We later discovered that they were merely the subcontractors; the main contractor for prison construction in the new Iraq was DynCorp, a Virginia-based company infamous for a scandal in Bosnia in the late nineties, in which its employees were accused of trafficking in underaged female sex slaves.

"There used to be an elaborate system of bribes," the general told us, continuing with her narrative of the bad old days. "There used to be vendors standing in the hallway, you had to pay for water, access to the mess hall, for food, showers, medicine." Doctor Majid shifted restlessly, looking from side to side.

"Do you have a special training program for new Iraqi prison guards?" I asked.

"Yes," said the general, "we do. It's a program geared towards human rights, handling prisoners in the right way, use of weapons, handcuffs, non-lethal methods of controlling prisoners ..." This program was also run by DynCorp advisers.

Now it was time for the pièce de résistance: a trip to the old death chambers. A short bus ride away, the area was eerily quiet, a museum of horrors the Americans hoped to mine for PR gold. First we had a brief look at the tiny death-row cell: one small toilet in the ground, a tiny window and walls lined with Arabic graffiti that read, among other things, "Death is better than shame," "Death is life for the believer" and the more prosaic, "2 September 2001, Ahmed Aziz al Najaf — with Jabar." Next we were led into the execution chambers.

The general walked up a ramp until she reached the gallows, where hangings had regularly taken place. "We've heard many tales of forced confessions here, right up until the time of execution. Many times people asked, 'What happened to all the bodies?' In fact, for the number of people buried here, there is simply no trace of many of the bodies. They just disappeared. We were told that one day Uday [Hussein] came out and said, 'The prison is far too crowded,' and he signed the death warrant of three thousand prisoners and they were executed that day. Just three thousand prisoners arbitrarily taken from a list."

"Are there any plans to set up execution facilities here, like they say might happen in Guantánamo?" I asked.

"No, none," said the general, rather taken aback. The security guys were paying close attention to me now; I hoped I would still get cookies and lemonade at the end of the tour.

"There is very good information," the general continued, "that if prisoners had not complied with the request to say that they were pro-Saddam, they would be tortured again before their hanging, and that in cases where hanging was not complete, they were cut down and taken into a gas chamber. I'm going to flip the lever now — the death toll, as we call it — and it's loud." The hanging platform came crashing down with a frightening sound.

After the general's dramatic display, we lingered a bit in the old death chamber to chat with Doctor Majid. "Were there no death certificates issued, doctor?" Robert asked.

"No," replied the doctor. "They had a nearby cemetery and they just buried them quickly." He also claimed that he'd never witnessed an execution, "because they happened at night. I didn't see anything, they would just pull up in black buses with tinted windows, special buses for the political prisoners. I usually asked one of the junior doctors to attend."

"Why did you stay in the same job here, doctor, do you like working at the prison?" I asked.

"We have plenty of poor prisoners — even they had no money to come to the doctor — so I try to help them," he replied. It was difficult to tell if he was speaking of the past or the present.

"Are you the only former employee still working here?"

"No, there are some others."

"The men that did the hangings, did you ever see them, did you know who they were?" Robert asked.

"I knew the people who did the hanging during the day, of the normal criminals," he replied. "But not the special security men who came at night for the political prisoners. They always disappeared. The political prisoners came here with special political judges. Cars came with dark windows, they send the prisoners inside, they make the hanging fast. Nobody heard anything." The doctor's eyes darted wildly as he spoke, so he looked both guilty and frightened at the same time. I wondered how much of a pay raise he'd received from the Americans.

As we were led back to the camouflage tarp where we'd started our tour, I could see the lemonade and cookies still sitting out. But we weren't offered any. The general and her entourage seemed relieved that it was all over, although many of them seemed a little sad to see us go; they didn't often receive "visitors." I half expected to hear a "Y'all come back now," from a particularly friendly Texan corporal.

The whole tour had barely taken two hours, but it felt like days. There was something incredibly draining about the whole experience. As we rejoined our driver, Mohammed, I commented on how the Americans seemed to have no sense of irony about their role as the new prison overlords. "Abu Ghraib," sighed Haidar as we drove out through the dust and dirt, "it's one of those places that will be here forever. After Saddam, after the Americans leave, this prison will still be standing."

WE DROVE BACK to the Hamra Hotel, my new base, which in its own way was a special kind of prison, a gilded jail for foreign hacks, a former honey- moon hotel with a shimmering pool protected by armed guards and yards of barbed wire. At night, as I swam cool lengths hoping to shake off the dust and despair of another day in Baghdad, I could see bats flying over the wire fence, barely missing the Australian soldiers standing on guard in full combat gear. But after the death chamber, it was sweet relief.

After a hard day of documenting suffering or planning the future of Iraq from the comfort of air-conditioned offices, the foreign journos, diplomats, military attachés, and aid workers who were staying at the Hamra met for drinks around the pool. Despite the car bombs and snipers, we all knew the truth: in Baghdad, it was much more dangerous to be an Iraqi than to be a foreigner. At dusk, our drivers and translators had to head home to lawless neighborhoods where you never knew who might decide to kill you for your car. Even the girl who ran the hotel's "business center" was terrified of missing her five o'clock ride home. Once, when I was desperate to file a story, I offered to have my driver take her home if she would just let me have an extra fifteen minutes of internet time. She refused, saying, "You have no idea what it's like to be a woman in Baghdad these days!" and almost burst into tears. Later I would learn that several of her friends had been abducted for ransom.

Some of the live-in staff, like the aging Iraqi hippie Samir Peter who played the piano in the dining room every night to a crowd of two, were trapped with us. "I am a prisoner here," he would tell me as he did his nightly yoga by the poolside in between sips of Johnny Walker and slow drags on a Lucky Strike, like some character from an Iraqi version of "Hotel California." "But soon I'll go to San Diego, I have a cousin there." Some nights after a few too many drinks Samir would tell me horror stories from the Iran–Iraq war. "I'm a Christian, you know, and my Muslim commander didn't like me so he sent me to the front lines," he told me once, pointing to the crucifix around his neck, which he was sure had saved his life, along with fervent prayers to the Virgin. Another time he came very close to me and made a loud throat-slitting gesture: "Gheeeeeek! I had to kill a man like this once!"

"I WONDER HOW MANY BOMBS we drive past every day?" Robert mused. It was the morning after Abu Ghraib and he and I were on our way to visit the main city morgue; he had a story to file and had asked me to accompany him and take photos. Considering how many bombs actually went off every week, it was a fair question. We had surely passed by a few soon-to-be-detonated ones in our travels so far. En route to the morgue we also passed a vacant lot that Haidar said was the site of old Abassid ruins; stores selling satellite dishes; the Mohammed Bakr al-Hakim mosque, where a Christian bishop had once met with Imam Ali and converted to Islam; and a corner music shop decorated with hanging drums and bugles. Life and death, ancient and modern, the morbid and the festive continued their dance unabated.

The morgue was full of grief-stricken relatives waiting to claim the bodies of their loved ones. Aunts, uncles, fathers, cousins, brothers stood or squatted, watching, waiting for their turn. The heat was oppressive and flies swarmed around pools of open sewage in the potholed pavement. Robert swung into full directorial mode, telling me whom and what to photograph, as I struggled to record as much as possible with my video and still cameras while trying to keep my hijab firmly in place.

We came across a toothless old man in a long white robe. His head was wrapped in a traditional kaffiyeh and thick glasses framed his ancient eyes, now red from tears. He told us his name was Sarhan Daoud and said, "I have come here to receive the bodies of my two sons." The night before his only sons, 27-year-old Ali and 19-year-old Ahmed, had been killed in their own home. It was the sad result of an old feud between families, we were told, "but there was never any bloodshed before." There had been the traditional formal apologies and monetary compensation and even mediation from mutual friends, but all, it seemed, to no avail. "My sons were eating dinner," the grieving father recounted with a quiet dignity, "and someone from the other family came and shot them."

"Could this have happened in the old Iraq?" I asked.

"No," replied Mr. Daoud, "because before there was the rule of law, a strong government, a strong Baath party ... Now we are just trapped in this tragedy. There were very few killings before. Now, guns are everywhere. Please let people know about this tragic situation."

I gave my sincere condolences to Mr. Daoud and thanked him for his time. In the photo, he is squatting on the ground, his hands held up, half in grief, half in supplication, his eyes lifted upwards.

The litany of tragedies continued. A woman in a long black abaya wept as she told me of her nephew, 27-year-old Hassan Ahmed, who had been shot to death the day before as he walked in the street near his home. Her sobs were drowned out for a moment by the ritual chanting of *wa la ilaha ilallah* as grieving relatives carried another coffin to a waiting minivan.

"My nephew lost his father in the Iran–Iraq war," the woman told me tearfully. "He died on the front in 1982." She showed me a photo of the boy she had raised, looking upright and serious in a grey windbreaker. "Who would want to kill him? He was innocent of any wrongdoing." The sound of an Apache helicopter filled the sky overhead. "We think it might have been a robbery, but we're not sure," said the aunt before breaking into a half sob, half chant: "Where are you, Hassan? What are you doing in such a place? This is not your place. Come back to me, Hassan."

Other families of shooting victims complained of the 15,000-dinar charge — ten U.S. dollars, a month's wages for some — which they had to pay to obtain an autopsy and a death certificate, while others spoke of ineffectual Iraqi police who did nothing to help them solve the murders.

We decided to pay a visit to the deputy head of the morgue, Abdullah Razak. In his nondescript office, Doctor Razak proudly told us that he had held his position for 29 years. He had a jolly disposition for a mortician, smiling and even telling the occasional joke. "We had 19 dead in here yesterday," he recounted, "and 11 were from gunshot wounds"; by way of comparison, the morgue had only had 21 gunshot victims in all of July 2002. Doctor Razak claimed that the fatalities were a result of both crime and revenge killings for political and other motives. He estimated that since the invasion, there had been a four hundred percent increase in deaths from violent crimes. Other estimates suggested that more than ten thousand Iraqis had been murdered since "liberation" four months earlier.

We returned to the courtyard, where even more grieving relatives had gathered. The male cousins of a man named Taleb Homtoush, who

Abdel Wahad holds up the death certificate issued after his son, Ali, was stillborn. His wife went into labor on the second night of Desert Fox bombing in December 1998.

had been shot to death in his doorway the day before, were among them. Taleb, they said, had been crippled while serving in the Iran–Iraq war, where he had also lost two brothers. The motive behind the killing was unclear. Robert cautioned me not to film the men or ask too many questions; afterwards he would tell me that because of their dress and appearance, he suspected they were members of the Badr Brigade, a local Shia militia.

One cousin, a very angry young man, told us, "You should know this. We are a Muslim nation and the Americans want to divide us between Sunni and Shia. But there will be no civil war here. People are dying because the Americans let this happen. You know that the Americans made many promises before they came here. They promised freedom and security and democracy. We were dreaming of these promises. Now we are just dreaming of blowing ourselves up in their faces."

It seemed like a good time to go, so we gave our condolences and bade them farewell. On the way to the car, I saw that just outside the morgue entrance, desperate relatives had placed posters of missing people. One read, "Beida Jaffer Sadr, 16 years old, blond hair, brown eyes, wearing a black skirt"; below her photo the girl's father had printed his phone number. I wondered if the number still worked. Another poster showed an older gentleman in a suit with the words, "We lost Mr. Abdul emir al-Noor al Moussawi last Wednesday, 11 June 2003, in Baghdad. He is 71 years old. White hair. Wearing a grey robe. A reward will be paid to anyone with information."

A few feet away, two women and a man squatted on the sidewalk, crying and swaying. I greeted the women and asked what was wrong. They indicated that it would be all right if I filmed them, but Robert, perhaps still spooked by the Badr Brigade guys, asked me not to. Their brother had been killed, they told me amid intermittent sobs, by a boarder in their home. He was someone they'd known casually from the neighborhood, they said, and it happened in a dispute over a cigarette. "My brother asked the boarder to put out his cigarette," said one of the sisters, named Fatima, "because it was bothering him and when he refused, my brother protested and said, 'But this is my home!'" The boarder had pulled out his gun and shot him. The sisters had given the police a good description, they said, but the boarder had run away and had not been found since. Fatima collapsed into sobs again and in an act of spontaneous solidarity, we embraced.

"I'm so sorry," I told her in English.

"He was an angel," she replied in Arabic, "such a good brother."

THERE WAS STILL ONE MORE morgue to attend to, this time at al-Yarmouk hospital, a ten-minute drive away. It was becoming increasingly difficult for journalists to access hospitals and morgues, as the CPA hoped to control information about health issues and mortality statistics. But luckily Haidar had the right connections. Here we met moon-faced Mortada Karim, dressed in a long white robe, and his colleague Abu Omar, more serious-looking and dressed in slacks and a long-sleeved shirt. They had already had quite a week. Revenge killings and murder/ robberies were becoming routine, they told us. But there were other kinds of killings as well.

"A few days ago," recounted Abu Omar, "we received the body of a 40-year-old woman who had been shot while trying to intervene in a fight between two men." They also told of a recent case where a father had killed his son; both were looters and they had had a violent quarrel over the spoils. In another horrific story, nine members of a family from Basra — five women and four brothers — had all died in the same incident. Apparently the brothers had found their sisters working in a Baghdad brothel and had killed the women for their "honor crimes," and were then killed themselves by the pimps.

They also dealt with the fallout of American violence against Iraqi civilians. "We've received more than two hundred people killed at checkpoints since the invasion," they said. Just the other day, they'd received the bodies of a mother and her child shot at a wedding party. When the traditional celebratory gunshots were fired into the air, the Americans had assumed they were being attacked and had opened fire, killing the woman and her baby.

"The problem," explained Mortada, "is that the American soldiers are nervous. They don't distinguish between aggressors and innocent bystanders."

As we bid goodbye to Mortada and Omar, I took a last look at the tiny white-walled room they worked in, with its cool blue trim and diaphanous curtains billowing in the breeze of a ceiling fan. There was something strangely peaceful about the place.

> A Stone said to another:
> I am not happy in this naked fence
> My place is in the palace of the sultan.
> The other said:
> You are sentenced to death
> Whether you are here or in the sultan's palace
> Tomorrow this palace will be destroyed
> As will this fence
> By an order from the sultan's men
> To repeat their game from the beginning
> And to exchange their masks.

> — "The Conversation of the Stone," by Iraqi poet Abdul Wahab Al-Bayaty, translated from the Arabic by Bassam Frangieh

Chapter 18: The Arts and the Orchestra

FOR THOSE IN SEARCH of visual metaphor in the "new" Iraq, there was truly a wealth of possibilities, ranging from the surreal to the purely literal: Baghdad streets lined with death shrouds announcing the names of the recently deceased mere yards from advertisements for the latest satellite dishes; the music and ballet school enclosed by barbed wire and bordered by an endless line of Iraqi soldiers waiting for their pay from American Marines; even barefoot children leading looted racehorses through traffic jams. But in front of the new Ministry of Social Affairs — painted Day-Glo pink for optimism by a Baghdad engineer with a 1960s color sense — a real whopper of a metaphor was unfolding. Twenty-six-year-old painter Esam Pasha was showing me his latest work: a whimsical mural of Baghdad painted over a former portrait of Saddam Hussein. This was the first Saddam mural to be formally painted over (if you didn't count the happy face I had seen defacing a Saddam portrait in Mansour). Beyond the "new Iraq" symbolism, there was an added plus: Amidst the garbage-strewn, weed-ridden patch of grass in front of the mural, a mangy yellow dog lounged fitfully in the afternoon sun. A few yards away lay the half-eaten carcass of its former canine companion. It seemed safe to say that in the new Iraq, it was a dog-eat-dog world.

You'd never have known this, however, by observing the local art scene. While bombs ripped through buildings, rival factions assassinated each other's leaders, and increasingly brutal occupation and resistance forces duked it out, Iraqi artists were playing it safe. This was in contrast to the scene under sanctions, when poignant tableaux spoke of the suffering of a populace under siege, playwrights pushed the political envelope with veiled criticisms of the regime's corruption, and composers wrote angry orchestral anthems with damning titles like *To the U.N.* (which was, after all, an embargo-enforcer).

Nowhere in Pasha's mural, for example, was there any reference to the recent invasion, current occupation, or continuing struggle of Iraqi civilians. Instead, his work was a tame ode to the treasures of "old Baghdad." Buildings from the city's glorious past declared themselves in Disneyesque forms and *Fantasia*-like colors. At best, it was decorative. At worst, it was irrelevant.

But such judgments were perhaps unfair. It had only been six months since "regime change" and it takes a while for artists to react to new situations. And the tension and uncertainty of continuing violence — more unsettling than inspiring — was as good a reason as any for cultural expression to become an escapist retreat from the pressures of survival.

A history of violence and oppression also contributed to an often automatic kind of self-censorship. By odd coincidence, Esam Pasha is the grandson of Nuri al-Said, King Faisal II's prime minister, who was literally ripped apart by a mob during the 1958 military coup that overthrew the monarchy. In his modest studio near Mansour, the handsome, bearded Esam confessed, "I don't really go in for politics much."

Esam's apolitical art comes out of a tradition of Iraqi abstract expressionism that has always avoided direct political commentary. Kurdish artists in the north, more influenced by a kind of graphic surrealism, have been an exception to this rule, as was the propagandistic war art that came out of Iraq's eight-year conflict with Iran.

But the relative timidity of post-invasion art may also have to do with harsh market realities. American military personnel had replaced U.N. employees and foreign diplomats as the biggest buyers of Iraqi art. And with hard-currency prices for paints and canvas still beyond the reach of many artists, the customer was always right. Luckily for Esam, he had been painting a series of eagle tableaux since before the invasion. "The soldiers love my work," he said, adding that he met many of his clients through his job as a translator for American forces.

Esam showed me a series of drawings he claimed he wouldn't have been allowed to exhibit under the old regime. One — seemingly innocuous — was of a chair with an arrow going through it. "This," he told me, "could have suggested a coup attempt against the government. The chair could have represented a throne, a seat of power." So why, I

Esam Pasha in front of his mural of old Baghdad, September 2003

asked, in the new era of "freedom," is no one painting, say, red, white, and blue thrones with arrows going through them?

He shrugged. "It's not a subject that really interests me," he said.

It seemed that resistance to the occupiers was only being expressed through violence, not art. How very un-Canadian, I thought. If American tanks rolled across our borders tomorrow there might not be as many home-made bombs, but I was sure there'd be plenty of ironic anti-American art. My thoughts were interrupted by the arrival of Steve, an American artist Esam had met while translating. Steve explained that he was an "embedded artist" who had been employed by the U.S. military to paint portraits of various Iraqi civilians and to sketch a battalion of Marines as they went about their daily duties. He looked like a slightly disturbed Marlboro man, but actually chain-smoked Lucky Strikes.

The three of us went to visit an old building recently acquired by the newly formed Union of Iraqi Artists. Esam thought it might make a good location for the Garden of Peace project. Located across the street from the large stretch of urban parkland that housed the Baghdad Zoo, the property was a bit run down but boasted an actual garden enclosed by a concrete wall. "We could do many things here," Esam said enthusiastically, pointing out a rusted swing set, an area where children could draw and paint and another where their mothers could plant the garden. But with American troops so close by, I was concerned that we'd need to cover the whole area in a bulletproof dome.

Still, our spirits were high as we climbed into the aging American sedan of my new driver, Osama. He was a wide-eyed boy who dressed like an Iraqi "Ali G," with a kind of wishful gangsta chic; his father had been a missile scientist under Saddam and his mother ran an association for developmentally delayed children. He was a Shia and he eyed the bearded Esam with slight suspicion; later he told me, "He is a Wahhabist, for sure," referring to the hard-line Sunni sect of Islam. In fact, Esam was nothing if not a free spirit, though there had been some bearded religious types hanging out at his studio; as with so many things in Iraq, it was hard to know exactly what was going on. Esam himself regaled us with a story of his ill-fated job as a translator for a journalist in Najaf. He and his employer had fled right after the bomb that killed Ayatollah Hakim and dozens of his followers. He was chased, he recounted, by an angry mob of Shias who called him a "Wahhabist," the very sect that many blamed for the attack.

After we had dropped off Esam and Steve, Osama confided to me, "You know, there was not so much a problem before between Shia and Sunni, but now … We all think it was the Wahhabists and the Americans behind the killing of Hakim, but things will stay cool … unless they come after Sadr." He meant Moqtada al Sadr, a leading Shia cleric with an impressive militia. "Then it will be civil war."

LATER THAT DAY, at the Akkad gallery in Abu Nawas, a Baghdad neighborhood on the Tigris, Haidar Wady, a 25-year-old sculptor, showed me his work. Elegant figures in bronze struck in dance-like postures. Many were winged angels with big feet. "That is to show the distance between our dreams and hopes and our reality," Wady reflected. One couple of angelic bigfoots seemed to swing in mid-air. "That one I did after the regime change," he explained. "It's about how we have this new freedom, but there's a danger there, too."

The gallery was about a hundred yards away from the Palestine Hotel, which, like the al-Rashid, had become an American fortress ringed by tanks and barbed wire. Immediately outside, a group of street children high on glue started a brawl. The gallery owner tut-tutted.

"These are Saddam's children," he said. I noticed that many of the ills once strenuously blamed on the embargo were now blamed on Saddam.

But then, social realism had never been popular in Iraq. As I looked around the gallery at the aesthetically pleasing if nondescript abstract paintings — stylized calligraphy here, Mesopotamian modernism there — the gallery owner complained about his lack of business. "Since the war, it's been really bad. Because of the crime and the curfew we don't have many visitors anymore. And the U.S. soldiers, they are only interested in the kind of bad, orientalist art we don't sell here." He was referring to the tableaux of harem girls smoking hookahs and desert sheikhs on black stallions sold out of makeshift galleries around the city.

Wady took me to the al-Hewar art gallery in Wazeriya, a prosperous residential neighborhood. Here he introduced me to Qasim al-Sabti, the wily bohemian owner who lived, worked, and exhibited in an old nineteenth-century villa and garden. Al-Sabti was a shrewd businessman as well as an artist, and boasted that both Paul Bremer and Saddam Hussein had been visitors to his gallery. "They were both here," he recounted, "they came and ate *mazgouf* with me in the garden." Once a popular spot for European diplomats and U.N. workers, the gallery still attracted dozens of young artists for afternoon tea in the ad hoc garden café. But there were fewer and fewer buyers these days; the Turkish embassy, which was right across the street, was bombed not long after my visit.

The artwork here was still very much in a decorative vein. A would-be Iraqi Chagall exhibited her painting of a lively gypsy dance. Al-Sabti's own work featured fantastical creatures dredged up from Sumerian mythology. The only works that offered even a hint of darkness were an abstract oil painting with suggestions of flames and smoke, and a sculpture of spy-like figures having a clandestine meeting. When pressed, he offered a cryptic interpretation. "We artists now are like a man holding a dove between two fires — one beside us and one in the distance. We cannot fight either fire, so we'd rather play with the dove."

People came to his gallery, said al-Sabti, to escape the violent reality of daily life and to celebrate the survival of Iraqi culture rather than to be reminded of the struggle to survive. I wondered if this might be the right spot for my "garden of peace" project — there were even doves and nightingales in the courtyard. I discussed the idea of holding a concert to launch the project at the gallery with al-Sabti, perhaps with some members of the orchestra. He was interested and invited me for a *mazgouf* lunch the following day. Exploding cars and deadly statistics did not seem to interrupt al-Sabti's genteel routine in the least.

I DECIDED THAT IT WAS TIME to check things out at the al-Rabat theater in al-Adhimiya, home to the Iraqi National Orchestra. I had a feeling I might find the orchestra there that evening, and luckily I did. But rather spookily, I also met up with Karim, who once again seemed to arrive at the exact same moment as me. With his shaved head and loaded gun holster he looked even more like a cop now, and when the security guards questioned him at the entrance, he shouted at them in

Arabic, "You don't know who I am? I'm in the Iraqi army!" But once inside, he quickly reverted to his old *artiste* ways, kissing old colleagues on both cheeks as if he were in a Parisian salon.

As we entered the theater, the orchestra was playing Bizet's *L'Arlésienne* and the mood was mildly triumphant. So what if the players had been receiving death threats and had to risk their lives to come to rehearsal? The orchestra's ranks were swelling — there were even two new recruits from the U.S. forces, a black female trumpet player and a skinny blond man on the timpani — and by the sounds of it, the players had bought new reeds and strings fairly recently. Ministry of Culture salaries, I would learn, had gone from $5 to $120 a month. But classical-music scores, recordings, and instrument parts were still expensive and hard to come by.

As the orchestra struck up another rousing run-through of Bizet, I remembered the first night I had attended rehearsal here, in 2000. The entranceway was home to a family of wild dogs, garbage and sewage leaked through the sidewalk, and the theater doors had lost their hinges. But the sound of violins had drawn me in. Many of the musicians were in dire economic straits, but the orchestra played on, continued plucking and bowing as they had throughout a decade of sanctions and bombings. For them, music was a lifeline.

Founded in the 1920s, the Iraqi National Orchestra is one of the oldest Western classical orchestras in the Arab world. Despite the frayed violin strings and cracked oboe reeds, it was still giving regular concerts at that time. Although their music was in a Western tradition, it was filled with an undeniably Iraqi passion and sense of urgency, especially when the musicians played their own compositions. One score — the aforementioned *To the U.N.* — was dramatic and angry, full of clashing cymbals and pounding drums. Another, the beautiful symphonic poem *Heartbeat of Baghdad*, celebrated the joys and sorrows of this ancient city. The composer of the latter piece was 26-year-old Iraqi Lance Conway, whose improbable name came from his Anglo-Irish grandfather, a soldier during the British occupation.

"My inspiration was Iraq through history," explained Lance. "I started with ideas about when Baghdad was first established, through to the time of Caliph Mansour, then when it was over-run by Mongols. And the last section is about the Gulf War. I'm expressing all my feelings about the city through my music." He lamented the fact that the war and embargo had prevented him from studying abroad, as many Iraqi music students had done prior to 1991, and that it had also severely limited the audience for his music, which he described as a "mixture of East and West."

"One day," he said, "I hope that there will be no borders or barriers, and my music can be heard internationally." But, he added, staying in Iraq had also been inspirational. "Sometimes I wonder if I would be as creative if I were abroad. Here I can feel more my own 'Iraqi-ness.' Sometimes I feel it's like a spring bubbling up from within."

The orchestra's conductor, Amin Ezzat, was enthusiastic about his job, despite the difficulties of being a musician and the sanctions-related tragedy he had experienced. In 1997 his wife had been killed when their gas stove — in poor repair because of the shortage of spare parts — exploded. Still, he continued to conduct and compose with great energy. "The hardest thing is lack of availability of instruments. And we also suffer from a shortage of players, because they have to work to support their families. They do different kinds of private-sector work: selling furniture, driving taxis. Before the embargo, they were all full-time classical musicians." But in some ways the artistic isolation had been a greater hardship. "Before the embargo," Ezzat said, "there were many more exchanges with foreign players and conductors."

Happily, American anti-sanctions advocates had brought in some scores of Gershwin classics the year before, including *Rhapsody in Blue*, which the orchestra had loved and performed the following season. They met the threat of renewed American military action with a resigned fatalism. "What can we do?" shrugged Ezzat. "We will just keep on playing," as they had most days, except for the worst moments of the Gulf War and Desert Fox bombings.

"When I'm conducting," Ezzat told me, his eyes shining with genuine delight, "I feel as if the whole world is in my hands and I can shape it in any way I like. I can express all my feelings through conducting, as well as the tragedy and the joy of my people. If I stopped doing this I wouldn't survive."

BUT NOW, ANOTHER KIND of survival issue was at play. Security concerns meant that rehearsals had to be held before dusk under the protection of Ministry-appointed armed guards. Despite these new dangers, the orchestra's "chairman" and alternate conductor, Abdel Razak al-Azawi, a plump, mustachioed man in his sixties, appeared quite happy. With the increased salaries more musicians showed up to work, and the orchestra was scheduled to take part in a State-Department-sponsored tour of the U.S. in December.

"We are also able to play some old songs that were banned before," he explained, such as nationalist anthems from the pre-Baathist, royalist age.

Amin Ezzat was not at the rehearsal, but Lance Conway was. He seemed less optimistic than his colleague. "I'm ambivalent about the American presence here," he said. "It's nice that they've taken an interest in us," but he felt "uncomfortable as an artist" accepting help from occupiers. Conway, who had once won the "Mother of all Battles" competition for his original compositions, said he was strangely uninspired by recent events. "I haven't composed anything lately. I just feel like staying in my room and thinking … and waiting," he explained.

Soon dusk would fall and so it was time to leave the theater. As the last few musicians packed up in the dwindling light, the sound of nearby gunfire began.

THE NEXT DAY, I RAN INTO Esam and Steve eating watermelon on the patio at al-Sabti's garden café. They were sitting with the sculptor Haidar Wady, who was wearing a baseball cap to hide his long, dark hair. "Why don't you let you hair down?" I joked.

"I can't," he replied. "At least not outside, on the street. People will think I'm either a homosexual or a foreigner." In post-invasion Baghdad, it was hard to tell which was worse. But here in the garden of the al-Hewar, it was safe for now. Soon I coaxed Haidar into taking off his cap, and as he swung his curly locks around we all laughed and clapped.

Esam walked me to the car afterwards and said, "Can I pass by the hotel later? I have something to tell you."

"*Ahlan wa sahclan,*" I replied in the traditional Arabic welcome.

Back at the hotel, I hung out poolside with a Turkish coffee, taking in the scene. At a nearby table, a motley crew including an Armenian-British mercenary ("working in security" was how he described it), an actual "tourist" from London, two American girls, and a German philosophy student were whooping it up. Over bottles of imported beer — one happy result of the invasion — the British "tourist" recounted how he and a pal had gone water-skiing on the Tigris that day. "We were down at Abu Nawas having lunch," he said, referring to the riverside area near the Palestine Hotel, "and there was an old man with a boat moored near by. Turned out he had some rickety old skis and some rope, so we decided to go for it!" Hard to believe the local snipers could resist the sight of two blond men water-skiing.

Soon Esam arrived and I invited him for a drink at a separate table. "I have to tell you something," he told me, his beautiful brown eyes suddenly serious. "In Iraq there are many people who will tell you stories, but ..." He looked around for inquisitive bystanders, "it's about Haidar."

"Yes, go on," I said.

"Well, you know, Haidar is a good artist and he was my best friend ... before. But then ..." Esam paused and looked around again. "I found out that he had been spying on me."

"What do you mean?" I asked, slightly taken aback.

"I mean in every community there were people reporting to the *mukhabarat*." Haidar, claimed Esam, was the "art world" spy. "Why do you think he was able to travel abroad, exhibit in Syria, meet with foreigners?" Esam asked. "He was working for security — this is why." The fact that Haidar was an accomplished sculptor had no bearing in Esam's argument. When I asked him later, Haidar would, of course, deny any connection to the old *mukhabarat*, but there were so many similar stories in Baghdad, so many layers of suspicion, that any or all of them seemed plausible. What was certain was that years of war, poverty and a police-state culture had conspired to turn friendships into betrayals, hopes into profound disillusionment. And now post-invasion realities were continuing to force neighbor to turn on neighbor, friend to inform on friend.

A YEAR LATER, I'D LOST TOUCH with Haidar but kept in e-mail contact with Esam. After a brief trip to Amman, which he found "too boring," he returned to his Baghdad apartment. I called him one day on his new mobile phone and he answered from the darkness of his studio. "We have no electricity," he said, "but I'm so glad to hear from you." He was still in touch with his American friends, he maintained, and when I asked him what he thought of the continuing U.S. presence in Iraq, he replied, "Well, even if they left, we'd still have the same problems. All I care about now is getting more electricity and seeing the security situation improve."

Esam was still painting, and even amidst chaos and violence, he said, soap operas were being filmed in Baghdad for new satellite channels from the Gulf. "The actors are getting paid in U.S. dollars," he recounted excitedly. But he saved the best for last.

"You know the other day I was out at Bab el-Sharj," he said, speaking of the downtown market that had now become a dangerous looters' den and drug-dealing center, "and I found a Miro etching." The work, called *Le Bagnard et sa Compagne*, had been looted from the Saddam Arts Center, and Esam had gone on a one-man mission to recover it, circulating descriptions among the hawkers until someone tipped him off. He'd bought it for $90 U.S. and intended to return it to a state-run arts center, whenever there might be one to return it to. He had also recovered several works by renowned Iraqi painter Dia Azzawi, and was now on the trail of two Picasso sketches.

Before signing off he said, "I'm going to attend an exhibit opening tomorrow. I wish you could be there."

A replica ziggurat in downtown Nasiriyah featuring a portrait of Saddam Hussein, spring 2000

Chapter 19: On the Road to Babylon

"WOULD YOU LIKE to go the museum?"

One evening my driver, Osama, asked me this as he dropped me off at the hotel. He was referring to the Iraqi National Museum, which had been savagely looted after the invasion, its contents gutted — and with them much of Iraq's ancient heritage.

"Is it open again?"

"I think so," said Osama. "At least, that's what the other drivers say."

"Okay, let's go tomorrow."

So the next morning, off we went for a drive through Karradah and down towards the city center. As we waited in the permanent traffic snarl, rusted-out cars with bits missing that might themselves have made interesting exhibits chugging along beside us, my thoughts turned to the museum. I remembered it from other trips to Baghdad, though I'd not spent much time there. It was never a big priority for stories, and I'd always sort of assumed it would be there the next time I was in town. Now it was gone, or at the very least, badly wrecked. But ever since Paul Bremer had re-opened the museum for one day in July — as a show of "goodwill" — rumors had surfaced that it was soon to re-open to the public.

I wondered which artifacts had been returned, snatched from the jaws of international-art-world thieves, and which ones were even now, as we drove in the scorching Baghdad sun, taking up space in a collector's salon in Geneva.

Sadly, I would not find out. The museum, we discovered, was still closed. As we drove past its battered but still defiant-looking entrance, I imagined what must have been a surreal and disturbing sight that fateful day in April 2003. Hundreds of opportunistic looters grasping at ancient treasures; other, more organized gangs — with inside help — going for the best stuff first. I tried to imagine a Canadian equivalent, but there wasn't one. The National Gallery didn't really compare — a gang running amok in Maple Leaf Gardens was closer, though I guess that had happened often enough. Perhaps a mob burning down Parliament Hill after stripping it of its precious metals?

But to have relics of ancient Sumeria and Babylon so savagely ripped off, as U.S. Marines stood idly by, was an insult not only to Iraqi but to world heritage. Unfortunately, this had been going on for quite a while. Even in 1997, when I first arrived in Iraq, the signs were there. I joined a busload of German pharmaceutical representatives, in town for a trade fair, on a trip to the site of Babylon, a couple miles south of Baghdad. Our guide soon made it clear that a few items from the ancient city were for sale.

As we walked around the ruins — reconstructed by Saddam with new "faux Babylonian" bricks inscribed with his name — the surrounding countryside felt like it might close in at any moment, greening over what was left of the original ancient city. After our tour, the guide — a middle-aged man with a Ph.D. in archaeology dressed in a threadbare suit — encouraged us to walk around a decrepit-looking souvenir shop that sold plastic molds of the famous Babylonian lion that had suckled Daniel and T-shirts emblazoned with Day-Glo images of King Nebuchadnezzar's chariots. Just outside the shop, he looked at me sharply and said, "Please miss. Something for my family. I am an educated man, you know ... but ..." — he made a sweeping gesture taking in the whole scene, the Germans boarding their bus and laughing about the "blue" movies they'd watched all the way in from the border, the reconstructed monuments emblazoned with dragons, the billboard of Saddam recast as Nebuchadnezzar — "this situation ..."

I gave him 2,000 dinars — then worth just over a dollar.

(Six years later, U.S. forces would build a military base here that seriously damaged part of the ancient site.)

WHILE TOURISM WAS ONCE a huge industry in the country, in the nineties, being a tourist in Iraq was kind of like being an assassin at Disneyworld; besides that nagging feeling of dread, there was always an acute sense of displacement, as if you'd accidentally stepped into the wrong movie. During my 2000 trip, nowhere in Iraq was that feeling more pronounced than in Ur, the birthplace of Abraham, the home of the Sumerian ziggurat and an Iraqi air base that made it a frequent target of American bombing. Much of the city's ancient ruins had been reconstructed with modern brick, so nothing was quite as it appeared to be, and the lone guide spewed forth hundreds of English words concerning ancient Sumerian culture in a dizzying monologue that he had clearly memorized phonetically. The main drag in the adjoining town of Nasiriyah, a hotbed of Shia unrest, featured a mini-ziggurat with a giant portrait of Saddam Hussein at the top.

During this visit to Iraq, English-speaking minders were in short supply, so unfortunately, my rudimentary Spanish landed me with a Spanish-speaking minder whose *español* was as rusty as mine. Kais, an affable bear of a man in his late forties whose face appeared decades older, was also one of the strictest minders on offer. He required written permission in triplicate before he would allow me to take a photograph, and his mere presence turned even the most verbose "man-on the-street" interview into nationalist platitudes or complete silence.

The ancient city of Ur is in the south of Iraq. It was one of the most important cities of Mesopotamia. The journey there is not uninteresting, as one must pass through the cities of Madain and Kut en route. There are undoubtedly fascinating stories to all these places. Unfortunately Kais knew none of them; or perhaps did but wouldn't disclose them. And every time I worked up enough psychic energy to ask a question in Spanish such as *cual es la poblacion de este pueblo?* he would look at me sideways and frown as if I'd asked about a state secret.

In all fairness, I couldn't blame him too much; after all we were entering the "no-fly zone," where daily British and American air sorties meant almost weekly civilian casualties. In addition, the grinding poverty was even worse outside city limits, and desperate highway robbers were not uncommon. It was little wonder Kais had been more worried than usual, and had little time for my questions. Eventually I just gave up and went to sleep in the back seat. It was all rural landscape, with the occasional gas station. Our driver, Ghassan, stopped at one rather suddenly, and I woke up.

We were not too far from Nasiriyah now. I walked to a nearby ditch and urinated with the utmost discretion. I looked up into the huge blue sky above me. There were no clouds and if a fighter plane had sped by at that moment, I felt sure I'd have been able to make eye contact with the pilot. Fortunately none did.

Three quarters of an hour later, we entered the town of Nasiriyah. It was almost one o'clock, and the dusty streets were empty of people. The architecture looked kind of post-revolutionary modernist. Ghassan drove to a sort of military headquarters — "*policia provincial,*" Kais explained — and a man who appeared to be in his mid fifties joined us in the car. He introduced himself as Mr. Karim.

Remembering the ditch, I asked where the nearest facilities might be. Mr. Karim directed Ghassan to a nearby hotel. "Many tourists come here," said Mr. Karim, smiling.

I walked inside the deserted hotel and met with a rather unfortunate bathroom. A kindly man dressed in an ancient dinner jacket and bow tie noticed my distress and brought in a plunger and a bucket of water. As he tried to fix the toilet, we chatted in broken English (by now, mine was broken too).

"You, Canada?" he asked in a friendly manner.

"Yes," I replied. "Me, Canada."

"Me, Iraq," he said. And then, putting down the plunger, he began to say, "Canada, Iraq ..." He put his fists together and moved them back and forth, "Same-same."

"Yes," I said, "kind of same-same, in some ways." I tried to think of some but couldn't muster any. We certainly hadn't been bombed by the Americans, not in quite a while at least. I had heard about the desperate water situation in the south; the damage done to basic infrastructure during the Gulf War had left its legacy. Cholera and amoebic dysentery were still common here even ten years later.

After the bathroom mission had been accomplished, I joined Mr. Karim, Kais, and Ghassan in the lobby. I bought everyone a round of Pepsis and we stood in silence, drinking them from the glass bottles we had to return. In Canada I may have been a poor writer, but here I was the Pepsi Queen. It felt weird to be the Big Spender among these mustachioed men twice my age and weight.

We got back into the car and drove a couple miles out of town. The flat, arid landscape was broken up by the occasional hill. Soon I could see the ziggurat, the ruins of which had been completely reconstructed. We drove right up to it, and feeling like a miscast extra in a Baathist B movie, I walked purposefully up the steep front steps. A guide appeared mysteriously out of the ether. His face was tanned and lined and his head was wrapped in a red kaffiyeh. He began to deliver a long spiel in the carefully memorized English script he had learned from his father and his grandfather — the original "guide" who had led English archaeologist Leonard Woolley to the ruins in the 1920s.

I learned that the ziggurat, a kind of stepped pyramid, had been built by Ur-Nammu, founder of the Third Dynasty of Ur (2124–2107 BC), and that its original height had been 56.6 feet. The favorite god of Ur was Sin or Nannar, the moon-god, and his ground temple had been nearby. Mr. Karim pointed absent-mindedly to a spot on the road in front of the ziggurat. "Over there," he said casually, "that's where the Swedish journalist was hit when a bomb was dropped here last month." Everyone looked unfazed by this comment.

"There used to be a lot more tourists here before the war," the guide told me, and he began reminiscing about the good old days when he could easily count on three dozen visitors a day. "Foreigners and Iraqis too. People would drive down from Baghdad and have picnics, play music, camp out under the stars." I wondered what songs they had sung.

He led us over to a huge pit a few hundred yards away. It was a cemetery, he explained, from 2500 BC. There were about two thousand graves there that had yielded an array of beautiful objects, including the famous Lyre of Ur, which would be damaged during the looting of the Baghdad Museum. The museum in Nasiriyah, I was told, was not open. Closed for lunch, or forever? I didn't bother asking.

Next to the pit was another cemetery, this one for the kings and princes of the Third Dynasty of Ur. Not far from it was a reconstructed ruin of what was supposed to have been Abraham's house. Abraham was from Ur, but I wasn't sure how they knew this had been his house. Perhaps it didn't really matter: the birthplace of the patriarch of three world religions was under siege, the details seemed frivolous.

We walked along the ziggurat's walls and, suddenly overcome by vertigo, I held onto the guide's arm for support. He seemed uncomfortable, as did the others. Everyone just wanted to go home. Ruins, schmuins. After decades of war and sanctions, their own lives were ruins. Who cared about Sumerians or Old Testament prophets when at any minute a bomb could fall from the sky and destroy your home, or your child could die from the drinking water, or a close relative could get taken away in the middle of the night?

I gave the guide some money and said goodbye. I wondered if his son would still be doing this in twenty years or if the ziggurat would get blown up. I supposed that even if it did, they could just re-build again; ruins upon ruins ...

After a quick tour of Nasiriyah, we hit the road again. Ghassan was desperate to get back to Baghdad before darkness fell and the highway bandits came out, and Kais seemed exhausted. I felt like crying. By then, I'd completely abandoned asking questions, but as the light faded, Kais started asking me about my family. In the fading light, he wistfully recalled his romance with a German girl he had met while studying in Spain in the early eighties. "*Carlotta, mi amor,*" he sighed, looking out the window at the barren landscape.

I didn't know what to say, and since talking was problematic anyway, I began to sing, in Spanish. "Besame mucho." Kais loved it. I imagined him dancing to the love song with Carlotta in some Madrid nightspot. Now he was married and fat and had two kids and earned a living spying on insufferable journalists.

"Do you know 'Guantanamera'?" he asked when I was done. We began to sing, and Ghassan hummed along.

Yo soy un hombre sincero
De donde crece la palma
Y antes de morirme quiero echar mis versos del alma

After a while, I fell asleep and dreamed of ruined cities all the way back to Baghdad.

Chapter 20: Tea with the "King"

ALTHOUGH I WASN'T ABLE TO SEE the remaining treasures at the Iraqi museum, I was somewhat consoled by having been granted an interview with "the King" — Sharif Ali Bin al Hussein. The pretender to the Hashemite throne that had been violently overthrown in 1958, this handsome descendant of King Faisal lived in a rented villa that evoked the romantic memories of the monarchist era, when stability and nobility reigned, at least officially. Although the reality had been a little different, a surprising number of Iraqis were nostalgic for the 1950s and the "King" was slowly garnering support among a diverse set of fans. He'd even begun a charitable foundation for poor Iraqis and had recently publicly criticized American policy in Iraq.

I had come to the King's headquarters several times before I managed to arrange a formal interview, and I always enjoyed the peaceful oasis of his garden with its statues and duck pond, remnants of a different era. This time I was ushered into the office of Sharif Ali's press secretary, an Iraqi man with a London accent, and offered tea. After a few minutes, I was taken into the makeshift "throne room," where a rather majestic-looking chair sat below a portrait of King Faisal II, Sharif Ali's cousin and Iraq's last king. After a brief security check, the King's arrival was announced and he walked in with a minder in tow. Looking very Savile Row and not unlike the investment banker that he was in "civilian" life in London, the dapper Ali proved quite charming and put me at ease as I fumbled with my video equipment. In the end his minder even acted as the sound man, holding the mike a few delicate inches from His Highness's elegantly trimmed moustache.

After the requisite tea and a brief chat about Canada, we began our formal interview. As the Baghdad sun streamed in through a window behind us, the King's calm composure and the coolness of the marble floor made me feel like I was speaking to someone from another time and place.

"Your Highness," I began, not quite knowing how to phrase the indelicate question, "Is Iraq headed for a civil war?"

"Well," he began, "I think there are divisions here, but Iraq is segmented not so much in terms of ethnic or religious lines, but in terms of social behavior. Some large parts of society have more in common with Mediterranean cultures like Egypt, Lebanon, and North Africa, while others parts are closer culturally to central Arabia. It is this underlying clash of cultures that creates a certain amount of social tension, as people come to terms with the twenty-first century."

"Why are people so nostalgic for the monarchy?" I asked.

"It's not so much nostalgia," he replied. "It's more of a comparison between the era of monarchies and the era of republics. The question ... is, which regime is best suited to preserve the unity of Iraq, to bringing justice, to prevent the rise of dictatorships, to treat all citizens equally, to create national institutions that are independent and not subject to the influence and domination of political parties. Who is going to prevent the rise of the secret police and stop them using the army against the people? It was the era of the monarchy in the past that insured that, and the republics were the ones that brought in civil war, external wars and dictatorships. So it's really a very pragmatic, practical outlook on which system is best suited for Iraq. And the majority of Iraqis ... support a return of the monarchy to Iraq."

I decided on a more philosophical question. "Your Highness," I started, "there's so much chaos and violence and uncertainty in Iraq right now, is there a place for nobility?"

"Yes," replied Sharif Ali, "I completely believe that there is. In fact, not only in Iraq, but generally in human nature; under oppression and tyranny, that is when nobility really arises. I mean nobility of the spirit, not nobility of the aristocracy ... which the Iraqi people have in great amounts. Let us not forget that the Iraqi people and civilization have been around for five thousand years and hopefully will continue to be around, based on the spirit and determination of our culture, our civilization, and our people. The traditional Iraqi values — of hospitality, chivalry, hard work, neighborliness — these were qualities deliberately undermined by Saddam's regime ... Now we have to rebalance the society, so the pressures of survival are reduced and we can foster that opportunity for Iraqis once again to create the society that we had before, which was one of solidarity and a sense of community." Ironically, I thought, these were the very values being fostered by the rising resistance movement.

I then asked His Highness how he envisaged his role in the new Iraq. Though he might have been the sentimental choice, the King had no real power. Even among monarchists, he was not necessarily the accepted heir to the throne, as he was related to King Faisal through his mother's side, a problem in a patriarchal society.

He replied that practically speaking, his party aimed to preserve Iraq's national institutions and to ensure that political parties were able to engage in democratic activity without fear of oppression or violence. He hoped to create a constitutional monarchy that could provide an independent foundation for political activity and prevent parties from exploiting the resources of government. His words were noble, but seemed worlds away from the reality of street gangs and Badr Brigades, not to mention trigger-happy troops and their associated paramilitaries. Might was right in Baghdad, and Sharif Ali's words had an almost old-world ring to them.

"People are talking about reconstruction in terms of physical infrastructure," I asked him, "but how long will 'spiritual reconstruction' take, in terms of the return of the Iraqi spirit?"

"The Iraqi people are tired," replied Sharif Ali. "They have no energy reserves left, after three terrible wars, civil wars, terrible oppression ... and so their spirits are low. We need to help Iraqis — all of us, together with the international community — to stand on their feet."

Asked how the American presence was influencing this process, the King replied that the U.S. policies were bad and had destroyed the initial optimism after the fall of the regime. Now people are much more pessimistic, he said, because "the Americans have completely failed to deliver on their promises, in terms of law and order, in terms of economy, standards of living, in terms of rebuilding a liberal, just, free society ... What they have delivered is a certain freedom of speech and a lack of persecution — but not much else. So Iraqis are fearful about their future.

And it's because of American policies."

"What was their greatest mistake?" I asked.

"Not including the Iraqis in the whole process, not trusting them, marginalizing them ... The Iraqi people feel they are being ignored; therefore they are not partners with the Americans in building a new Iraq. They now see Americans as occupiers, cut off from Iraqi society, immune to the pleas of the Iraqi people, uninterested in the opinion of the people — isolated in an ivory tower, a bubble."

"How can this be remedied? Through an increased U.N. presence in Iraq?"

"The core issue is that the coalition has achieved its war aims, the regime is gone, the weapons of mass destruction are no longer an issue, there's no connection to September 11, therefore there really should be a rapid return of sovereignty and independence to the free Iraqi people — under the supervision of the U.N. This can be done in a few months, and this will save American taxpayers tens of billions of dollars. It will get American troops out of Iraq, and will free Iraq's people. The American presence now is becoming the problem — their presence has created a self-fulfilling fear. We should focus on the fact that the Iraqi people are not a colony or a breakaway province. We are a sovereign, independent country of free people and we need to take our country back now." But how safe would the King and his entourage be, I wondered, without the presence of the Americans?

I knew that the King was concerned about women's issues, so I asked him about the role of women in Iraq. "Iraqi women are important members of society," he responded, "and have many different roles: professionally, in the labor force, in all aspects of life. That role needs to be recognized. It's not taken into account now. Their salaries are lower than men's, yet they are still playing an important function. We aren't at that level yet where Iraqi women are secluded or left at home, but they aren't accorded equal rights, economically or socially. That will come only if the political role of women is enhanced and if they can take on important political positions."

We then talked about his plans to restore the royal tombs in Khadamiya. The tomb of Faisal I, the founder of modern Iraq, was the first place he had visited on his return to Iraq in June 2003, the King explained, because "it's important to remind people of what our forefathers managed to do — how they gained our sovereignty and independence, and how now it's our turn to do the same."

"Didn't Saddam play the royalist card at one point?" I asked.

"There is a great deal of support for the monarchy and even under Saddam, the royals were always popular. Saddam tried to exploit that affection by his renovation of the royal tombs [in the 1980s]. And at one point, there was even talk of him trying to appoint himself 'King.'"

"But your vision is for a party above politics?"

"Yes, and above ethnic and religious affiliations too. The royal family should be a unifying factor, not associated with any geographic, ethnic, or religious community, and should be the neutral arbiter, a symbol of Iraq's tolerance and sense of community. Essentially, we'd leave politics to the politicians."

What the Iraqi people needed most, the King believed, was peace and security. That would be the basis for developing all aspects of society. By security, he said, he meant peace of mind, economic security, protection from being abused by those who are more powerful: "This is what Iraqis need now; they need to know that they're safe, that their future is not worse than their past — and when we get that, then we can build our country with confidence."

We discussed the damage being done by Bremer's neo-liberal agenda. His Highness complained that the IGC was more interested in allowing foreigners to buy up bits of Iraq than in restoring electricity, clean water, a functioning health-care system, and law and order. "The risk to Iraqi sovereignty," he said, "is that our priorities as a people are being undermined by commercial objectives."

In the short term, Sharif Ali said that he was pessimistic. He thought that crime and basic infrastructure would get much worse. But after that he was optimistic: "I'm completely confident in the abilities of the Iraqi people to improve things. We've been around for thousands of years — God willing, we'll be around for thousands of years more. I'm sure that we will surmount all these obstacles and create an Iraq that's free, democratic, and a credit to the region."

Iraqis always seemed to be longing for a golden age, whether it was that of Babylon, Haroun al-Rashid, or King Faisal. Perhaps in a place imbued with such history, imagining a future required more effort than falling back on one's illustrious past. Perhaps the real struggle in Iraq — its spiritual jihad — was to free itself from the sheer weight of inertia.

"Would you care for more tea?" Sharif Ali's soothing tones interrupted my imaginings.

"Thank you," I replied, thinking what a decent chap this wannabe monarch was. The man who would be King might never be, but his lack of real power seemed to account for his good nature. Instead of the arrogant posturing I had come to expect from Iraqi politicos, I found he had a genuine sense of humor and a rather dandified aesthetic sensibility. As we sipped chai in the "throne room" after the formal part of our interview was over, he smiled at me and asked, "Wherever did you find such fabulous earrings?"

The King soon confessed that he was rather bored and lonely in his rented "palace," virtually trapped there most nights because of security concerns, a pampered prisoner among his flock of followers and ever-increasing retinue, all hoping for some kind of messianic salvation, or at the very least, a dip in his swimming pool. Sharif Ali's world seemed to exist only in Baghdad. When I inquired about his contact details in London, I was given only a telephone number in Kensington that connected to a mumbled message and an e-mail address to which no one ever replied. He was almost a dreamland monarch, whose kingdom was not of the outside world.

"Would you like to stay and meet some people from my charitable foundation?" offered Sharif Ali. There would be some orphans coming to visit, he explained; they were being sponsored by a local NGO that was hoping for "royal" patronage. I agreed and within minutes, a flood of children and half a dozen adult caretakers burst into the "throne room." I retreated to the sidelines as Sharif Ali greeted each child personally and gave him or her a coloring book and crayons. Girls of six, their bodies wrapped in traditional hijab, giggled shyly as I filmed them. One asked me, "Are you the Queen?"

*Sharif Ali Bin al Hussein in the "throne room" of his Baghdad villa,
below a portrait of Iraq's last king, Faisal II, September 2003*

As the King posed with the children for a photo in front of a portrait of King Faisal, I noticed one little boy wearing an orange sweatshirt with the word "Gap" on the front. Another boy, perhaps seven, perhaps eleven — so many had been stunted by malnutrition, it was hard to tell — never smiled. The kids, I would learn, were from a working-class Shia slum in the north of Baghdad. Some were orphans and others were part of a community of displaced people, living in an old abandoned swimming pool.

Soon they spilled out into the foyer of the villa, decorated by an aging chandelier and an Iraqi flag draped on the wall behind it, and full of hangers-on drinking chai and men in business suits or camouflage fatigues. The children spread out on the patio, holding makeshift signs that said WE ARE HOMELESS ORPHENS WE NEED HOME HELP US PLEASE. I guessed these were for the Western media types, though I was their only representative.

The whole scene lasted for maybe three minutes. As the children dispersed, I arranged with Ali — the young, bearded organizer of the NGO, called the Educational Society for Homeless Children — to visit his office and one of their projects. The children were being given basic literacy classes, as well as some instruction in music, and had prepared an operetta about their lives, I was told, that they were hoping to perform soon. This gave me an idea.

Chapter 21: In Hospital

"SHE WANTED TO BE A DOCTOR when she grew up," said Mohammed, the father of six-year-old leukemia victim Sarah, "but now she just wants to grow up."

I sighed as I heard the familiar refrain of yet another desperate parent, this time in a rundown cancer ward in Baghdad's main pediatric hospital. Six months after "liberation," the state of children's health was even worse than it had been under sanctions.

I remembered visiting what was then called the Saddam Hussein Pediatric Hospital in 2000. In addition to being the foremost public pediatric facility in Iraq, it was also a teaching hospital, so I'd been given a tour and a briefing by two young interns. You could tell by their manner and dress that the two interns were from well-to-do families, while most of the patients were poor. There was compassion in the interns' eyes, but you had the sense that as soon as they finished their internship, they would move to a private clinic or — if they were lucky enough to have a relative outside — perhaps even to America. Their state salaries were almost worthless now, and by all accounts the public hospitals were devoid of even basic medicines. These really did seem to be places where, as an Iraqi friend once told me, the poor came to die.

We were taken on a tour of a ward where several babies and young children lay ill, their mothers and fathers hovering over them, many in great distress. I felt like a voyeur rather than a journalist. How could I talk to these people? What questions could I possibly ask them?

I approached one lady whose baby was suffering from an acute upper-respiratory infection as well as severe malnutrition. As she cradled her tiny infant in her arms, I introduced myself and asked her where she was from. "Saddam City," she replied. She told me that her name was Hadidjah and she had eight other children at home, where her husband, who hadn't worked since he had a heart attack in 1997, was waiting. Hadidjah wore a pinkish headscarf that only seemed to highlight her sallow complexion and the dark circles under her sunken eyes. The intern told me that some women who came into this ward were so malnourished they couldn't produce breast milk to feed their babies.

Hadidjah's neighbor, Rashida, had come from the outskirts of Baghdad with her seven-year old daughter, who was suffering from a form of meningitis. Rashida told me she had five other children at home and her husband had died during the Gulf War. The hospital did not have the antibiotics needed for a secondary infection the girl had developed, so the prognosis was not good. What, I asked her, did your daughter like to do when she was well?

"She always dreamed," said Rashida, "of going to school. But she never had the chance. She had to work in the market with me."

In the far corner of the ward, a baby boy was dying. Surrounded by the mother and father and several relatives, the doctors attempted to resuscitate the infant, who had stopped breathing. A woman in the bed beside him was quietly weeping.

Suddenly the scene turned from tragedy to farce. I looked outside and saw an Iraqi security man staring at me with a walkie-talkie in his hand. Seconds later, the Chinese deputy foreign minister, in town for a meeting with Tariq Aziz, walked into the ward surrounded by his entourage and a camera crew from a Beijing TV station. There was a whirl of lights and flashes and official photographs and people talking in Chinese and Arabic. And then, within perhaps a minute and a half, they were gone.

A few minutes later, the baby was dead and his female relatives were weeping with long, wailing sobs. As the interns ushered us out of the ward, we saw the father, a young man with a moustache and a blue cotton shirt, standing outside, shouting angrily. "Who was responsible?" he cried. "Who let this happen?"

TWO YEARS EARLIER I had spent a day in a private Christian hospital in Karradah. It was December 1998, shortly after Desert Fox, and I had gone there minder-free on the pretext that I was ill. At 9:00 a.m. that morning,

Doctor Akram was already hard at work. Making out a prescription in crisp typewritten Arabic, he pounded away at his trusty old Olivetti like an Iraqi Don Quixote. But he was hardly fighting windmills.

"Amoebic dysentery," said the aging, white-haired doctor. "The third case this week. [It was only Tuesday.] And she is from a good family too," he said of his patient, an old woman from the neighborhood.

Karradah had once been a good part of Baghdad, but it had fallen on hard times. Once a stylish area for the middle classes, it was now home to street kids and beggars who lived in the abandoned houses of the failing bourgeoisie. Garbage and open sewers surrounded the palm-fronded villas, crumbling with neglect, rusting with memory. This was winter in Baghdad, seven years after the Gulf War, and the sanctions were hurting.

"First it was the Iran–Iraq war," explained Doctor Akram. "That's when it started ... The refugees from the south, they started to come ... Their lifestyle was ..." — he was searching for a polite way to express the contrast between urban sophistication and the rural simplicity of the migrants — "*different* than ours."

"But it wasn't really until the embargo that things got difficult." The doctor paused for reflection as a child wailed in the background. "I mean, in the eighties, a family of five could live well on a salary of thirty dinars a month. Eat at restaurants, go to the cinema, even take a holiday abroad. Now people don't have enough to eat." He shrugged his shoulders and offered a resigned "*haram.*"

As for the omnipresent threat of American bombing, Dr. Akram asked, "What can we do? There is nowhere to go." His own children lived abroad, but he preferred to stay where his work was. "People depend on me," he explained. "I can't just leave."

"The situation here reminds me of an American movie I once saw," the doctor continued. "It took place on the island of Manhattan. The whole place was turned into a giant prison that no one could escape from. It was controlled by different gangs who were always fighting with each other. I can't remember the name though."

He was talking about *Escape from New York*.

"That's what Iraq has become now," he said. "A jungle."

I asked him about the photograph on the wall, from which Dr. Akram as a young man smiled back at me. It was taken in the fifties, and in it he resembled Burt Lancaster.

The doctor was happy to change the subject and reminisce about his youth. "I had quite a reputation in those days," he confided. "I was always chatting up the English girls." That was before the 1958 revolution, when King Faisal still ruled and the British presence was tangible.

Just then a worried-looking young man burst into his office and inquired about some test results.

"Is he sick?" I inquired.

"No, it's his wife. She's eight months' pregnant."

A detached explanation followed. "She is severely anemic, from malnutrition. This is her first child." According to U.N. agencies, thirty percent of the adult population was suffering from malnutrition. This mother-to-be looked exhausted, the little lipstick she wore only serving to highlight her drawn mouth. She was 21.

Her husband introduced himself as Hassan and accepted a cigarette. His story was not uncommon. He had been a soldier during the last six years of the Iran–Iraq war. His brief career as a peddler in the market was interrupted by the Gulf War, and for the past five years he had been unable to find any steady work. He and his wife subsisted on the meager rations of the "food basket" allowed to Iraqis under the U.N. "oil-for-food" plan. The per-capita distribution worked out to about 25 cents a day, and included no fruits, vegetables, animal proteins, or vitamin or mineral supplements.

I asked Hassan if he had had to sell any of his possessions to survive. He laughed and pointed to his shirt: "Everything but this." He recited a list that read like a consumerist wish-list: "My car, fridge, TV, radio, furniture, even my dishes."

When the doctor heard the story he refunded Hassan half his fee: 1,000 dinars, less than a dollar, but still equivalent to a third of a worker's monthly salary. As the couple left the building he confided, "It's hard to tell, you know, which ones are really starving. They may be clean and well-dressed, and you'd never know that they were in dire straits. Too proud to say anything."

Later that day, Dr. Akram introduced me to a favorite patient. Seated demurely in his office underneath the photo of the doctor as a young man was a woman in her eighties. Her hair has been dyed black and her eyebrows painted on, but her skin revealed her age.

"This is my old friend and a great singing star of Baghdad," the doctor said graciously. "She comes to visit me and also for arthritis medicine," he whispered. "I give her a discount."

The old woman smiled, showing a few gold teeth.

"She used to sing in all the best cabarets in town," the doctor continued proudly, "and at night, on Iraqi TV." He meant that she used to perform nationalist songs, hymns to Iraq and its "great leader," on the nightly broadcasts.

But it was the cabarets she wanted to talk about. "Baghdad used to be so beautiful" she said longingly, "so glamorous. You should have seen the dresses I used to wear. Everything's changed now," she continued. "No one respects good music any more."

"Do you remember this one?" she asked the doctor, as she started to sing an old Umm Kulthum song. Her voice was scratchy but still strong, as the serpentine melody unfolded. "My darling," she sang, "my beauty, my life / remember those nights / with the smell of jasmine in the air ..."

For a moment, the present dissolved. There was no more embargo, no more military threats, no iconographic presidents, just pure, unadulterated memory. The old woman's eyes were young again as she sang, "Your face was like the moon shining at night."

Then we heard the knock of another patient at the door and her voice faltered.

"I can't remember the rest," she sighed, "but it was a beautiful song."

THAT SAME DAY I WAS introduced to Sister Marie, the hospital administrator, a determined-looking woman in a uniform that was half nurse and half nun. She greeted me in French and invited me into her office. In the twenty or so yards it took to get there, she was stopped several times by patients, anxious relatives, and nurses looking for medicine. Once inside, she shut the door and offered me some tea.

"This is a private Catholic hospital," explained the middle-aged nun in perfect French, "but we treat everyone. Rich, poor, Muslim, Christian. It doesn't matter. Those who pay a supplement, those who can't. We get some very well-dressed people coming in, professional people who can't even afford the price of a blood test [less than a dollar]. And sometimes, some uneducated *bazari* [merchants] will walk in with a bundle of dollars."

The sanctions had even created situations where nuns were obliged to barter on the black market. "That's where we get our drugs," admitted Marie. "It's really the only option."

As if on cue, the door to her office opened and a young man in jeans and a T-shirt walked in with a discreetly placed bundle of bills. He was Sister Marie's contact for black-market currency exchange. When buying penicillin, only dollars would do.

The door opened again and two doctors from a neighboring clinic walked in. It seemed they'd come for some hard-to-find heart medication they thought Sister Marie might have. When they found out where I was from, they politely grilled me for news from the outside.

"What do Americans know about our situation here, under the embargo?" asked one, a heart surgeon who had completed his studies in California. "Do they know how we're suffering?"

His colleague interjected, "Do you know we can't even get medical textbooks? Or find out anything from the latest medical journals? We're operating with decade-old knowledge. Why do they not allow these things under the embargo? What kind of threat could they pose?"

I pleaded observer status, and their tone softened.

The heart surgeon offered me a Marlboro and talked fondly about his student days in Los Angeles.

"Well," he said resignedly, "I guess the only way I could get back there is if I marry an American girl."

Everyone laughed, but the doctor protested. "I know, I'm already married, but my wife doesn't mind. You know, she encourages me. She says, 'Anything is better than sitting here in this mess. She thinks that once I got to California, I could send for her and the children and …" He paused in mid-sentence, lost in his imaginary escape to Orange County.

A plump, middle-aged woman walked in. She was wearing a pseudo-Chanel jacket and high heels. She looked a little pale. Beside her was a young boy who greeted Sister Marie with a kiss.

"This is my nephew and his teacher," Marie told me in French. "She is not well."

"What's wrong?" I asked, as the teacher left the office.

"She's here for an abortion," Sister Marie said, quite openly.

The idea of a nun directing abortions at a Catholic hospital in a predominantly Muslim nation was mildly mind-blowing. But Iraq was, after all, a nominally secular country where abortions were probably more common than in the U.S.

In any case, for the moment, the moral issue burning in Sister Marie's mind was not the rights of the unborn; she was busy cursing the embargo and those responsible for it. "It's a struggle just to find sterilized instruments to perform operations with," she complained. "We risk arrest just to buy medicine. Sometimes, I don't know how we can run a hospital in these conditions."

Asked about the threat of American bombing, Sister Marie repeated her favorite phrase of condemnation: "*Comment vont-ils être jugés, les responsables?*" — "Those responsible, how will they be judged?"

FIVE YEARS LATER, IN 2003, Iraq, which had once boasted the best medical system in the Arab world, still maintained infant-mortality rates on a par with sub-Saharan Africa. Some say that sanctions were just a particularly brutal form of globalization and privatization, as state-run services deteriorated and even middle-class families were forced into ruin to pay their loved ones' medical bills. But if the embargo resulted in a form of extreme capitalism, the U.S. invasion created a kind of mercenary free-market system and encouraged violent class warfare. Under sanctions, the black market in medicine still benefited from a certain kind of control, thanks to state involvement in smuggling. Now, wild-eyed street children got high on valium and all kinds of unregulated pharmaceuticals bought from street vendors, while the parents of children like Sarah were unable to find chemotherapy drugs anywhere in Iraq.

I discovered all this when I returned to the pediatric hospital in 2003. Ironically, it was now hard for journalists to gain access. The same hospital that had served the propaganda purposes of Saddam's regime by showing foreign media the terrible price Iraqi civilians were paying under sanctions had now become a public-relations nightmare for the new regime. Technically, I needed official permission from the new Ministry of Health to visit the wards, but fortunately I was able to get in by sweet-talking a good-natured guard, who ushered me and my translator in to meet the doctor in charge.

As we walked down a long, dimly lit corridor, I noticed the absence of the usual hospital smell of ammonia. I would later learn that the hospital lacked even basic cleaning products.

We were soon sitting inside the office of one Dr. Mohammed, a bearded man who looked to be in his mid-thirties. His demeanor was calm, but his face betrayed his obvious exhaustion. He spoke concisely, but in a low-level monotone.

"I was here many times before the war," I said. "Is the situation in terms of pediatric health any better than it was before?"

"Well," said the doctor, "I want to welcome you first and thank you for your interest." Even in times of great distress, Iraqis seemed never to lose their sense of hospitality, even if it was to welcome you to a place of death and dying. "I want to tell you that, in fact, it's worse now than before, but much better than during the war itself. That was the worst time — with no power, water, bombs falling everywhere. But if you want to know the state of pediatric health now, it's worse than before, definitely." He explained that since the fall of the government, the Ministry of Health was barely functioning and they were dependent on NGOs such as CARE, as well as UNICEF and the World Health Organization.

"But now that the U.N. and many aid organizations are leaving, how will this affect your hospital?"

"We hope that they will stay. They were the best help for us in terms of health care. There is no real government. It's as if we've been set adrift now, all by ourselves."

"Has this lack of budget contributed to more deaths of children under five?"

"Definitely, yes, and the number-one killer is gastroenteritis, because of the bad water supply after the war. The many displaced people have put extra stress on Baghdad's water system. Also, many kids came back from having lived rough outside during the bombing with water-borne illnesses. The second biggest killer is cancer. The cancer cases are increasing daily and each one needs special care. But we have no proper facilities." The doctor looked like he was ready to wring his hands, but he kept his calm tone throughout our interview.

"Every three days," he told me, "we get seven new cases, especially leukemia. Since 1991 we have had a big increase in the number of children with leukemia."

"Why do you think there has been such an increase?"

"Well, I have no documented reports." In fact, the equipment needed to test radiation levels was also banned under the embargo, but British troops, who had surely been exposed to less radiation than Iraqis who had lived through three wars in less than two decades, were already being treated for DU (depleted uranium) poisoning. "But I do believe there is a strong relation between DU and cancer, especially since most of the kids with cancer come from the south, and studies have found more uranium in the rivers, in the atmosphere there, even in the food supplies."

"With the latest bombings during the invasion, will you see an increase in leukemia?"

"Yes, I'm sure of it. I have already seen more cases coming in."

"Is it easier now to get cancer drugs — or just as hard as it was under the embargo?"

"Before the war, the embargo made it difficult. Now, there is no one to pay for the drugs, even if they are on the market. Patients can't afford them and neither can the hospitals. Some NGOs come with drugs, but it's very haphazard. We need quality, not just quantity, and we need consistency in the drug supply. We need a central health authority to take care of this, and at the moment there really isn't one."

"With so many problems, what is your greatest need now?"

"We need a continuous supply of oxygen, which means we need a better generator and more electricity to keep it stored properly, in a cool atmosphere. Now we have electricity altogether maybe 15 hours out of 24."

"What happens during the rest of the time?"

"The generator is there — but it's only enough for light and some air conditioning, and not for special machines like dialysis."

"Are your patients' lives at risk when there is no power?"

"We refer kids to other hospitals when our machines don't work. One time the electricity cut at 3:00 a.m. and we had to refer fifteen children to other hospitals. At this time the U.S. forces did not allow anyone out, and one of the ambulances was stopped and detained by them, and that child died, waiting at the checkpoint."

"What is it like being a doctor now in Iraq? To see patients die because of bad water, lack of medication, electricity?"

"It's hard for me, and all the time I blame the agencies, the Americans — all of them. As they delay things, the children die. We wait weeks, months … for basic medicine and equipment … Is it really true that the U.S. can't do anything in six months? I am working day and night to save my patients. I don't know how things will improve in the future but right now it's terrible. We have some supplies in stock now, but not enough. And what will we do when they run out? Right now, we don't even have enough painkillers."

A hospital full of dying children and no morphine. That was one of the worst horrors of this place.

Chapter 22: Old Boys

THE NEXT DAY I DELVED FURTHER into the safe realm of nostalgia. I accepted the gracious offer of a certain Mr. S, whose family owned the Hamra Hotel, to drive around the neighborhood of Kadhimiya, where he had grown up in the 1950s. It was a beautiful Friday morning when we began our tour, driving past quaint riverside streets that had changed little in five decades as well as brand-new villas that had sprung up more recently. The white-haired but still handsome Mr S. spoke longingly of the carefree days when his nanny would get up early to bring him a kind of sugared bread filled with the cream of buffalo milk from the market, and of pheasant-hunting expeditions during his golden youth. We drove past his former family estate, the bones of which now ran the length of three different single-family dwellings. "Look, that's where the courtyard garden was," said Mr. S, pointing out a huge area that was now most of someone's house.

Kadhimiya had a rich monarchist past, and the tombs of the royal family were only a few minutes away, though they were now virtually inaccessible because of American roadblocks. "I used to see the King," recalled Mr. S, "riding in his carriage on the street near where we lived. I was always very impressed to see him in person." As we drove past a riverside fish restaurant where Mr. S used to dine with his parents — now flanked by palm trees and pools of leaky sewage — he sighed and told me, "They were better days before, you know. We lived better than our sons." He turned to Mohammed, the twenty-something driver of his luxury SUV. "Look, Mohammed here, what has he experienced so far? Military service, war, bad schools, economic disaster. I had a better education, lifestyle. I had more freedom. I lived better than my children are living now." This was the Generation-X dilemma, Iraqi style — only Baghdad GenXers were really angry, and increasingly armed and dangerous.

"All these revolutions, all these wars," continued Mr. S. "What have we gained? Nothing. Saddam destroyed so much of this country. It would be more settled here if there were a king. Iraqis need constancy, continuity, not the American-style democracy of electing someone new every four years."

Soon we ventured into the old downtown area of Baghdad, the center of things in the 1950s. All along Rashid Street, crumbling buildings displayed the tell-tale traces of their former glory days — an elegant archway here, a remnant of gold leaf there. We passed the old parliament buildings, flanked by rubble and children begging in the street. Not far from here, in 1959, a young Saddam Huseein had made an ill-fated assassination attempt on Prime Minister Abdul Karim Qassim (the general who had lead the 1958 coup that overthrew the monarchy) and then fled the city on horseback disguised as a Bedouin. Then we arrived at the Shabandar café on al-Mutanabbi street, once a hotbed of political and intellectual discussion, now a bit of a museum where toothless old professors came to meet foreigners and practice their English. Mr. S was extremely nervous about leaving his driver and SUV waiting for long outside, but allowed me a few minutes to check things out. He pointed out the photos of old Baghdad that lined the café walls, black-and-white images of elegant picnics and boats on the Tigris. These were pictures of a golden age, conspicuously devoid of any reference to RAF planes dropping poison gas on tribal villages or the British control and intrigue that had marked the monarchist era.

"This neighborhood is very dangerous now," Mr S. told me as he ushered me out of the café. "I hardly ever come down here any more." He looked rather pale as he spoke, a ghost trapped in the ruins of his memory.

I HAD MET OTHER EXILES who had returned since the invasion. One night at the Bourg al Hayat, I happened upon a poolside table of them, mainly men in their late sixties who had been part of the Baghdad *nomenklatura* before the 1958 coup that overthrew the monarchy. The entire group of half a dozen portly gentlemen dressed in sports jackets and chinos was clean-shaven; not one had the trademark Baathist moustache. Instead their faces betrayed a certain patrician ease, born of privilege and frequent dinners at fine restaurants in London and Washington D.C. They were all contemporaries of Iraqi National Congress (INC) leader and then IGC chairman Ahmad Chalabi. Speaking of such pro-invasion exiles who had come like carpetbaggers to stake a claim in the new Iraq, an Iraqi woman journalist had muttered to me, "They seem to hate us more than the Americans."

In fact, the former exiles' often contemptuous attitude towards their fellow countrymen was more a product of retro-classism from another era than any overt political differences. In turn, Iraqis who had remained in their country and suffered decades of hardship were disdainful of their returning brethren, who had enjoyed the "good life" abroad. They were particularly incensed by the fact that these were the Iraqis given power and position — although arguably rather token — by the Americans. "What do *they* know about a country they left thirty years ago?" was a common refrain.

One thing was certain: the exiles still knew how to have a good time. Their table strewn with half-empty bottles of arak and whisky and the ashes of Cuban cigars, the men joined in the rousing chorus of a song from the 1950s. The whole scene had the vague air of a high-school reunion. As one rotund former ambassador put it, "The old boys are back!" This was a reunion of "old boys" who had grown up together, gone to school together and married into each others' families. Some of these merchant families had been trading together since the ancient days of the Silk Road.

And the "old boys" figured that they were well-equipped to deal with the new Iraq. Over glasses of arak, they told me of their rose-colored plans. "The American invasion is the best thing that has happened to Iraq in a long time!" exclaimed one member of a prominent merchant family whose family had done business on the banks of the Tigris for thousands of years. "It will turn the economy around and in five or six years, our economy will be on a par with Saudi Arabia." As we spoke, the unmistakable smell of sewage wafted up from some forlorn hotel pipes and we heard the distant sound of mortar fire.

The "boys" waxed enthusiastic about the billions of dollars that the

U.S. would spend in reconstruction efforts. This was several days before Bremer's announcement that even state-run companies like the Ministry of Petroleum were open to private investors, essentially proclaiming that the whole country was up for grabs and reducing the survival chances of the old family monopolies — which had even persisted in various forms under the Baathists — to zero. There was no way the old boys could compete with the multinationals; there were even rumors that the growing insurgency was being funded by old boys disgruntled about being cut out of the loop. But tonight, the mood was euphoric.

"I know there are still problems here," admitted the businessman from the old merchant family who, it turned out, owned the hotel. "But, within a year, once the economy has picked up and people have jobs, the resistance will die down, I'm sure of it." He leaned towards me. "My family are merchants, we have never been *political*. But if you're clever, you know, you can turn politics into money. We Iraqis are the best businessmen in the Middle East. It's the Israelis who will lose out — soon we'll be able to compete with Japan and Germany."

A former diplomat, who had once been the Iraqi ambassador to the U.S. and who had resided happily in North Carolina for decades, was equally optimistic. "There are four million Iraqis abroad," he said, "and they will return here once there is a viable political system and the security situation has improved." Ah, there was the rub. But the ambassador did not foresee these things taking long: "Soon Iraq will be a beacon of democracy in the Middle East." He spoke of Iraq building a relationship with Europe and helping to "rid the region of terrorism," of the creation of a Middle Eastern NAFTA-style trade agreement. He did not seem insincere or deluded as much as nostalgic for his youth, those easy days playing on the banks of the Tigris, when a few families ran things and all was *luxe, calme et volupté* rather than poverty, chaos and terror. After a few more sips of arak, the sound of loud gunfire drew us inside and we bid each other good night.

A WEEK LATER, I FOUND MYSELF having lunch with Mr. Mehdi, another returning exile (and the father of Rend Francke, who would later be appointed Iraqi ambassador to the U.S.). He had invited me to the

Alwiyah Club, a venerable institution of the Baghdad establishment that had first opened as a British officers' club in 1924. It had survived military coups, revolutions, and regime changes, and just months earlier had been a favorite hangout of Tariq Aziz. Now Aziz was in an American jail and it had become the club for returning exiles, many of whom used to frequent it in the 1950s. Hardly any foreigners came here, despite its location some two hundred yards away from the Palestine Hotel and directly opposite Firdos Square, where Saddam's statue had been toppled. Lately the square, now graced by a Goddess of Liberty statue as wobbly as the new government, had become a place of protest, where everyone from soldiers waiting to be paid to mothers missing sons came to hold banners and hope for a brief appearance on CNN. The muezzin's cry rang out five times a day from the Fourteenth of Ramadan Mosque across the street, and right outside the club, street kids sniffed glue and moneychangers camped out with stacks of dinars. But inside the high iron gates, another world awaited.

I walked through the polished granite entrance and entered a foyer that reeked of dusty old colonial gentility. The lights were out — probably because there was no electricity — but the interior was marked by heavy wood paneling, grandfather clocks, dark draperies, and an air of hushed privilege. I wandered into a kind of sitting area, where old men lounged on plush sofas, smoking cigars or playing backgammon on wooden tables. The manager then led me into the dining area, where businessmen sat under ornate chandeliers negotiating deals, with a view to the garden and tennis courts. This place was still a bastion of the Sunni elite. Mr. Mehdi, sitting at a table laid out with elaborate linens, crystal, and cutlery, rose to greet me.

"My dear," he said, "so glad you could make it." Mr. Mehdi resided at the Palestine Hotel, but came to the club often to unwind. Devoid of taxi drivers and soldiers and trinket sellers and with its orange trees and rolling lawns, it did seem like a relaxing place. The food was also quite good, and over a *mezza* of hummus and tabouleh, Mr. Mehdi told me what a wonderful time he had been having visiting his old haunts and catching up with friends. But he was concerned about the new foreign-investment laws that had just been introduced; it seemed that his plans for a nice, quiet retirement in his hometown might not be working out.

We retreated to the garden, and sat in the shade. "It used to be the best social club in Baghdad," he told me, gazing out at the tennis courts. "But it's deteriorated a bit lately. I hope it will come to life again in the near future. But the quality of people, you know, it's not quite the same. Baghdad now, it's a city run by villagers. You know, when the club started in 1924, it was mainly for the British expatriates. Before the revolution of 1958 there were perhaps a hundred Iraqis out of a membership of one thousand. After '58, it opened up to Iraqis, and now there are more than twenty thousand Iraqis with less than a hundred foreigners." This last statement was made with a certain sense of pride.

"What do you remember about the heyday of this club?"

"Well, it used to be very lively, a lot of parties, music on Saturday and Thursday nights, dancing — a lot of Iraqi and foreign couples mixing together. There used to be a residential area adjacent to the club, it's gone now, where British officers and their families stayed ... Before '58 and even for some time afterwards, people were still living well. Of course, everybody was sorry that the royal family was killed, but that's part of Iraqi history. Iraq remained a good country to live in, an enjoyable place to stay, until '68, when the Baath regime came to power, and then we started to go downhill from that date on, until we reached almost the point of no return in 1990. We reached the bottom of the barrel."

Even when he recounted details of personal or national tragedy, Mr. Mehdi's voice remained calm and he continued to speak with the same patrician air, even as his city lay imploding all around him. It was his first time back in his homeland in 25 years.

"I left Iraq first in 1964, when they nationalized the banks and the insurance companies, as well as many industries," he told me. "I was involved in many of them, as chairman, as managing director or as a member of the board. I was very disappointed — I mean everything that we'd built was taken away with almost no compensation at all. And then I came back in 1968 and started a paint factory. Finally, in 1978, I decided that was it. It was time to leave my country for good. In fact, I left broken-hearted." Here, he showed some real emotion.

Animated discussion at the Shabandar café, Baghdad, September 2003

"Thank God and thanks to the Americans they got rid of Saddam for the Iraqis. Otherwise he would have ruled Iraq for two centuries — him and his descendants. So we can never forget what the Americans have done for us."

"What made you decide to leave in 1978?"

"Well, as I said, the situation was not safe for liberal people, people who weren't members of the Baath party. They sometimes asked you to co-operate with them, or forced you into becoming a member, which I refused to do. So they took my passport away for one year, and I tried to put some pressure on the authorities here to give it back to me, through some friends I had here, and my friends said, 'Don't insist because you might be put in prison if you do that. Just keep quiet, until this cloud will pass.' After one year they returned my passport and I left Iraq with no intention of returning. But now with Saddam gone, I'm happy to be back in my own country. I'm not a practicing Muslim, but nevertheless I used to always pray, 'Let me live until I see the end of Saddam's regime.' And thank God I have," he said, smiling.

But would he also be witnessing the end of his country?

"Yes, I know what you mean, but after thirty-five years of such an oppressive regime, don't expect things to be back to normal in a couple of months. There are a lot of people who were in an advantageous situation under Saddam, who were influential, who had positions in the government or made money through Saddam, and they cannot accept that they have no more power. So they are fighting, hoping to get back what they lost. I believe that even if it takes one year to get things back in order, that will be very reasonable." But what kind of "order" would it be? Increasingly, as deals were hashed out between the Americans and the Shia clerics, it was not likely to be one that favored Mehdi and his cronies.

"Do you think there's a future for democracy in Iraq?"

"I think Iraq in five year's time will be an example in the region. In fact, democracy is not foreign to Iraqis. From when King Faisal first came to Iraq until 1958, we had a semi-democratic regime with elections, albeit with some intervention from the government to influence the results. But still, there were elections, people making political speeches openly, editorials in the newspapers critical of the government. Democracy does not come overnight. It's something you build up little by little. With the four million Iraqis living abroad, I hope that maybe two or three million will come back and this will be a big boost to the country, because they have experience living in democratic countries in the West. I'm very hopeful that we will have democracy, not as the British know it but at least better than any democracy around us."

"How did you feel coming back here after 25 years?"

"Well, I was always in contact by telephone with my two brothers who stayed here, and I met people coming from Baghdad in London or Washington or Beirut. So I wasn't so shocked, I already knew that the situation was bad. The first day I came back, I was welcomed by all my old friends. I have so many invitations now, with old relations and contacts."

"Did you feel sad about all the destruction?" I was referring to the invasion but he took it more generally.

"Yes, every Iraqi will feel sad when he sees what's happened to his country. Iraq is now fifty years behind in terms of development. It was much better in '78 when I left ... We went from being one of the richest countries in the region to the poorest."

"So will you go back into business now? Do you feel confident enough about the situation?"

"Yes, definitely. I don't want to retire, sitting at home waiting to die. We are starting to apply to open a bank here in Iraq, with myself as chairman ... and we are thinking of starting an insurance company. And other ideas ... I have many in my head. I can't tell you everything."

I shuddered slightly as I tried to imagine someone selling life insurance to Iraqi families in the current climate. Were Mehdi's dreams just fantasy? I was torn between laughing and feeling sorry for this old man who had come back to reclaim part of his childhood. He was as tied up in this whole tragedy as the street kids outside the club. They were just in different places on Iraq's giant wheel of suffering.

Mehdi excused himself to go for a swim, so I rejoined my translator, Galen, and did some filming in the garden of the Alwiyah Club and then in Firdos Square. As I stood in front of the Goddess of Liberty statue,

I noticed an American tank a few hundred yards away with a gun pointed straight at me. I couldn't decide if it made me feel secure or exposed. But when a wild-eyed man began to circle around us and shout in Arabic, the gunner didn't bat an eyelid. "What's going on?" I asked Galen.

"Shhh," he said, "just don't say anything. Let's get out of here."

As we packed up our gear and headed for the car, he explained that the man, who was still following us, was shouting, "Are you foreign journalists? Come to my house, come to my house! See what the Americans have done! See the damage they've caused!" While his story could have been legitimate, his aggressive demeanor made it seem more likely that this was just a ploy: lure a foreign journalist into a back street and steal from them, or worse.

"But what about the Americans?" I asked Galen. "I mean, they're right there. Aren't we safe because of their presence?"

"Are you kidding?" Galen replied. "They don't intervene in Iraqi-on-Iraqi crime." It hit me that even in the middle of the day, in the middle of Firdos Square, I was totally vulnerable. To the average Iraqi criminal I looked like fair game, and to the average American soldier I was nothing but another Iraqi casualty. Just then Mehdi wandered out of the club gate, fresh from his swim. "Hello, Hadani," he waved. "I'm walking back to the hotel."

"Maybe you'd better come with us," I told him as he took in the scary guy and suddenly clicked as to what was going on. In an instant, Mehdi was in the back seat and we were off, even as our menacing new friend ran after us. The whole drama had lasted maybe a minute and a half but seemed, in that suspended-animation way, much longer. And Mehdi seemed to take it all in stride. He was still in the honeymoon stage of his return.

After we dropped him off at the Palestine, I asked the driver to stop a few hundred yards from the entrance so I could film a lovely old villa. As I videotaped the intricate wrought-iron gate, my camera gaze caught a scene happening fifty yards away. Some street kids high on glue were having an argument. As two of them sat slumped over the threshold of an old hotel, another three gaunt creatures of indeterminate age bobbed and weaved in a doped stupor in the middle of the dusty road. Their spindly legs looked like they were about to crack under their weight. One boy squatted down, right in the middle of the road, and put his face in his hands. It looked as though he were crying, but I was too far away to tell. The two other boys moved their arms wildly, in gestures that were half embrace, half assault. I watched, transfixed, as the boy on the ground grew bored of his despair and slowly stood up. A few seconds later, he turned around and stared straight at the camera. Suddenly, all five kids were on their feet and running towards me, shouting and raising their fists in the air.

I turned on my heels and ran towards the car. Galen and the driver jumped in and we managed to get away just as one of the boys' fists smashed down hard on the hood. It was perhaps my most terrifying moment in Baghdad. The city that I'd grown to love seemed to be turning against me. I knew it was time to go.

Twelve-year-old Shada and her two-year-old sister in front of their makeshift home in an abandoned swimming pool in Baghdad, October 2003

Chapter 23: The Pool People

WITH MY BUDGET, ENERGY, and general enthusiasm for Baghdad waning, I decided it was a good time to inquire about a flight out. In an expensive mistake, I had only purchased a one-way ticket from Jordan, and now the price of a flight back to Amman had more than doubled. In addition, the rules about who could fly were increasingly fuzzy, and the road conditions ever more dangerous. I was starting to feel desperate when a letter arrived for me at the hotel, sealed in wax. It was an invitation to dinner at L's that same evening.

"Don't worry," said L over a gourmet dinner at his villa. "There's a flight on Monday, I'll have one of my assistants take care of it."

The next day I met up with Ali, the NGO worker I had seen at the King's villa, who had promised to lead us to an abandoned swimming pool in a northern suburb of Baghdad to meet some of the people displaced by the invasion. After an hour of driving we arrived in a working-class, predominantly Shia neighborhood where about three dozen people were living in a squalid old aquatic center. Children greeted us as we pulled up to the entrance, and we were led through the old changing areas that had now been converted into makeshift homes. Laundry hung haphazardly over grungy tiled floors; a pet cat lapped dirty water near a rusted drain; a portrait of Imam Ali graced a cracked cement wall. Outside, tents made of wire and dirty towels masqueraded as houses for several families.

I made my way into the courtyard, whose overgrown garden and muddy earth offset the brown water of a huge Olympic-sized swimming pool with a diving board. A twelve-year-old girl named Shada approached me and smiled sweetly. In her arms she held her two-year-old sister, Houda. Shada had a vaguely Bedouin look about her and told me she came from Sheeshan, a desert area outside of Baghdad. "After Baghdad fell, we came here," she said, "because our house was bombed and we

had nowhere to live. Now we have no clothes, no house, no money."
Her family, she said, had been reduced to begging and seeking aid from
foreign humanitarian groups.

Ali explained that he had established his NGO shortly after the
invasion. With help from some of his wealthier neighbors, and after
selling his own car, he had managed to raise enough funds to rent the
pool complex as a transitional shelter for homeless children and their
families. The rent was 150,000 dinars — about a hundred U.S. dollars
— a month. There were also some children here from two former
orphanages that had been looted after the invasion. "Their house was
occupied by thieves," he explained, "and the children had no one to
care for them." Some of the orphans now slept in a mosque in Sadr
City that Ali had secured for them. During the day, many of the kids
worked as street hawkers in the market, selling pop, cigarettes,
vegetables, whatever they could manage.

Shada, already a little woman in her headscarf and long cotton dress,
told me a little more of her story. "When our house was bombed," she
said, "my father was badly wounded and now he can't work any more.
We began to wander, to try and find a place to live, and we ended up
here." That had been six months ago. Her disabled father had stayed
with Shada and her sister at the swimming pool, but her mother had
gone to seek work as a peddler in another city. When she wasn't taking
care of her sister, Shada also worked in the markets.

Shada was sharp and spoke frankly of her situation. "Life here is
very bad, we don't feel comfortable. It's dirty, there's no electricity, no
clean water, no safety or security. But it's better than nothing. Before
things were better because we had a place to live — it was ours — and
we had good security. Now there is kidnapping and thievery
everywhere. I'm glad that the regime is gone, but things were better
before." The sound of gunfire punctuated her last remark.

"Did you ever go to school?" I asked.

"No," she replied, "I would like to study but my family is too poor
and I have to work to help them." Later, she told me that she wanted
to be a doctor.

I was then introduced to four kids, all siblings: Malik, Karim, Abda, and Sara. "We used to live in Sheeshan," said Malik, the eldest at twelve. "We rented a small house there, but during the war we left our house and came here because we couldn't pay for the rent."

"We didn't have much money before the war," added his sister Sara, whose hair was cut short and who I had taken for a boy at first. "But before the war my father was in good health and used to work every day." During the bombing, she said, her father had sustained head injuries and suffered brain damage.

Just then her father, forty-year-old Ala Abdullah, emerged from one of the interior rooms. He explained that his injury had occurred the night before the fall of Baghdad, although he had no memory of exactly what had transpired. "I suffered a lot during the war," he lamented, "and now I have no house." He said he'd lost his job selling furniture, although it wasn't clear if this was due to his injury or to the recent economic downturn. His brother had lent him some money and he had come to Baghdad seeking work, although his condition made this difficult. "I don't remember things," he told me. "I feel nervous sometimes and I have fits. I fall into rages, and sometimes I hit my children. I've been to see some doctors but I don't have enough money for proper medical treatment."

Indeed, Ala didn't even have enough money to feed his children and relied on help from local people, who donated rice and lentils. He was not aware of any agency that could help him. "Three months ago," he said, "a group of French aid workers came here saying they were doing a study on homelessness and that they would help us. But so far, nothing," he shrugged. I sensed I was one of many well-intentioned foreigners who had visited the "pool people."

"Things were better before the war," Ala concluded, "because there was free medical treatment for everyone. I don't want a lot — just a small, simple house and good medical care, that's all."

"If you had the opportunity to tell Paul Bremer something," I asked, "what would it be?"

"I'd like him to visit this place to see what kind of conditions Iraqi people are living in."

"You wouldn't tell him to get out of Iraq?" I asked.

"I have nothing to say about these matters." It was hard to tell if he was being circumspect or just resigned and fatalistic.

By now, the group I had come with had left and it was just me and Ali and my translator, Galen. I walked around to the other side of the "change rooms" and saw a small boy drinking a trickle of dirty water from a hose that had been lying in the mud. Around the corner, more laundry hung above sewage and a woman in black abaya stood holding her baby daughter. The girl was skinny, with big black eyes that stared distractedly but with great intent. She wore an orange and purple sweater. She had TB, her mother told me. They didn't have money for medicine, but "we depend on God."

Ali now began to plead with me to leave. "It's getting dangerous," he hissed. "Five minutes," I said, "only five."

The mother continued with her story. "We are from al-Husseinyieh," she said, "and we were one of the first families who came here to live." There was a hint of pride in her voice. They had rented a house in al-Husseiniyeh, she explained, but left because of the bombing during the invasion. When they went back afterwards they found that the owner had come to reclaim it. "We lost all our furniture and possessions," she said.

Her husband, she recounted, was severely handicapped from his time on the front lines in the Iran–Iraq war. He had received a small pension and sold spare parts, but now his stipend — like his job and his house — had disappeared, shortly after Operation Freedom began.

"It was much better before," said the sad mother with the sick child in her arms, "because of the security situation. Now no one can work easily because it's too dangerous to even go out on the streets."

With that final caution, Ali practically dragged me back to the car. I left the old swimming-pool complex with a blur of images behind me: children waving goodbye, an old man in a tribal headdress, a woman scooping water from a barrel, the faint blue outline of a dolphin painted onto the entrance. As we drove away, I saw a blackened building across the street and two girls staring through a barbed-wire fence.

Chapter 24: Dinner at the al-Rashid

THAT SAME AFTERNOON, I met with Hank and Shortridge once again, this time at their new home, the al-Rashid Hotel. Before the invasion I had regularly stayed at this grand hotel, but it had since been requisitioned by the Americans and it was now very hard to get inside. As we arrived at the armed compound, we were motioned over to a large parking lot. I didn't know how long our meeting would be, so I asked Galen, the young English-language student who was now acting as my driver and translator, to wait for me. It was now about five minutes to six, our scheduled meeting time, and as I walked through the maze of security checkpoints, I kept my fingers crossed that there wouldn't be too much of a delay. After all, there had been a mortar attack on the hotel that morning and security was probably tight.

To further complicate matters, there hadn't been time to change since my visit to the pool people. In an effort to keep cool and modest, and with my clean laundry supply dwindling, I had worn my last baggy white t-shirt. But the large image of Che Guevara emblazoned on it, combined with the effect of my black, sun-blocking cap, conspired to help me resemble a mad Bolivian revolutionary. But luckily for me, the soldiers at the main checkpoint were Hondurans. "*Hola!*" I smiled, and they simply waved me through. *Hasta la Victoria siempre compañeros!*, I wanted to say, and I hope you don't have to die for your green card.

After a few more checkpoints, I finally crossed the threshold of a familiar, yet drastically changed, Baghdad landmark. In the 1990s, visitors to the hotel had walked across an infamous mosaic that graced the entranceway, a large likeness of George Bush Senior with the words BUSH IS CRIMINAL written beneath it. I was eager to see if it was still there, but it seemed that it had been whitewashed. The same gargantuan chandelier still hung in the marble-floored lobby, but the familiar portraits of Saddam were missing. Instead of mustachioed

Baathist notables, the place was now teeming with tall Americans, both soldiers and CPA apparatchiks. I walked towards the front desk, where Hank and Major Shortridge were waiting for me.

"Hello there," said Shortridge. "We weren't sure if you were going to make it."

It was only 6:15, which, I thought, wasn't bad for Baghdad. But I soon realized that these two gentlemen were pretty clueless about life outside their little fortress. Their Baghdad — the one of armed escorts, air-conditioned, bulletproof vehicles, decent food, working telephones — was miles away from mine. How much farther removed were they, I thought, from the life of the average Iraqi?

On the way to the restaurant, I noticed that most of the same shops were there, selling Bedouin trinkets and antique silver pawned off by old families heading discreetly for financial ruin. None of the waiters at the coffee shop looked familiar. I inquired after Adel, a charming old Egyptian man who had worked there for years, but learned that he'd been demoted to room service. I sat down with the increasingly wary looking American/Australian pair, whose eyes were glued to my t-shirt. "You know I spent some time in Bolivia," said Hank, the old US-AID hand, somewhat bemused. I tried out some Spanish on him and he responded quite convincingly, if with a somewhat Nicaraguan *sabor*. I explained that I'd just been to visit a displaced persons camp and that there'd been no time to change. Hank and Major Shortridge were dressed in casual khaki, but looked infinitely cooler than most of Baghdad. As we spoke, what seemed like a whole battalion of Marines sat down two tables to our right.

The conversation soon turned to the subject of Iraqi women. Hank readily admitted that he didn't know that much about them, but figured that oppression of women was something "endemic in the Arab world." Then, oddly, he recounted the story of his tall, blond, mountain-climbing niece who was planning to rollerblade through Cairo on an upcoming trip to Egypt. "I had to kind of take her aside," he said, "and say, 'Look, honey, it's not going to work.'"

I pondered this as some Spanish officers spoke *madrilleno* vowels to our left and the almost identical-looking Marines to our right slurped onion soup.

"Well, it's time to order dinner, I reckon," said Major Shortridge. It seemed a little early to eat — most Iraqis have supper well after eight p.m. — but we were in Fortress America on military time. I had a six-dollar chicken escalope, which was surprisingly delicious, as if a different grade of fowl was being airlifted into the green zone.

As we ate our dinner among soldiers, I suggested that the garden-of-peace project might be a way to bridge the gap between the new Iraq and the old, between returning exiles and those who'd remained, even between upper and lower classes. The ladies who lunch, I argued, might well take up the cause of the gardening mums and their kids. Hank and Shortridge looked vaguely convinced, but I knew deep down that my idea was probably as naive as trying to rollerblade through Cairo.

I asked Hank if he had heard of Captain Stacey Simms, who, I'd been told, was in charge of orphanages. "We don't know him," said Hank. "He's part of the army. They kill, we rebuild. They usually create the orphans and we build the orphanages." I was surprised by Hank's frankness and thrilled that he had such a black sense of humor — it was almost Iraqi.

As our meal wound down and we were served cups of hot chai, it was time for some bottom-line reckoning.

"You know, Hadani," began Hank, "your project is of interest to us, but, at the end of the day, it must have some political and economic benefit for us." I wondered how that might work. I imagined the headlines in one of the new U.S.-backed newspapers: HAPPY CHILDREN PLAY IN U.S.-AID FUNDED GARDEN, AS THEIR FATHERS ARE DETAINED AT ABU GHRAIB.

While we were chatting, I happened to mention that my driver was waiting for me in the parking lot and that his car was rather run down, with hardly any functioning lights, heat, or air conditioning. I explained that my other driver, Hassan, couldn't make it that day because of some deadline that had passed for getting new licence plates, which he couldn't afford. All this news was foreign to Hank and Shortridge, and Hank said, "You know, we could use someone like you — as a spy." It was hard to tell if he was serious or not, but he continued, "We need someone who blends in with the local population ... and we could probably afford, say, $15 a day."

"Plus security?" I asked, playing along.

"No way," they laughed. Most Iraqi CPA employees earned about $5 a day and risked their lives doing so.

I said my goodbyes to Hank, then Major Shortridge escorted me out. He walked me to the edge of the first checkpoint, from where I was to walk some hundred yards alone in pitch darkness to the parking lot. But it was so dark and scary-looking — and such a prime target for mortar fire or pot shots — that we decided it would be too much of a risk. Shortridge himself seemed slightly disoriented and I was beginning to feel rather woozy myself. There was an eerie silence as we walked briskly back into the somewhat safer realm of the al-Rashid. But the reality was that the Americans would have to seal off a part of the sky and build some kind of Star Wars-style impenetrable shield if they ever wanted to feel safe in Iraq.

Within a few minutes, Shortridge had arranged for an "official vehicle" to escort me back to the parking lot. I thanked the Australian major and went off with two guys named Cesar and Spence in a spanking new air-conditioned GMC. Cesar didn't talk much, but Spence, an all-American guy in his mid-twenties, told me he was from New Hampshire.

"How long have you been here?" I asked, as we meandered the long way around the green zone.

"Three months," replied Spence.

"And how has it been so far?"

"Wonderful," he said, with great sarcasm. Some Americans, it seemed, did have a sense of irony; I'd always thought it was such a Canadian thing.

"What were you doing in there for so long?" asked Galen when I finally reached him. It was now 8:00 p.m. "That parking lot was a very dangerous place! My father will be very worried about me!" Unlike Osama, who boasted that he drove to even the most dangerous of places, Galen had clearly not gone far without his father. "There are thieves everywhere!" he said.

"Even with all those tanks around, you were still worried?" I asked.

"Of course," he said. "Thieves don't care about tanks. Besides, the Americans will not intervene."

As we passed more American tanks on the way back to the hotel, Galen confided, "You don't know how much I hate them. They promised us so much."

Chapter 25: Garden of Peace

TWO DAYS BEFORE MY DEPARTURE from Iraq, I was busy preparing invitations for an inaugural fund-raising concert for the Garden of Peace project, to be held in the terrace of Qasim al-Sabti's gallery. I could not change the course of history, I could not end the occupation or produce a new, corruption- and violence-free Iraq, but I could organize a concert in a garden with some musicians and a few children. I had talked to Ali of the homeless children's NGO and he had agreed to have the kids perform their operetta. Karim seemed interested, and the playwright Sayegh had promised to come. Even my old driver Osama said he would be there.

Nadia at the hotel internet café enthusiastically helped me choose fonts and decorative flower motifs for the invitations. Then, with rather manic energy, I set about hand-delivering the invitations: to the National Theater, where workers were busy digging up the sewers; to the "King's" palace, where the hangers-on were busy looking busy; to the Palestine Hotel, where mercenaries and CNN correspondents rubbed shoulders. I was on a mission.

I returned to the Hamra to find Karim waiting for me in the lobby. He looked a little more like his old *artiste* self. Why hadn't he called me? "I've been depressed," he replied. "This country, it hasn't changed at all." I agreed, but was more interested to know how he had changed. Happily, Karim was game to perform with me at the concert and promised to pass by the next evening for a rehearsal.

That evening I also received an invitation to attend a little get-together at Mr. S's apartment. Not quite knowing what to expect, I walked into a roomful of singing, dancing, and oud-playing Iraqis performing *makam*, traditional love poetry set to music. Among the guests were Karim's cousin Mohammed and a couple of old musicians who had played in the cabarets that once flourished in Baghdad. Spirits were high and soon I found myself dancing too, moving my hips and hands in serpentine rhythms to the delight of the Iraqis. It was a great evening, full of pure joy and release. No one talked about what was going on outside in the night, where some American soldier was surely being shot at or was himself shooting some poor curfew-breaker, out there in the darkness where some terrified family was hearing the sound of their front door being broken down or a mother was trying to comfort a dying child. We did not speak of invasion or occupation, of presidents or regimes, of the past or the future. After a while, we did not speak at all. We just sang and danced.

THE DAY OF THE CONCERT, Karim arrived, cello in tow, in a sharp new suit. He had borrowed a friend's BMW especially for the occasion. Things started off well, but inevitably we began to argue after a few minutes, bickering about a wrong turn he'd taken and the ensuing traffic snarl like some suburban couple on their way to a bridge game. Soon, Karim started one of his increasingly frequent anti-foreigner rants. By the time we arrived we were barely speaking to each other.

Happily, lots of people turned up for the concert. Most were Iraqi, with the exception of Steve, the "embedded artist," and a *Houston Chronicle* photographer Osama had brought along. The kids from the homeless children's society were there, looking wide-eyed and excited. When I asked Karim to come over to meet them, he refused, saying, "Kids make me nervous." Thankfully, good old Sadiq Ali Shaheen the actor arrived and charmed them with a few parlor tricks. The painter Esam Pasha turned up as well, with a poem to read about the "glories of Baghdad" — historical glories, but glories nonetheless. Eventually, after it became clear that no "foreign dignitaries" or "international media" would be coming, we decided to begin.

I thanked everyone for coming, thanked al-Sabti for lending us his gallery, and introduced Karim as "one of Baghdad's best cellists." Then we began Gounod's "Ave Maria." As Steve filmed with my video camera, the mellow tones of Karim's cello drifted into the late afternoon air. One of the resident doves flew overhead. I began to sing, "*Ave Maria, Grazia plena, Dominus tecum / Benedicta tu in mulieribus.*" The children smiled as the song unfurled; Sadiq sat in the front row with his eyes closed. "*Sancta Maria, sancta Maria, Maria / Ora pro nobis, nobis peccatoribus / Nunc et in hora, in hora mortis nostrae Amen.*"

For a moment even Karim smiled at me, as if the beauty of the music had erased whatever animosity existed between us. But when I introduced Esam, who was to read his poem accompanied by Karim, there was some sort of disagreement. Karim picked up his cello, put it in his case and, as Esam began to read, walked off towards his borrowed BMW. I would never see him again.

After Esam finished reading, shyly and in very formal Arabic, it was time for the children's operetta. They appeared on the balcony, three boys and one girl aged from seven to twelve, and began to sing a combination of traditional folk songs and original melodies. It was deeply moving, especially knowing that the boy with the loveliest voice had suffered untold horrors.

The first song was an old patriotic anthem from the Iran–Iraq war, whose lyrics — "Those who are not on our side, should not drink water from the Tigris / because the water is clean and pure, but they are not / we only live once, we only die once / so it is a blessing to die for one's country" — could well be applied to the current occupation.

Next, one of the boys sang a song about a student and his teacher. "Take this book and notepad," he warbled, "I don't need them any more, because there is no time to study / Happy are those who can leave this country of suffering / Please, teacher, let me go to work, give me a chance to bring food to my family / I like what you teach / But the family is hungry / When I give them food, I will feel I am a good student."

Then another boy, with sad eyes and a lovely lilting voice, sang a nationalist Kurdish song, mixed with some Arabic: "How can I forget / I feel it in my blood." Next the girl, a tiny creature called Ibtisam, sang a haunting melody, an old lullaby transformed into a song of mourning for a dead child. The purity of her voice contrasted with the gravity of the lyrics: "I am going to the graveyard to visit my dear one / In my life I only ever asked God for a boy, not for money or anything else / My tears are a song, my crying is a melody / We are crying but some people think we are singing / But no, it is not a song but a lament for our suffering."

A boy with a more robust voice then began to recite a poem by the dissident poet Arian al Sayed Khalaf, a Communist who had been imprisoned by Saddam in the '70s. (He later gave up writing and survived as a merchant.) "I hope someone will bring me good news, about peace, about love," the boy, Hassan, sang; "If anyone doesn't believe how I've suffered, just look at my wounds / We have to try, we have to hope / If you think your efforts are for nothing, don't despair / Nobody will forget Che Guevara / No one will forget Ho Chi Minh." It was a far cry from Teletubbies or Walt Disney.

Soon the Khalaf poem fused into a more fluid classical Arabic poem, "Birds are flying so free / We wish we were like them / They sing their song as the sun rises." The operetta ended with a rousing anthem whose lyrics combined nationalism, hope, and a bit of John Lennon:

> Look straight ahead
> Don't look back
> The time for fear is over
> The time of difficulty is over
> The time of injustice is over
> From the graveyards, from the prisons we are coming
> From among the injured
> Rise up people, come together
> People from the north and the south
> War is over now
> Come together, work together
> The mountains are dancing with the plains
> Don't look back, we have to move forward and work together
> No more death, no more wars
> Let us live in peace and harmony.

It seemed amazing that after all Iraq had been through it could still offer up four cherubic children singing of hope and harmony. These children, who had witnessed war and pillage and worse, were somehow able to stand and sing proudly of their country and their dreams. Where did such resilience come from, and how long could it last?

*Assem, a twelve-year-old diabetic boy who works in a
shoe factory to pay for his insulin, October 2003*

Two of the boys and the girl were cousins, I discovered, who were being raised together by their grandparents because their parents had died in the war. None of them could go to school because they had to work in the markets to help support their families, so the society was their only recreational and educational resource. Despite their hardships, they looked relatively happy and healthy, but there was something about their companion Assem, a twelve-year-old boy with sad eyes, that made me want to probe further.

It turned out that Assem was from Al Shaab, a tough neighborhood in the north of Baghdad, that he was a diabetic, and that he had to work twelve-hour shifts in a shoe factory to pay for his insulin. His pay was only 6,000 dinars a week, less than five bucks. His parents were elderly and unwell, he said, and since his older brother was killed by the *fedayeen* militia in the early days of the invasion, he had become the family breadwinner. His tale was out of Dickens, but his eyes spoke of Iraq's recent trials.

"My boss doesn't beat me because he knows I'm sick," Assem told me in a whisper. He'd never been to school, he said in a monotone, but he'd like to be an engineer. When I asked him if he'd like to study music, his eyes lit up and he nodded enthusiastically. The singer Kazem al-Saher was his idol, he said. As an ambulance screamed in the background, he told me that his neighborhood had been bombed during the invasion and that he still had nightmares about it, as well as a recurring dream that Saddam was coming to get him. I asked him if he ever had any good dreams, but he said he couldn't remember any.

Saying goodbye to the children wasn't easy. I hugged them all and congratulated them again on their performance. I told them I would think of them in Canada and wished them the best in their lives. Taking Assem aside, I gave him $20 U.S., which he refused at first but finally accepted when I told him it was for his insulin. I also gave Ali a small contribution for the association. He and the kids accompanied us to the car. Ibtisam held my hand and they all waved goodbye as we drove off. I wondered if I would ever see them again, if I would ever return here. What would Iraq be like in a year from now? Was there even a slim hope of a decent future for these kids?

Epilogue

THE NEXT MORNING, I rose early to finish my packing and say my goodbyes. Soon Ehab, the young man who worked for Custer Battles, came to take me to the airport. "We'd better hurry," he said. "We don't want to be late."

Luckily we made good time on the highway, so Ehab indulged my request to film one last stand-up, this time for a story I hoped to do on Iraqi women. We stopped at a house along the route, where some women in long black abayas sat outside a white stone wall. They very good-naturedly agreed to be filmed. "Iraqi women have borne the brunt," I began, as the women sat beside me with a quiet dignity, "of two decades of war, sanctions, and uncertainty." We only had to do two takes. "Perfect," said Ehab. "I got you, the two ladies, the whole picture. Perfect."

Safely ensconced in my suite at the Amman Intercontinental, I would play over and over the haunting image of the two women standing against the white wall, staring straight at the camera, daring the viewer to return the honesty of their gaze. Their weathered but handsome faces seemed to tell the story of this long-suffering place.

As we approached the airport, waves of nostalgia and regret began to wash over me. I could see the old terminal, which had been converted into a gulag and now housed a Burger King. Ehab stopped to check in at the Custer Battles "security camp" and left me alone for a moment in the back of the GMC. The faces of the children came back to me, the sounds of Karim's cello playing *Ave Maria*, the scenes in the hospital, the street kids, the soldiers at the al-Rashid, the dark corridors of Abu Ghraib, the cruelty of friends and the kindness of strangers, promises kept and broken, the soothing chants of the Sufis, Haidar's lead-footed angels.

I barely made it on to the tiny plane as a huge crowd of Iraqis and foreigners jostled for position in the wildly snaking line. This time my seat mate turned out to be a special forces man who had once dreamed of becoming an opera star. Flying over the land that I had come to know and love, urban traces slowly gave way to vast desert expanse. As I stared out at a broken nation, its distant landscape turned luminescent. For a moment it sang with light.

A women with her children in Nasiriyah, spring 2000

Acknowledgments

THERE ARE SO MANY special people and strange circumstances that brought me to the place of writing this book. Perhaps it all started the day I missed my wake up call at the al-Rashid and never made it on the "secret" bus tour to Saddam's palaces organized by the minders at the Ministry of Information. Instead I spent the day hanging out in markets with a young translator who was also a student of English literature and a cousin of Tariq Aziz. Amid cardamom sellers and cartfuls of oranges we discussed Samuel Beckett and Naguib Mahfouz. Somewhere on a winding street in Karradah, while my colleagues were hot on the "official" trail, it hit me. I had to write a book about Iraq. Frustrated by the confines of 1,000-word dispatches, I realized that this was the only way to approach anything remotely resembling Iraqi reality.

The problem was, no one was really interested in Iraqi reality, or in the nation's staggering history, glorious culture, or long-suffering populace. Instead most North Americans seemed obsessed with Saddam — one Iraqi out of twenty-four million. Rather absurdly, it took an American invasion for the world to notice Iraq.

I met Scott Steedman, my editor at Raincoast Books, by chance in the spring of 2003, while hosting the presentation of a National Film Board documentary on a Canadian artist in Baghdad. Within a few months, I was off to post-invasion Iraq, not sure what to expect.

So here's to happenstance and fortuitous meetings. I'd like to extend my thanks to those Iraqi border guards who first let me through in 1997, even though they thought I was a Kurdish separatist and not a Canadian writer; to the Iraqi National Orchestra and composer Lance Conway, who opened up a world of music to me in a seemingly tuneless place; to Sadiq Ali Shaheen and Muhsen el-Ali, who introduced me to Iraqi theater; to the Sufi *tariqa*, who took me in; to Wania Yusef, who let me sing Aznavour songs with him in Baghdad; to Ahlam and Karim, who invited me into their homes; and to Sabah and Dalal, who helped me make sense of things. I'd like to thank my publisher and the team that helped produce this book. Special thanks to Scott, who commissioned my book and believed in it.

Without the support of other editors over the years, this book would not have been: Leonard Doyle, foreign editor at the *Independent*, who published my dispatches on orchestras and oil-for-food resignations; Andrew Tuck at the *Independent Magazine*, who was mad enough to send me to Baghdad to do a story on musical comedy; Stephen Engelberg at the *New York Times*, who commissioned a series of features on topics not too many people were covering at the time, and who asked me what an "ululation" was, and listened calmly as I demonstrated it in ear-splitting tones over the bugged phone lines at the Press Center, while bemused minders looked on. Thanks to Tyler Brule, who sent me on an amazing assignment to cover architecture and so much more for *Wallpaper**; to Mark Abel, the fabulous former foreign editor at the *San Francisco Chronicle*, who seemed to understand Iraqi humor right away; and to Gloria Jacobs at *Ms. Magazine*, who commissioned and lovingly edited my feature on Iraqi women.

My time in Iraq was made richer by the grace of many wonderful colleagues: Robert Fisk, with whom I enjoyed romantic trips to prisons and morgues; Stuart Freedman, whose bad jokes and compelling images sustained me; and Olivia Ward, whose friendship I was lucky to gain during a bombing campaign.

I'd like to thank my old minders. Thanks to Ali for being so dogged in your attempts to control me — it was a lot of fun. And thanks to those guys who helped me translate midnight Iraqi wire-service copy during Desert Fox; to Ziad, who expelled me ever so nicely; and to Jabar, whose hospitality knew no bounds. Thanks also to a plethora of long-suffering drivers who may or may not have been keeping files on me; and to Adel at the al-Rashid, who always brought me the good pomegranate juice when I asked for it.

And thanks to the hundreds of Iraqis I met, interviewed, broke bread, and danced with over seven years. Your spirit and your stories will stay with me always.